Developing Urban Entertainment Centers

Principal Authors

Michael D. Beyard

Raymond E. Braun

Herbert McLaughlin

Patrick L. Phillips

Michael S. Rubin

Contributing Authors

Gayle L. Berens

John Casazza

Steven W. Fader

David A. Mulvihill

Mary B. Schwartz

Jay D. Wheatley

**Urban Land
Institute**

About ULI–the Urban Land Institute

ULI–the Urban Land Institute is a nonprofit education and research institute that is supported and directed by its members. Its mission is to provide responsible leadership in the use of land in order to enhance the total environment.

ULI sponsors educational programs and forums to encourage an open international exchange of ideas and sharing of experience; initiates research that anticipates emerging land use trends and issues and proposes creative solutions based on this research; provides advisory services; and publishes a wide variety of materials to disseminate information on land use and development.

Established in 1936, the Institute today has more than 13,000 members and associates from more than 50 countries representing the entire spectrum of the land use and development disciplines. They include developers, builders, property owners, investors, architects, public officials, planners, real estate brokers, appraisers, attorneys, engineers, financiers, academics, students, and librarians. ULI members contribute to higher standards of land use by sharing their knowledge and experience. The Institute has long been recognized as one of America's most respected and widely quoted sources of objective information on urban planning, growth, and development.

Richard M. Rosan
Executive Vice President

Cover: *Las Rozas retail/entertainment center in Madrid, Spain. Design by KMD Architects.*

Project Staff

Senior Vice President, Policy and Practice
Rachelle L. Levitt

Project Director
Vice President, Strategic Development
Michael D. Beyard

Director, Book Program
Nancy Stewart

Manuscript Editor
Eileen Hughes

Book Design/Layout
Helene Y. Redmond, HYR Graphics

Cover Design
Betsy Van Buskirk

Associate Director of Publishing Operations
Diann Stanley-Austin

Word Processor
Joanne Nanez

Executive Assistant
Ronnie Van Alstyne

Recommended bibliographic listing:
Beyard, Michael D.; Raymond E. Braun; Herbert McLaughlin; Patrick L. Phillips; Michael S. Rubin. *Developing Urban Entertainment Centers.* Washington, D.C.: ULI–the Urban Land Institute, 1998.

ULI Catalog Number: U11
International Standard Book Number: 0-87420-824-6
Library of Congress Catalog Number: 98-60123

©1998 by ULI–the Urban Land Institute
1025 Thomas Jefferson Street, N.W.
Suite 500 West
Washington, D.C. 20007-5201

SPONSORS

ULI would like to thank the following companies for their generous sponsorship, which has permitted us to publish this book in full color. ULI especially appreciates the support of Kenneth Wong, President, Walt Disney Imagineering, for coordinating the sponsorship effort.

rockwellgroup

TrizecHahn

ACKNOWLEDGMENTS

Many individuals contributed their time and talent to this effort, and to each one of them I say a heartfelt thank you. I particularly would like to thank my coauthors—Ray Braun, Patrick Phillips, Herb McLaughlin, and Mike Rubin. Without their incredible breadth of knowledge, experience, and insight into this new topic, the book would not have been possible. Perhaps more amazing was their willingness to devote time on weekends and during the evenings to an effort that offered only professional, not monetary, rewards. The authors of the case studies—Gayle Berens, John Casazza, Steven Fader, David Mulvihill, Mary Schwartz, and Jay Wheatley—also deserve thanks and special recognition for their thorough research and their commitment to digging for information that often is hard to get. Mary Schwartz merits special mention for her dogged efforts to update case study information for projects that were moving targets.

I would also like to thank the many project developers, designers, architects, and public officials who spent time with the case study authors and provided written materials and photographs, often on very short notice. They always seemed to be available for our questions as we double- and triple-checked information, and they were equally accommodating of our sometimes demanding production schedules. Nora Lee and Jean Turner of the *Entertainment Zone* both have been remarkably generous with their time, information, sources of information, photographs, and moral support along the way, and I deeply appreciate their kindness.

Several other people contributed feature boxes on specialized topics that add much to the flavor of the book. Thanks go to Jill Bensley, Daniel J. Brotman, Dennis Carlberg, Steve Thomas Emberson, Michael C. Getlin, Robert S. Holt, Daniel C. Sheffey, Peter Slatin, Richard Yuan, and Andrew Zarnet. Tsilah Burman pointed out the need for a glossary, and I want to thank her for pulling it together.

I also want to thank the members of ULI's Entertainment Council for their ideas and support during the lengthy development process for this book. Andy Halliday, Bill Kistler, Peter Rummell, Mel Simon, Frank Stanek, Lee Wagman, and Ken Wong are just some of the people who have been invaluable assets as we try to figure out how ULI can provide both the information and the forum that the urban entertainment industry needs as it matures.

Finally, I would like to thank the Urban Land Institute staff for its skill and dedication in bringing this book together: Ronnie Van Alstyne for trying to keep me organized, never complaining as the work piled on, and taking care of so many important assignments; Joanne Nanez for processing all of the text, including major edits, with such attention to detail; Helene Redmond for doing a beautiful job of designing and laying out the book (often in the middle of the night!) under extraordinarily tight deadlines; Eileen Hughes for doing a wonderful and lively edit of the text; and Nancy Stewart for managing the entire editing and production process so that every detail was taken care of—and to perfection, as always. I also would like to thank Betsy Van Buskirk for designing the book's cover, Diann Stanley Austin for coordinating the book's publication, Joan Campbell for searching her databases for obscure information that I needed, and Rachelle Levitt for her unwavering support (and nudging) throughout the book's lengthy gestation period.

And to all others who had a hand in this work but could not be mentioned in this limited space, I extend my sincere appreciation.

Michael D. Beyard
Project Director

PRINCIPAL AUTHORS

Michael D. Beyard

Michael D. Beyard is vice president, strategic development, at the Urban Land Institute. In addition to conceptualizing and developing new strategic directions for the Institute, he directs ULI's research and conference planning in commercial real estate development. His specialties include urban entertainment, shopping centers, and downtown development. Beyard is the author, coauthor, or project director for numerous ULI publications, including the *Dollars & Cents of Shopping Centers* series, *Downtown Development Handbook*, *Remaking the Shopping Center, Developing Power Centers*, and *The Retailing Revolution*. He created and is the director of ULI's trailblazing conference series on urban entertainment development as well as other conferences in the United States and Europe. For three years, he directed ULI's work with the United States Agency for International Development (USAID) in central Europe. Prior to his long tenure at ULI, Beyard was a senior management consultant with Booz Allen & Hamilton. He earned an undergraduate degree in international economics from Rutgers College and a graduate degree in urban planning and development from Cornell University.

Raymond E. Braun

Raymond E. Braun is a senior vice president at Economics Research Associates (ERA), Los Angeles, specializing in leisure and tourism economics and recreation attraction development consulting. He is head of the firm's entertainment and recreation practice group.

ERA's clients in the theme park industry have included major operating companies such as Disney, Universal Studios, Time Warner/Six Flags, Paramount Parks, and others. Major urban entertainment projects have included Mall of America, Yerba Buena Gardens, Universal CityWalk, MCI Center, and numerous others. Braun also has served as planning consultant for the new J. Paul Getty Center in Los Angeles. He has extensive experience in the United Kingdom, Europe, Australia, Japan, China, Singapore, Canada, and Mexico.

Braun has participated in the following organizations as member, speaker, and publications contributor: International Association of Amusement Parks and Attractions (IAAPA); International Association of Fairs and Expositions (IAFE); Urban Land Institute (ULI); and International Council of Shopping Centers (ICSC). He holds a B.A. degree in economics from Claremont McKenna College and an M.B.A. degree from the University of California at Los Angeles.

Herbert McLaughlin

Herbert McLaughlin oversees design and research at KMD. The firm has won more than 100 design awards, including 30 AIA awards. In the last five years, KMD has won the following international design competitions: Cheil, Seoul; Han Nam Dong, Seoul; International Design Center, Nagoya; Jayaland Master Plans, Indonesia; Kookmin Bank Headquarters, Seoul; Lu Wan Development, Shanghai; Nasan Metro Plaza, Seoul; New Shanghai International Plaza, Shanghai; New Shanghai International Center, Shanghai; Panambi, São Paulo; Plaza Merdeka, Kuala Lumpur; Royal Washington, Hiroshima; Turtle Creek, Dallas; and Malaysian Embassy, Washington.

McLaughlin has been a visiting critic or lecturer at Harvard; Columbia; UCLA; University of California, Berkeley; University of Illinois; University of Wisconsin; and Stanford. He also has lectured at conferences and seminars for the National Trust for Historic Preservation, the Urban Land Institute, National Real Estate Development Center, *Architectural Record,* National Endowment for the Arts, Smithsonian Institute, San Francisco Museum of Modern Art, U.S. Department of Housing & Urban Development, and NEOCON.

Patrick L. Phillips

Patrick L. Phillips is a senior vice president at Economics Research Associates (ERA), where he is responsible for the development and delivery of ERA's services throughout the eastern United States. He coordinates the firm's activities in the area of urban real estate and also serves on its board of directors. ERA is a private consulting practice focusing on economic and feasibility analysis, strategic planning, and transaction-related services for real estate investors and developers, public agencies, financial institutions, and nonprofit organizations. Recent focus has been on the market, economic, and financial aspects of a new generation of downtown, visitor-oriented projects that combine retail, entertainment, lodging, and other uses.

Phillips is a frequent speaker on urban development issues, and he is the author or coauthor of five books and numerous articles. He is a member of the Urban Land Institute and is active on ULI's Urban Development and Mixed-Use Council. He also teaches at the Berman Real Estate Institute at Johns Hopkins University. Phillips's academic training includes a graduate degree in public management and finance from Syracuse University's Maxwell School of Citizenship and Public Affairs. Before joining ERA, he was a senior manager with the real estate consulting group of Ernst & Young.

Michael S. Rubin

Michael S. Rubin, Ph.D., is president and cofounder of MRA International. Rubin is a pioneer in the field of entertainment-enhanced development, having first introduced the concept of the urban entertainment center and having been the innovator behind many of the more creative location-based entertainment concepts. His experience includes 15 years of consulting and venture creation with diverse entertainment companies, hospitality companies, development firms, and financial institutions.

Rubin earned master of architecture and master of science degrees from the University of Pennsylvania and a Ph.D. from the the Wharton School of Business. He has been an adjunct professor at the Fels Institute, the Wharton School, and the Graduate School of Fine Arts (Architecture and Planning) at the University of Pennsylvania and is a frequent speaker at entertainment and real estate industry forums. He has received professional awards from the AIA, AIP, PEI, and HUD, as well as *Progressive Architecture*'s Award for Excellence and the Urban Land Institute's Apgar Award.

CONTENTS

PREFACE

The Urban Land Institute is pleased to offer the first comprehensive, case study–based book on urban entertainment development. The goal of the book is to strengthen the understanding of this new form of development and to help move the industry forward as it matures. To do this, ULI has documented through case studies and the insights of industry experts how the current range of urban entertainment projects is being created; identified the industry's critical development issues; reported how they are being resolved; and highlighted the challenges that still need to be met. ULI believes that entertainment companies, real estate developers, and public officials—the partners in most urban entertainment projects—need this information as they explore uncharted territory to create projects that meet public as well as private goals.

ULI believes that this new form of development has unusual potential to change the way that people think about downtowns and to generate additional economic and social activity there, benefiting both project creators and the public. We also believe that it provides an important way for shopping centers to strike back against non-store shopping alternatives and to reinvent themselves to meet the rapidly changing demands of the world's consumers.

Downtown and major suburban "downtown" locations are being targeted for the largest and most ambitious urban entertainment centers. ULI sees these locations as having the identity, image, access, and related cultural activities that are the key requirements for successful urban entertainment developments.

Throughout history, downtowns have been centers of entertainment and culture for societies throughout the world. Until World War II, that was true in the United States as well; before then, almost all public entertainment, amusements, and cultural facilities were located downtown. The nature of these activities, however, has evolved rapidly in the last 100 years: Crystal Palaces and expositions were the hallmarks of the Victorian era; vaudeville houses and amusement parks were the stars in the 1900s and 1910s; the first motion pictures with sound were featured in the great movie palaces of the 1920s and 1930s. Legitimate playhouses and concert halls endured throughout all of these eras, but by the 1970s they were the only major forms of entertainment left in

KMD Architects

3

(Preceding page:
The future of urban
entertainment? The
proposed Las Rozas
retail entertainment
center in Madrid.)

most downtown areas except for those in a handful of our largest cities, such as New York and Chicago.

David Nasaw describes this trend in his book *Going Out: The Rise and Fall of Public Amusements:* "The era of public amusements that was born in the later decades of the nineteenth century has come to an end. We have lost not simply buildings and parks but also the sense of civic sociability they nourished and sustained. Once, [these] amusement spaces defined the city as a place of glamour and glitter, of fun and sociability. But they have vanished forever."[1] It is no secret why this occurred: rapid suburbanization in the post–World War II era; retail decentralization; the decline of the industrial economy and the rise of a technological and service economy not tied to central cities; and middle-class flight impoverished central cities and left them devoid of their largest and richest market segment.

In response, during the past 40 years, the nature of entertainment shifted largely from the public to the private realm. Entertainment had been a very public experience, sought after in the heart of great cities, where all classes of society mingled in close proximity. Beginning in the 1950s, it began to take two different but curiously related forms.

The availability of private entertainment in the form of television and later, VCRs, home theaters, computer games, and the Internet meant that Americans could be entertained in the privacy of their own home. At the same time, public entertainment gradually shifted to a more controlled private environment in the form of movies and arcades at regional shopping malls; family amusement parks; ballparks that were largely removed from cities; and distant resorts, all of which were far from downtowns and their diverse populations.

David Nasaw accurately laments this trend: "The huge and heterogenous crowds that gathered [downtown] have been dispersed. The audience at a shopping center theater; the spectators at suburban ballparks;

and the visitors to theme parks, festival marketplaces, and enclosed shopping malls are, by comparison, frighteningly homogenous."[2]

Can excitement and social inclusion and interaction be reestablished in America's cities, or is it a phenomenon of the past? The resurgence of downtowns has been reported regularly over the past 20 years, and comeback cities are routinely designated, but much of this news has related to the rebirth of small segments of the city. Fundamental problems that seem intractable still remain, but recently an encouraging trend—the reemergence of urban entertainment in the form of galleries, clubs, restaurants, civic and cultural facilities, sports, and multimedia—has taken root along with alternative living spaces and seems to offer real opportunity for downtown revitalization.

An entire generation of Americans has now grown up in a largely homogeneous suburban environment, and they are looking for something more to entertain themselves. When the consumer has been everywhere, seen everything, and done everything, the old entertainment options simply will not do anymore. People are becoming blasé about the technological wizardry that is available

Urban entertainment past and present: The New Amsterdam Theater on 42nd Street in New York City.

to them at home and work. And the old-style shopping mall, the epicenter of suburban culture and entertainment, seems pretty dull in comparison to the promise of a spectacular collection of new, out-of-home entertainment options that if creatively bundled and executed can capture the interest of the most jaded consumer.

What is this spectacular collection of entertainment options? The Urban Land Institute defines an urban entertainment center as a new form of shopping center that must contain three basic components: at least one pure entertainment attraction, usually a new-generation cinema complex; theme restaurants; and entertainment-oriented shops in a coordinated, intensely sociable environ-

ment that draws large and diverse audiences throughout the day to activate the space. Gated amusement parks and attractions that charge an entrance fee for the entire attraction do not qualify. (However, there can be gated attractions within urban entertainment centers.) The Urban Land Institute considers gated attractions fundamentally different forms of development from urban entertainment centers, where customers are under no obligation to spend any money and must pay for only those attractions that they are interested in on an individual basis.

Urban entertainment often requires some form of public/private partnership to be successful. The Urban Land Institute strongly supports these partnerships: they provide an efficient way to achieve both public and private goals. From the public perspective, downtowns need to be revitalized and suburban centers need to be energized in order to generate tax revenues and enhance their marketability for spinoff residential development and employment-generating activities. From the private perspective, urban entertainment developers usually need the public sector to share the financial burden of development due to high development and operating costs, particularly in downtown locations. And links with public facilities such as museums, performing arts centers, sports facilities, and convention centers greatly enhance the prospect that urban entertainment centers will be successful.

Urban entertainment projects require higher visitation levels than traditional shopping centers because their construction and operating costs are higher and because customers spend less per capita for entertainment than they do for the more essential goods sold by traditional retailers. This highlights the challenge that the industry faces as it tries to determine what locations, mix of activities, financing structures, and partnerships will make the concept work.

Chapter 1 explores why urban entertainment center development is taking off not only in North America but around the world. It describes the confluence of forces that are driving the trend and how these forces will shape its future. Chapter 2 describes what urban entertainment development is, including the types of activity it encompasses and the configurations it takes. Chapter 3 describes how entertainment centers are put together in a business sense, including project positioning, programming, financing, and execution. Chapter 4 describes the unique planning and design issues that must be addressed.

Chapter 5 presents the most comprehensive collection of entertainment center case studies that has been assembled to date. This chapter includes most of the centers that have an operating track record, from stand-alone entertainment centers to shopping centers that have been infused with entertainment attractions. Chapter 6 presents a discussion of where the urban entertainment industry is heading and includes some predictions about future directions and opportunities. The book concludes with a glossary of terms used by the players in the urban entertainment development industry. Some are in common use for all real estate projects but may be unfamiliar to the entertainment industry; others are commonly used in the entertainment industry but may be unfamiliar to real estate developers. In an industry that merges

The modern forerunner of today's emerging urban entertainment districts: Baltimore's Inner Harbor.

two very different industries—entertainment and real estate development—it is essential that everyone speak the same language.

This book is not the last word on the development of location-based urban entertainment centers. It is the first comprehensive look at these new types of development from a real estate perspective, and it provides experiential, practical information on how these projects have been conceived, planned, designed, programmed, structured, and financed. Where data were available, project economics and performance also are presented, including construction and operating costs, rents, and sales per square foot. The Urban Land Institute believes that the lessons that have been learned from the market experience of these pioneering projects is invaluable to the entertainment and development industries and the public sector as they work together to create the next generation of urban entertainment projects.

The Urban Land Institute usually creates books that highlight best practices in the development industry, and this book is no exception. However, it is still too early to know all the answers. Undoubtedly, some of what is covered in this book will need to be modified and updated as more projects are completed and more definitive economic and financial data are made public. The entertainment companies, developers, retailers, and restaurateurs who are pioneering this exciting new form of development are expanding the realm of what is possible by experimenting with new attractions, combinations of activities, and configurations. The Urban Land Institute hopes that the information provided in this book will help move that experimentation process forward successfully into the 21st century.

An urban entertainment fantasy: the Forum Shops at Caesars Palace in Las Vegas.

Notes

1. David Nasaw, *Going Out: The Rise and Fall of Public Amusements* (New York, NY: Basic Books, 1993), p.1.

2. Ibid., p. 1.

CHAPTER 1

FORCES DRIVING URBAN ENTERTAINMENT

What forces have led to the emergence of urban entertainment centers (UECs) in the 1990s? The proliferation of UECs has resulted from the convergence of trends involving the entertainment industry, retail and real estate development, and municipal revitalization. In UECs, entertainment, dining, and retail components are being bundled together by a variety of players to form synergistic leisure destinations. Developers are seeking new strategic real estate models to compete against the burgeoning value-oriented retail sector while municipalities are hoping to promote urban revitalization by attracting suitable developments to downtowns. Meanwhile, entertainment companies are seeking new opportunities to exploit regional entertainment and retail initiatives. As a whole, UECs are a response to changing patterns favoring closer, more accessible leisure options that can be enjoyed more frequently.

Interestingly, UECs are a result of both positive and negative economic conditions over the past few decades. To a great extent, the heart of the UEC concept is the prevailing importance of leisure in American society, which is an expression of a strong economy. At present, people of all ages and most economic strata have a significant amount of disposable income. Thus, pleasure, indulgence, relaxation, stimulation, and entertainment have emerged in the modern era as inalienable rights. The UEC comes at a time when consumers can afford to buy superfluous merchandise like logo ballcaps from NASCAR Cafe, miniature versions of Frank Lloyd Wright–designed stained-glass windows from the Museum Co., and magnetic poetry kits for the refrigerator door. They also can afford gratuitous foods like smoothies and cappuccinos, which they consume not because they are hungry but because they have a specific craving. Entertainment, too—like a five-minute motion-simulator ride priced at a dollar per minute or a spin on a human gyroscope—is similarly accessible and justifiable.

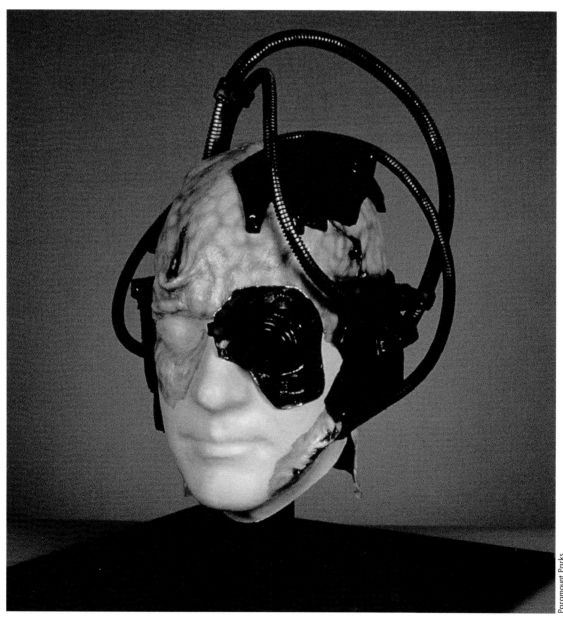

Yet the UEC also owes its origin to the economic constraints of recent decades, especially the recessions of the 1970s and early 1990s. The strained economy inspired the development of off-price and outlet retailers. These shopping alternatives have competed against shopping malls, thereby spurring the transformation of malls into UECs as they seek a competitive niche. Meanwhile, the explosion of two-income families, which has largely fueled the growth of out-of-home dining, also has been a result of economic necessity. And the blighted condition of the nation's inner cities, which has made revitalization necessary, is similarly a byproduct of long-term economic conditions outlined in the preface.

INTENSE RETAIL COMPETITION

In recent years a variety of circumstances have created a highly competitive retail environment for regional and super regional shopping centers, or "malls." Overbuilding of retail in general has been a significant factor. While the amount of retail square footage was between 12 and 14 square feet per capita at the beginning of the 1980s—conforming to general guidelines for sustainability—by 1994 there was nearly 19 square feet of space per capita. Much of that excess space is found in malls. According to the ULI's *Dollars & Cents of Shopping Centers: 1997*, regional shopping centers have, at 12 percent, the highest vacancy rate of all center types, nearly twice that of the runner up, super regional shopping centers.

The decline in mall performance has been due in part to the degraded conditions of many of the centers, a large number of which are 15 to 30 years old. In addition, many department store chains that have long served as anchor tenants in these developments have consolidated, closing many stores. Further undermining shopping malls is the recent proliferation of new value-oriented retailers such as stand-alone discount stores and off-price, outlet, and power centers. These concepts—which offer maximized breadth and depth of product lines; a no-frills environment; and high-volume, low-markup sales strategies—exploded during the recession of the early 1990s. According to the National Research Bureau's Winter '97 issue of *Shopping Center Directions*, for every regional en-

The spectacular marquees and entrance to the Warner Bros. cinema complex at Centro Oberhausen help draw customers away from the competition. (Preceding page: Consumers can buy superfluous merchandise like the Borg mask based on the popular TV show at "Star Trek: The Experience" at the Las Vegas Hilton for a mere $4,500.)

Photogenics

closed mall that opened in 1996, 17 power centers opened.

The threat posed by value retailers to regional shopping centers, whose tenants typically cannot match the off-price retailers in either price or scope of product line, is exacerbated by the fact that value retailers have succeeded in capturing higher-income shoppers as well as the expected lower-income shoppers. According to a Roper Starch Worldwide Study, the types of store that affluent Americans—those with more than $100,000 in household income—are significantly more likely to patronize than the total U.S. public are florists, gourmet food stores, greeting card stores, jewelry stores, kitchenware specialty stores, and *warehouse clubs*. Moreover, although the proportion is less than that of the total public, about half of affluent Americans surveyed had made a purchase at a discount store in the previous month.

Further competition with shopping malls has come from remote, technology-based shopping conduits. Although geocentric shopping is certain to remain dominant long into the future, alternative commerce systems such as television and on-line shopping as well as mail-order catalogs promise to create additional competition for traditional shopping centers. The U.S. Department of Commerce estimated in 1997 that these alternatives currently account for only 4 percent of consumer sales, yet the phenomenal growth rate of on-line activity certainly will have a profound effect in the longer term.[1]

According to the February 1997 *Urban Land*, the number of households online reportedly went from nearly zero in 1990 to more than 15 million by fall 1996, with 43 percent of households with personal computers (PCs) online. By 2000, the number of households online is expected to double to 30 million, which represents slightly less than one-third of U.S. households. Furthermore, technological advances allowing for more sophisticated and personalized browsing—like computer models of shoppers' bodies that allow them to select clothing that is

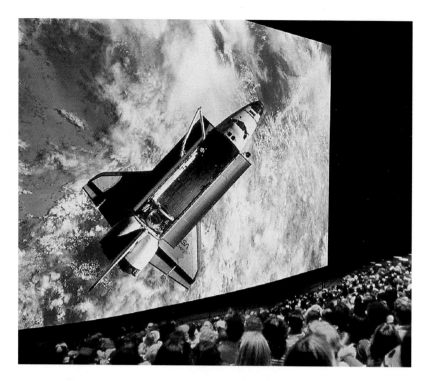

guaranteed to fit, as well as efficient parcel delivery systems and encryption techniques to safeguard financial transactions—will make electronic shopping more convenient.

These pressures have led mall developers to embrace the UEC concept as a way to remain competitive. By adding entertainment and dining amenities and by shifting toward entertainment-oriented retailers, these projects broaden the realm of commerce from commodities that are physical, such as clothing, books, and jewelry, to those that are experiential, such as fun, excitement, social interaction, and education.

Education as entertainment. IMAX shows *Destiny in Space* on its large-format screen.

THE RISE OF LIFESTYLE RETAILING

With the emergence of lifestyle retailing, stores have become more leisure oriented and more experiential—characteristics that are intrinsic to UECs. While people historically have been identified by their trade, even taking it as their surname—Cooper, Baker, and Smith are examples—they increasingly are identifying themselves by their lifestyle, and even more specifically by their leisure in-

Robert Pisano

Robert Pisano

terests. These days, "I'm a skier," "I'm a vegetarian," or "I'm an avid reader" are common personal summations. Perhaps even more important is the appeal to values and aspirations that creates demand for the types of products and activities found in new entertainment-oriented stores and attractions. In the current competitive retail environment, retailers have sought to differentiate themselves by catering to the needs of people with specific lifestyle profiles. In fact, in many cases, businesses are specializing in a particular type of *consumer* rather than a particular type of *product*.

Starbucks, for instance, is forming strategic alliances with retailers in various fields, including Crate & Barrel, Barnes & Noble, and Nordstrom, whose patrons fit the same lifestyle profile as those of the gourmet coffee bar chain. And by selling private-label coffee makers, mugs, compact discs, and thermal carafes, Starbucks does not aim to sell coffee to everyone so much as to sell "coffee-drinker" lifestyle products to its upscale target market. As department stores retain only the most profitable services and departments—cloth-

ing and home furnishings—specialty retailers are expanding their domain to include new product categories in boutique departments. Eddie Bauer, for instance, has expanded from its emphasis on men's clothing to include women's wear, luggage, housewares, and so forth. What makes these ventures successful is that they are leveraging the cachet of their brand name and style. Acting in essence as fashion consultants, these stores shelve only those goods that fit their customers' lifestyle profile, rather than stocking "the universe under one roof," as did traditional department stores.

With lifestyle retailing, patrons are more inclined to identify with a particular store. However, this intimacy is not merely product based, as there also is a growing emphasis among retailers on integration of experiential pursuits. Some stores have incorporated entertainment-oriented activities within their stores, inducing consumers to spend their leisure time in a retail environment. Gourmet coffee bars and live jazz at Barnes & Noble and Borders bookstores and Playlands at McDonald's illustrate this strategy.

Educational experiences also can become a link between retailer and consumer. Home Depot patrons, for instance, can learn how to lay tile and install plumbing in the store's home improvement classes. In such cases, retailers assume the role of advocate for, or consultant to, the consumer, passing on their expertise and more or less impartial opinion about the goods for sale. An extreme example of this personalized attention is Levi Strauss and Co.'s made-to-order Personalized Pair blue jeans, which are manufactured to the customer's measurements taken at a retail boutique.

However, the distinction between entertainment and education in the retail setting frequently is blurred. Sporting goods and music stores offer "play-before-you-pay" or "try-before-you-buy" opportunities whereby consumers can test merchandise in the store before purchasing it. At Bass Pro Shops Outdoor World in Springfield, Missouri, for example, shoppers can learn how to tie fishing flies and then test them out at the store's indoor trout pond as well as use rifle and bow ranges. At Oshman's Sporting Goods customers can give athletic equipment a trial run on in-store courts. Similarly, the REI (Recreation Equipment Inc.) flagship store in Seattle has a 475-foot dirt mountain-bike test track, a rain room in which to test waterproof clothing, a *faux* hiking trail on which to test boots, and a 65-foot indoor rock-climbing pinnacle. Meanwhile, Virgin Records Megastores lets patrons listen to compact discs before purchasing them. True, in these instances customers are learning about the merchandise, but because the merchandise is typically leisure related, they are clearly enjoying it as well. The strategy, then, is to increase consumer exposure to the merchandise in anticipation that the goods will sell themselves.

One result of lifestyle retailing is that stores are coming to emphasize the experience as much as the merchandise. In this new breed of retailing, one could confuse the store with an entertainment center that has a store theme and the merchandise with souvenirs

with which to commemorate the experience. John Naisbitt, author of *Megatrends*, has described this in his newsletter *Trend Letter* (December 12, 1996), as a new era in the "experience economy":

> In the present era of mass customization, companies find they need to repackage their products and services to deliver unique experiences. Previously, when the industrial economy shifted to the service economy, mass production required companies to wrap *services* around their products to attract customers. In the experience economy, company services are linked together to form memorable events that personally engage the customer.
>
> Consider, for example, a birthday cake. If you buy the individual ingredients required to make a cake, *commodities* such as flour and sugar, you might pay about $1 at your grocery store. A prepackaged cake mix (a *product* made from commodities) might cost about $4. If you order a ready-made cake at a bakery, you can expect to pay around $10 to $15 for the *service* of preparing and decorating it. A total package—an *experience*—of a Discovery Zone party costs in the range of $50 to $75.

Retailers at UECs—Virgin Records Megastore and the Disney Store, for instance— are able to compete with discount stores like Wal-Mart, which sell many of the same goods, by offering just such experiences. Furthermore, these experiences are being bundled together to create highly synergistic relationships. One recently proposed UEC was to have an IMAX specialty-format film theater showing educational films next to educational retailers like Nature Company and the Museum Co. Meanwhile, sports bars and athletic gear retailers could be located in their own jock-oriented area. These sorts of arrangement bear a striking resemblance to theme parks such as Disneyland, which have theme areas like Frontierland and Fantasyland in which all components, including attractions, food and beverage outlets, and shops, reinforce the theme.

Strength of Out-of-Home Dining

Dining is an essential component of the UEC mix. The current strength of out-of-home dining is due to lack of time and fundamental social changes that have occurred during the last half century, including rising divorce rates, the increase of single-parent and dual-income households, and the reduction in family size. While restaurant business constituted 29.7 percent of total food expenditures in 1982, the figure had climbed to 34.6 percent by 1992. In 1997, the National Restaurant Association's *Restaurant Industry Forecast* predicted that the industry would reach an all-time sales high of $320.4 billion, representing a 4.3 percent increase over the prior year.

As the traditional family has eroded, so too has the traditional family dinner. An entire generation has grown up without traditional sit-down meals. More and more, consumers grab a bite to eat on the run, giving rise to myriad out-of-home dining options. With increased demand and the emergence of new suburban communities, which offer ripe territory for expansion, fast-food and casual restaurant chains have experienced rapid growth. This has allowed them to amortize the costs of developing centrally manufactured food products, distribution systems, preparation techniques, and brand identities through wide-scale marketing. Furthermore, they have perfected environmental designs, menus, and operating systems to accommodate single diners or groups of diners paying separately. These strategies include compact seating, single-person portion sizes, and counter service.

This has led to more efficient restaurants —and credible corporate tenants—that can be located virtually anywhere, including in neighborhood, community, and convenience shopping centers; shopping malls; and UECs (frequently within food courts) as well as in alternative locations like airports and college campuses. Thus, dining out has become a convenient adjunct to other activities, including shopping and entertainment.

Americans view eating out as the number-one way to unwind and relax. Theme restaurants like the Rainforest Cafe offer even more —leisure dining as entertainment.

At the same time, dining—which is intrinsically pleasurable—also has remained a leisure activity, a role it has played since ancient times. This is confirmed by the *1994 Master Card Dining Out Study*, which found that Americans view eating out as the number-one way to unwind and relax. Gourmet coffee bars, popcorn wagons, frozen yogurt shops, pretzel carts, fruit juice bars, and the like illustrate the wide range of indulgence-oriented restaurants that satisfy consumers' cravings more than their hunger. And theme restaurants, sports bars, jazz clubs, and dinner theaters offer an even higher level of leisure dining that acts, in essence, as entertainment.

Consumers' demand—or willingness—to enjoy food with other attractions is an essential source of the synergy that fuels UEC development. For those patrons who visit a UEC primarily to dine, the various concomitant retail and entertainment amenities complement their experience. Conversely, customers who visit a UEC mainly for retail or entertainment purposes will find a range of dining opportunities to satisfy their hunger or to indulge their taste for something special.

There has been some fluctuation in restaurant business in recent years—due mainly to economic contractions, which promote more conscientious spending patterns; an overabundance of facilities in some markets; increasingly convenient packaged food items at supermarkets; and the new fashionableness of home cooking—but the long-term trend is strong for out-of-home dining. The trend is further strengthened by the fact that Generation X is the first to be raised eating restaurant food on a regular basis. Critical social phenomena, like dual-income households and single parenthood, are likely to continue to exert their influence as well.

Ubiquitous Entertainment

Paralleling the growth of out-of-home dining and the consequent proliferation of restaurants is a similar ubiquity of entertainment due

Race Rock is a popular motor sports memorabilia and celebrity restaurant that fires on all four cylinders: food, beverage, entertainment, and merchandise.

to a related combination of sociological and technological developments. Among them are the domestic constraints that have emerged in the past few decades, altering leisure patterns. The rise in dual-income households, single parenthood, job insecurity, and children's conflicting school schedules have fueled demand for economical, frequent, flexible, and brief leisure pursuits that are close to home instead of the costly, infrequent, preplanned, and extended vacations of the past. Contributing to this demand is an increase in disposable income among youth, who tend to be predisposed toward discretionary spending on entertainment and have the means to travel to local destinations yet are less able to venture outside the region. More than ever, consumers are seeking leisure experiences in convenient doses on a weekly basis, inspiring the development of new regional and community-level entertainment destinations, including UECs.

The repeat visitation pattern typical at these locales is facilitated by refreshed forms of traditional entertainment like cinemas, live performance theaters, music venues, and sporting events, all of which draw patrons back again by offering ever-changing presentations. At the same time, dramatic new tech-

The spectacular art nouveau interior of the New Amsterdam Theater was restored by Walt Disney Company to house its theatrical productions in New York City.

video games, for instance, have long made them an ever-present diversion in places as different as convenience stores, pizza parlors, and student unions.

Yet ubiquitous entertainment has taken the form of more than dedicated entertainment amenities. Partly due to consumers' real or perceived "time poverty," there also is a demand for entertainment that supplements or accentuates existing activities, many of which are central to UECs. Thus, the concept of entertainment-value, as a qualification of how entertaining something is, has emerged as a competitive factor in everything from restaurants ("eatertainment") to museums ("edutainment"). Retail stores, or more specifically, entertainment-oriented retail stores, also have embraced entertainment as a value-added commodity and a way to differentiate themselves from the competition. Store design themes, dynamic audio and visual presentations, elaborate visual merchandising displays, interactive "play-before-you-pay" stations, and in-store cafés are some of the ways retailers have transformed shopping into a leisure experience.

ENTERTAINMENT INDUSTRY EXPANSION

The ubiquity of entertainment is due in part to the expansion of the entertainment industry. Early in its history, companies like Paramount Pictures, under founder W.W. Hodkins and later Adolf Zukor, understood the power of vertical integration. By collapsing the industry's three distinct functions—production, distribution, and exhibition—into a single organization, these innovators were able to exploit fully the value of cinema at each stage, from scripting to screening.

Similarly, in recent years, entertainment companies like Disney, Time Warner, Universal Studios, and Sony have pursued rampant expansion, mergers, and acquisitions to enable them to capitalize on their core assets—the ephemeral intellectual "properties" that

nological advancements have brought about unique modes of entertainment like video and virtual reality games that encourage repeat, interactive play. Meanwhile, new, physically compact, technology-based attractions like motion simulators have emerged. Requiring only a few hundred square feet, these rides fit within the UEC's retail-scale environment yet are able to offer dynamic theme park–caliber experiences on a par with that of a roller coaster. Because many of these attractions use changeable media and software, they tend to be uniquely suited to meeting UEC's need to promote repeat visitation. Many of them also can be installed and removed with ease, and some are even portable, allowing them to be located virtually anywhere. The compact size and widespread appeal of are the stories, characters, and brands that they own. To illustrate, in 1955 the Walt Disney Company (then called Walt Disney Productions) described in its annual report involvement in theatrical production and, beginning that year, distribution; television production in the form of two shows; Disneyland, which opened that summer; and licensing of characters and music. In contrast, by 1996 the company's activities included film production and distribution; home video; television and cable production, syndication, and broadcasting; radio production, syndication, and broadcasting; music publishing, production, distribution, and licensing; live theatrical production; character merchandise and licensing; retailing; newspaper, technical, book, and magazine publishing; development and marketing of multimedia computer products; ownership and interests in theme-park resort developments worldwide, with a cruise ship line underway; and ownership of and interest in professional sports teams.

The resulting synergy among such activities has allowed these companies to amortize marketing expenses across multiple product types, achieve higher levels of awareness through multimodal penetration, and insulate themselves from economic downturns in particular business areas. For instance, a rise in oil prices may hurt Disney's destination theme parks but leave box office earnings unaffected. The converse, however, is that when properties fail—especially when a film "bombs" at the box office, because films frequently introduce other properties—it can hurt the theme parks (which may have parades and attractions tied to the movie) as well as licensed consumer products and retail stores (which sell products based on the movie). For instance, Disney reported in its *1996 Annual Report* that comparable store sales in its Disney Stores were down 2 percent "primarily due to the strength of *The Lion King* [an animated feature film] merchandise in the prior year," which is another way of saying that the follow-up animated film the next year was not as strong a property. Thus, vertical integration makes strong properties all the more critical.

The impact of entertainment industry expansion on UECs is both direct and indirect.

ENTERTAINMENT COMPANY BUSINESS AREAS

Film/Television

Film Production
Film Distribution
TV Production
TV Syndication
Home Video
Animation

Music

Recording
Publishing
Distribution

Broadcasting

Network Television
Cable Channels
Radio Stations

Publishing

Books
Magazines
Newspapers

Theme Parks

Design and Operations

Consumer Products

Licensing
Product Development
Multimedia
Retail Stores
Catalogs

Other

Professional Sports Teams
Cruise Lines
Live Theatrical Shows
Online Games and
    Entertainment

Source: Economics Research Associates.

Fueling the success of urban leisure developments is the emerging popularity of the imagery and ideals of "city life" among the generation of consumers who grew up in the sub- urbs. Music video portrayals of gritty downtown settings, the popularity of thrift-store apparel, and angst- filled "grunge" subcultures like that of skateboarders are evidence of an "urban chic" aesthetic. While this mode originated as a vernacular ex- pression of Generation X pessimism about prevailing economic and social conditions—which the deteriorated inner-cities amply symbolized—it has since been absorbed by the commer- cial design, fashion, and media indus- tries. Burgeoning lifestyle retail chains like Urban Outfitters, Junkyard, and Hot Topic and the GameWorks en- tertainment centers—which share a dystopian motif of scrap metal, graf- fiti graphics, dilapidated architecture, and industrial grime—exemplify the surging fashionableness of urbanism.

As this aesthetic is shaping as well as expressing people's perceptions of "the city," mitigating or capitalizing on it may be part of cities' strategic efforts to attract visitors downtown. For instance, old industrial warehouses and abandoned factories may be given new life through adaptive use rather than be demolished. Thus, cities retain their historic roots while the structures provide visitors with an "authentic" experience distinct from what they find in the suburbs. Accord- ing to the July 1997 issue of the *Entertainment Real Estate Report*, the number of industrial building to be transformed into UECs has doubled in the past five years. One example is

GameWorks entertainment centers share a design motif that exemplifies the surging fashionableness of urbanism.

As the saturation point for theme parks in the United States is approached, entertainment companies are looking for new opportunities to exploit intellectual properties as well as apply their design and operational expertise through regional or community projects.

Disney, which recently formed a new di- vision dedicated to regional entertainment, has announced plans to open a chain of up to 30 of its 100,000-square-foot DisneyQuest high- tech game centers in cities worldwide. Mean- while, Disney's involvement in the 42nd Street revitalization effort in New York City's Times Square is an example of the company's participation in a more comprehensive UEC development. The company also is develop-the Power Plant in Baltimore's Inner Harbor, which is being converted by the Cordish Company into a UEC with a Hard Rock Cafe, Barnes & Noble, and Starbucks, plus virtual reality centers, music venues, and other amenities. At the same time, London's Battersea Power Station reportedly is undergoing a $296 million redevelopment by the landowner, Hong Kong-based Parkview International, and United States–based development partner the Gordon Group. The 60-year-old art deco building will include a 32-screen cinema complex by Warner Bros. International Theaters and Village Roadshow of Australia. Eventually, the center will add theme-park attractions, retail, hotels, and various other commercial and residential amenities.

The interest in "city life" is as much about urban living as urban aesthetics. Consumers crave the functionality of the city: dense, eclectic, spontaneous, pedestrian environments where entertainment, dining, and retail options are in close proximity. This comes as a rejection of the sprawling and homogeneous suburbs, which have proven to be entirely inhospitable to pedestrians as well as lacking in character. Thus the city has become the model for UEC design.

The Loading Dock at GameWorks, one of numerous, specialized interactive game rooms designed to resemble urban loft space.

In some cases UECs aim to recreate historic or romanticized Old World streetscapes: promenades, piazzas, benches, fountains, merchant carts, and kiosks. CocoWalk, for example, a successful 138,000-square-foot UEC in Miami's Coconut Grove district, features brick pavers, potted flowers, colorful awnings, and a central plaza. In other cases, and with revitalization in particular, there may be an attempt to restore the original flavor of an area. The design guidelines for the revitalization of 42nd Street in New York, for instance, call for oversized billboards, tacky facades, and "vulgar heterogeniety" by architect Robert A.M. Stern.

Source: Patrick Phillips and Jay D. Wheatley, Economics Research Associates (ERA).

ing a UEC complex as part of its planned expansion on its Anaheim property. The project, which will feature name-brand tenants within a dynamic pedestrian environment, will serve to link the Disney hotel complex with Disneyland and the forthcoming Disney California Adventure theme park, which will be situated on the current parking lot.

In large part, the model for this project is Universal CityWalk, a prototypical UEC that Universal Studios Hollywood opened next to its theme park in Universal City, California in 1993. In addition, Universal Studios, DreamWorks SKG, and Sega Enterprises have begun opening the first few of their planned chain of 100 GameWorks centers, each of which will include hundreds of video games, several proprietary game experiences, a compact counter-service café, a pub, and a retail boutique selling logo items, all distributed throughout a 30,000- to 50,000-square-foot industrial-theme space laden with sensory stimuli. Sony Retail Entertainment, too, is exploring the regional entertainment field with its multifaceted complex, Metreon, at Yerba Buena Gardens in San Francisco. Along with a cinema complex similar to that at its Lincoln Square, New York site, the Yerba Buena Gardens project will include innovative restaurants, retail, and a play facility based on *Where the Wild Things Are*, a book by famed children's author and illustrator Maurice Sendak.

Entertainment industry retail chains like the Disney Store and Warner Bros. Studio Store have raised consumers' expectations of the retail experience. These stores' extensive design features—like intensely themed facades and interiors, projection screens showing film and television properties, and elaborate and evolving visual merchandising displays—are being imitated by the many nonessential, fashion, gift, and impulse merchandisers that are typical of UECs, as they come to see experiential retailing as a viable competitive edge over value-oriented off-price, big-box, and outlet stores.

URBAN REVITALIZATION

The drive to revitalize blighted downtowns has created remarkable development opportunities for UECs. Following World War II, growing families seeking the middle-class luxury of homeownership—aided by government mortgage policies and transportation initiatives—led the movement of America's population to the suburbs, leaving the nation's cities in despair. In the decades that followed, private investment likewise flowed into the sprawling communities that ringed the cities, resulting in new development forms like shopping centers and industrial and business parks, which further contrib-

uted to the obsolescence of many downtowns. In general, there became fewer reasons for people to venture into the city. Meanwhile, the residents who were left in the inner cities —primarily the disadvantaged—found themselves in the center of an economic donut in which wealth continued to ripple outward.

Realizing that the vitality of the downtown is essential to the economic health and image of the entire region, governments at all levels have become actively involved in resuscitating America's cities through a spectrum of legislative and economic actions aimed at encouraging redevelopment, revitalization, adaptive use, and infill development. The goals of these revitalization efforts typically have included raising property values and taxes, increasing sales tax revenues, stemming crime, creating construction and permanent jobs, improving civic image, and attracting tourists.

To stimulate the private investment necessary to accomplish these goals, such mechanisms as cash contributions, financing aid, tax abatements, zoning and building code variances, new or improved infrastructure, and the creation of dedicated taxes for physical improvements have been commonly and strategically employed.[2] Some cities have initiated business improvement districts as well, which provide street maintenance, security, parking, marketing, and tenant recruitment services in much the same way that shopping centers do.[3]

However, cities have reevaluated the types of development that can be sustained in the inner cities, as manufacturing and even professional services become less reliant on urban locations. In large part, development related to leisure pursuits has been most attractive. Cities have sought to accentuate their remaining assets: their geographic centrality; their ability to attract tourists and business travelers; their pedestrian orientation and architectural integrity; and their established symbolic, historic, and cultural role as the heart of the region. As a result, they have largely repositioned themselves as

leisure destinations through an emphasis on arts and entertainment; dining and retail amenities; and special venues like convention centers, stadiums, and sports arenas. Importantly, they have become the exotic "nearby getaways" for consumers who desire a fleeting escape from the homogeneous suburbs (see the feature box on pages 18–19).

Sometimes urban revitalization efforts revolve around a large UEC complex like E-Walk on 42nd Street in New York's Times Square; Metreon in San Francisco, which has been developed by New York–based Millennium Partners and Sony Retail Entertainment; and the Power & Light District in Kansas City, Missouri, which is being developed by hometown theater company AMC. In other locations, the revitalization effort takes the form

of UEC districts that involve public efforts and myriad developers, such as in Old Pasadena and Santa Monica's Third Street Promenade, both in California.

Notes

1. See ULI's 1997 publication *The Retailing Revolution: The Impact of Nonstore Retailing on Shopping Centers* for a detailed discussion of this trend.

2. See ULI's *Downtown Development Handbook* for an in-depth discussion of these mechanisms.

3. See ULI's new book, *Business Improvement Districts,* for an in-depth discussion of how these districts operate and the types of functions they perform.

The introduction of cultural and entertainment activities at Navy Pier represents the revitalization of a major historic resource in downtown Chicago.

CHAPTER 2

WHAT ARE URBAN ENTERTAINMENT CENTERS?

Attempting to define urban entertainment centers is a treacherous task, as the definition is destined to be either uselessly broad or myopically focused. From small, shopping center–scale complexes such as CocoWalk in Miami's Coconut Grove to expansive revitalized urban districts like Old Pasadena in California, the projects that fall under the UEC banner are widely diverse in size, content, and context. This comes as no surprise, however. With a multitude of participants working to put these projects together—retail developers, entertainment companies, and local governments—there is no shortage of strategies or creativity.

For each of these participants, UECs are likely to mean something different. Retail developers may see them as the new-wave shopping mall. However, entertainment companies might be looking at them as the next-generation theme park. Local governments, meanwhile, are apt to view them as a fresh take on urban revitalization. The truth is that they can represent all these things. Yet that does not suggest that these diverse manifestations have nothing in common. There are, in fact, characteristics that link UECs and serve to describe—if not define—what they are.

THE TRINITY OF SYNERGY

In general, urban entertainment projects tend to offer a combination of entertainment, dining, and retail—the "trinity of synergy"—within a pedestrian-oriented environment. These amenities act independently but primarily in unison, drawing visitors from a variety of overlapping markets. This is what distinguishes urban entertainment centers from other forms of retail development. Cinemas, for instance, will attract patrons from an area three times as large as a traditional community "film zone"; food courts and restaurants can draw employees of nearby businesses at lunch time or after work; and the development as a whole may pull in visitors from an hour or more away depending on the regional competition. In addition, as well, the development often will count a number of tourists among its visitors, particularly if the development is located in an area such as Orlando or Las Vegas.

Third Street Promenade is the heart of a maturing urban entertainment district in downtown Santa Monica, California, that was developed through public/private collaboration. (Preceding page: The Entertainment Center at Irvine Spectrum.)

In the few operating UECs visitors tend to stay for a few hours and return regularly in a pattern that more closely resembles that found at shopping malls than at theme parks, although there is greater emphasis on evening activity. Regardless of the word "urban" in the name, UECs are not restricted to downtowns. They are found anywhere that enough people are found, including the suburbs and tourist spots. Nevertheless, no matter where the project happens to be, the conceptual qualities of urbanism—the density, vitality, and eclecticism of amenities—are essential.

TYPES OF URBAN ENTERTAINMENT CENTERS

Urban entertainment centers generally fall into two broad categories: districts and complexes, the latter of which includes a variety of notable subtypes. What distinguishes these categories are the processes and players responsible for their development as well as differences in form, operation, and location.

Urban Entertainment Center Districts

UEC districts are urban areas that have been revitalized and/or repositioned as leisure destinations through the development and renovation of properties and public spaces and the attraction of desirable tenants. For the most part, the urban structure of streets, sidewalks, and buildings remains intact, yet sometimes the street is closed to vehicular traffic and transformed into a pedestrian promenade, either permanently or during the evening. Examples include One Colorado in Pasadena and Santa Monica's Third Street Promenade, both in California, and Times Square in New York City.

In major metropolitan areas, the "anchor" for such redevelopment may take the form of regional destinations like stadiums, arenas, and convention centers, many of which are entertainment oriented. Often, smaller-scale amenities like cinema complexes that draw from a smaller market area are sufficient to spur rejuvenation in smaller communities. Although UEC districts can emerge organi-

	Third Street Promenade	Times Square	General
Location	Third Street between Broadway and Wilshire Boulevard in Santa Monica, California	New York City's famed Times Square	Downtown districts, many of which were formally blighted
Players	Various property owners; cinema, restaurant, and retail companies; city of Santa Monica	Tishman Urban Development Corporation; Disney; Forest City Ratner; entertainment, restaurant, and retail companies; Urban Development Corporation (UDC) of the state and city of New York	Property owners; retail developers; entertainment, restaurant, and retail companies; municipalities and government agencies
Size	Six blocks with positive effects on adjacent streets	Thirteen acres	One block and larger
Features	Cinema complexes; restaurant and retail tenants including brand chains; megaplex cinema; live performances	Hotels; live theaters; entertainment venues; 200,000-square-foot E-Walk UEC complex with theme and brand restaurants and retailers	Theme and brand restaurant and retail tenants; megaplex cinema or other destination entertainment venue, such as a stadium or arena; hotels, offices, or other mixed-uses
Summary	The area, which was an underperforming pedestrian promenade, was revitalized in three distinct phases; several cinema complexes moved in and spurred restaurant business, which in turn fueled retail business.	New York State condemned 52 properties on blighted 42nd Street and initiated redevelopment. Developers were awarded rights to develop entertainment-oriented projects.	UEC districts are seen by cities as a way to revitalize downtowns and attract business activities that have been lost to the suburbs during recent decades. Requires involvement by public and private participants.

Source: Economics Research Associates.

cally through what could be described as a "snowball effect" as businesses are a drawn to other businesses in a synergistic interaction, in most cases they owe their existence to municipal efforts to revitalize blighted areas. The authority and economic resources governments may employ in such initiatives are varied and potent. Through such mechanisms as cash contributions, financing aid, tax abatements, zoning and building code variances, new or improved infrastructure, and the creation of dedicated taxes for physical improvements, cities can create highly attractive development environments. The public benefits of revitalizing urban areas can be phenomenal: raised property values and taxes, increases in sales tax revenues, stemmed crime, creation of inner-city jobs,

As the market for theme parks in the United States nears the saturation point, companies involved in theme park development are seeking new ways to exploit their well-known brands and design and operational expertise while addressing changing leisure patterns favoring closer, more accessible leisure options. The result is massive investment in regional entertainment ventures such as the family-oriented DisneyQuest facilities and the expanding GameWorks chain, both of which are high-tech game centers developed by large and vertically integrated entertainment companies known for their premier theme parks.

DisneyQuest is the creation of the company's recently formed regional entertainment division. The company plans to build up to 30 of the 100,000-square-foot centers in cities worldwide over ten years, including sites at the company's existing resorts in Orlando, Anaheim, Tokyo, and Paris. The first center is scheduled to open at Walt Disney World in 1998, followed by one in Chicago in 1999.

At DisneyQuest, which will charge a gate fee and use a proprietary "smartcard" stored-value card system developed by American Express, there will be four distinct theme environments: the Explore Zone, a virtual adventureland where guests are immersed in exotic and ancient locales; the Score Zone, a superhero competition city where guests can match their game-playing skills against the best; the Create Zone, a private "Imagineering" studio for artistic self-expression and invention; and the Replay Zone, a carnival on the moon where guests experience a retro-futuristic spin on classic rides and games. There will be two dining areas as well, the Wired Wonderland Cafe, combining indulgent desserts and an Internet-based attraction, and FoodQuest, a quick-service café.

Meanwhile, a joint venture among Sega Enterprises, DreamWorks SKG, and Universal Studios plans to open up to 100 GameWorks centers world-wide over a five-year period that began with the opening of sites in Seattle, Las Vegas, and Ontario, California, among other locations, in 1997. Each 30,000- to 50,000-square-foot facility includes top-of-the-line video games by myriad manufacturers, several proprietary games inspired by Steven Spielberg, an Internet lounge with laptop-equipped easy chairs, food and beverage counters, and a retail boutique selling logo-emblazoned goods. The environmental theme consists of a grungy "urban chic" aesthetic of rusty metal, exposed brick walls, and grime-covered pipes evocative of a gritty MTV video.

Unlike FECs, which tend to be located along freeways in suburban communities, these high-profile regional entertainment facilities often are part of UEC complexes or districts. As with theme restaurants, the investment represented by these centers requires them to be in high-traffic and tourist-oriented areas. Such is the case with each of the first three GameWorks centers. The Seattle site is located within a block of a Planet Hollywood, Nike Town, FAO Schwarz, and Cineplex Odeon multiplex in a burgeoning UEC district. The Las Vegas site is within the Showcase UEC on the Strip. And the Ontario Mills site, outside of Los Angeles, is in a 1,700,000-square-foot off-price entertainment/retail megamall developed by the Mills Corporation and the Simon DeBartolo Group.

Source: Raymond E. Braun and Jay D. Wheatley, Economics Research Associates (ERA).

The Waverunner environment at GameWorks.

improved civic image, and amenities for tourists are a noteworthy few.

Urban Entertainment Center Complexes

UEC complexes are distinguished from districts in a number of regards. The primary difference is that instead of representing the revitalization of an *area* that encompasses numerous autonomous property owners and developers, complexes are cohesive, managed *properties* with tenants, not unlike a traditional retail center, or "mall." This means that complexes can be located outside urban areas—on "greenfield" sites in the suburbs or at resort locations, for instance—as well as in the city. Not surprisingly, complexes have emerged as natural components of districts. An illustration of this is the 200,000-square-foot E-Walk being developed by Tishman Urban Development Corporation on 42nd Street, which is a cornerstone of the 13-acre Times Square redevelopment in New York City.

As with retail centers, UEC complexes typically are the result of a retail or leisure developer acting independently or in partnership to develop a new facility or adaptively use an existing building such as a factory. In terms of operations, many of the same landlord-tenant relationships found in retail centers are found in complexes. Management usually is responsible for the upkeep of structures, parking facilities, and common areas; insurance; utilities, systems, and services; overseeing design codes; scheduling common area uses and entertainment; center marketing; mediation of intertenant disputes; and recruitment of suitable tenants. In compensation, ancillary charges in addition to rent, such as common area management (CAM) fees, are paid by the tenants. Charges tend to be higher than at typical shopping malls due mainly to UECs' higher quality of environmental design, tendency to occupy more costly real estate, and more pervasive common area entertainment.

E-Walk, a spectacular retail/entertainment/hotel project, is under construction on 42nd Street in New York City's Times Square district.

However, UEC complexes do differ from traditional retail centers in several ways. Not only do UECs have a greater emphasis on entertainment, dining, and entertainment-oriented retail in terms of tenant mix, but they also require a higher level of reinvestment and refreshment of amenities to maintain excitement. The long-term success of a complex depends on management's ability to attract tenants that create the synergistic relationships characteristic of UECs. In addition, ongoing common area entertainment as well as dynamic marketing will usually require greater attention and investment than is typical with retail centers.

	Ontario Mills	Universal CityWalk	Entertainment Center at Irvine Spectrum	General
Location	Near the juncture of Interstates 10 and 15 in Ontario, California	Outside the gates of Universal Studios Hollywood, Universal City, California	Near the juncture of Interstates 5 and 405 in Irvine, California	Highly populated urban and suburban areas; tourist spots
Players	The Mills Corporation	Universal Studios, Inc.	The Irvine Company	Entertainment companies, retail developers
Subtype	Retail destination–driven (off-price mall)	Entertainment destination–driven (theme park)	Freestanding	Regional retail or entertainment destination or freestanding
Size	1,700,000 square feet	222,000 square feet (100,000-square-foot expansion underway)	260,000 square feet (250,000-square-foot expansion underway)	150,000 square feet and larger
Features	Off-price and brand retail tenants; food court; megaplex cinema; specialty-format theater; GameWorks; Dave & Busters; American Wilderness Experience	Retail and restaurant tenants including theme and brand chains and unique local businesses; megaplex cinema; motion simulator; live performances; humorous California theme	Retail and restaurant tenants including theme and brand chains; megaplex cinema; live performances; exotic Moroccan theme	Theme and brand retail and restaurant tenants; megaplex cinema; high-tech game centers; and other entertainment venues
Summary	Ontario Mills is a large off-price retail development with nighttime-oriented entertainment amenities. The result is that Ontario Mills is a complete leisure destination, drawing visitors from throughout the Los Angeles/San Bernardino region.	Universal CityWalk was intended to bridge the existing theme park, amphitheater, and cinema complex. The project capitalizes on the large number of amphitheater and theme park visitors already being drawn to the site.	The project originated as an attempt to meet the dining needs of employees in the nearby business park. Entertainment, particularly the cinema, was included to generate nighttime and local resident business.	New-generation leisure development. UEC complexes that draw tourists or regional visitors typically include destination retail or entertainment amenities, while those without such components generally appeal to a limited market area.

Source: Economics Research Associates.

Among UEC complexes there are a number of notable subtypes:

▼ Those attached to regional suburban retail destinations.
▼ Those attached to regional entertainment destinations such as theme parks, sports venues, resort hotel casinos, and cultural or public institutions.
▼ Those that are freestanding.
▼ Those in downtowns, including Pacific Place, the Shops at Sunset Place, and Hollywood and Highland.

Retail Destinations

The competition from value-oriented retailers and the increasing demand for localized leisure options have prompted an increasing number of developers and operators of retail centers to turn to the UEC concept. In contrast to retail centers, which focus on selling tangible *merchandise*, UECs bundle entertainment, dining, and retail to create a leisure *experience*. At such large-scale retail developments as Ontario Mills in Ontario, California, and Mall of America in Bloomington, Minnesota, the inclusion of unique entertainment and dining amenities was planned from the beginning. Meanwhile, owners of existing centers—many of which date from the 1960s and 1970s and are in need of rejuvenation—have elected to transform them into UECs. Through the addition of entertainment, dining, and entertainment-oriented retail amenities, these facilities seek to expand their market area, extend visitors' length of stay, and extract more spending per capita by offering a wider range of spending opportunities. In the future such additions may fill spaces vacated by anchor department stores because of chain consolidation. For instance, in 1995, Horton Plaza in downtown San Diego

Yerba Buena Gardens is an emerging cultural and entertainment destination in San Francisco. The San Francisco Convention Center (foreground) and Museum of Modern Art (center rear) soon will be joined by Sony's Metreon entertainment center.

Photogenics

resort hotel casinos, like Caesars Palace in Las Vegas; and cultural and public institutions, like Yerba Buena Gardens in San Francisco (which is home to the city's museum of modern art as well as the nearby Moscone convention center) all have emerged as potent anchors for UEC development. Adding dining and retail amenities to a major entertainment venue is not dissimilar to infusing a retail site with entertainment and dining, as described above. In either case, the goal is to capitalize on the drawing power of a destination, lengthen patrons' visits, and broaden their spending profile.

Freestanding Destinations

UEC complexes also have been built as freestanding developments, exemplified by the Entertainment Center at Irvine Spectrum in Irvine, California, and CocoWalk in Miami's Coconut Grove. Without regional retail or entertainment drawing power, these projects tend to rely on frequent visitation from a tight resident market. This makes particular types of amenities more, or less, appropriate. In general, regardless of whether the amenity is entertainment, dining, or retail, it must generate a high level of repeat visitation. Cinema complexes, along with video game arcades and nightclubs, are highly effective at doing this, in contrast to novelty experiences such as motion simulators. Similarly, one-time-only dining place like dinner theaters or exotic theme restaurants are eschewed in favor of brand-name casual restaurants and fast-food outlets with broad appeal. Appropriate retailers include "big books" stores such as Barnes & Noble and "big music" stores such as Virgin Megastore that cater to a broad demographic range, including tourists and residents, rather than "studio stores" and niche specialty shops.

bolstered its entertainment appeal by filling a vacated Robinsons-May department store with a Planet Hollywood and the largest Sam Goody in the country and by expanding the existing United Artists Theater to 14 screens.

Entertainment Destinations

UEC complexes also frequently are developed adjacent to, or as components of, regional entertainment destinations. Theme parks, like Universal Studios Hollywood; sports venues, like the MCI Center arena in Washington, D.C.;

TYPES OF COMPONENTS

Entertainment, dining, and retail amenities are, in essence, the subatomic particles of the UEC universe, each representing a fundamental mode of consumption. Entertainment, for instance, is a type of *experiential consumption* in which the consumer pays for the opportunity to experience something that is pleasurable, yet ephemeral. Dining is a type of *literal consumption* in which the consumer pays to consume food or drink on the spot. And shopping is a type of *acquisition consumption* in which the consumer pays to acquire an object to take home for long-lasting or later enjoyment.

In UECs, not only are these modes compatible, they are complementary. Theme restaurants like Hard Rock Cafe have retail boutiques while Borders Books & Music stores have in-store cafés. Movie theaters sell snacks and beverages from concession counters while Planet Hollywood portrays Hollywood glamour by projecting movie clips on its walls. Virtual reality centers like Virtual World sell brand-name souvenir merchandise while the REI (Recreational Equipment Inc.) flagship store in Seattle offers a virtual hiking trail and a rain simulation room in which to test outdoor gear. The point is that in UECs the three components—entertainment, dining, and retail—are intertwined and nested in one another in every conceivable way. This, of course, makes categorizing components somewhat challenging. For instance, should a dinner theater be classified as dining or entertainment? But it is this sort of *dynamic ambiguity* that is the soul of the UEC development type. Some of the most common components of UECs follow below.

Entertainment

Various types of dedicated entertainment can be found in UECs, each one effective in its own way. *Ambient entertainment*, in the form of festive architecture and free street performances, for instance, is a passive yet powerful tool in disarming patrons and cueing them into the center's leisure focus. Meanwhile, *impulse entertainment*, like carousels and rock-climbing walls, provide visitors with opportunities for spontaneous experiences. Finally, *destination entertainment*, including cinema complexes, live theaters, and sports venues, serve to draw traffic to the center,

---

UEC CONSUMPTION MODES: "TRINITY OF SYNERGY"

Entertainment

Experiential Consumption

Experience that is pleasurable yet ephemeral

Dining

Literal Consumption

Food of beverage to be consumed on the spot

Retail

Acquisition Consumption

Objects to take home for long-term or later enjoyment

Source: Economics Research Associates.

NESTING OF ENTERTAINMENT, DINING, AND RETAIL

Entertainment	Dining	Retail
GameWorks	**Planet Hollywood**	**Borders Books & Music**
Entertainment video games, Internet access, theming	**Entertainment** movie memorabilia, video screens, theming	**Entertainment** live jazz, reading chairs
Dining brewpub/café/coffee bar	**Dining** full-service restaurant	**Dining** café/coffee bar
Retail boutique with logo t-shirts, hats, jackets	**Retail** boutique with logo t-shirts, hats, jackets	**Retail** books/recorded music

Source: Economics Research Associates.

leading to spillover business for adjoining restaurants, retailers, and other entertainment venues.

Ambient Entertainment

Ambient entertainment, in many respects, is the lowest common denominator of UEC entertainment. Through environmental design themes and public performances in common areas, ambient entertainment serves to set the mood, establishing the UEC's role as a leisure destination in which merely visiting the center is enjoyable regardless of the stores one patronizes. By extending the duration of guests' visits and inducing them to linger and browse, ambient entertainment works to the special advantage of the UEC's retailers, restaurants, and providers of impulse entertainment.

Environmental design is a customary embodiment of ambient entertainment. Whereas traditional shopping malls built in the 1960s and 1970s tended by comparison to be rational and functional in design, today's UECs are designed to exude excitement, energy, and creativity. This is achieved through the unconventional manipulation of design variables like materials, scale, composition, and context. Such features as theme architecture, dynamic signage, bold landscaping, unique lighting, and interesting "street" fixtures like fountains and kiosks are part and parcel of the UEC landscape. For instance, the dazzling streetscape of Universal CityWalk combines fantasy architecture, surreal signage—including a towering King Kong scaling a building facade—interactive fountains, and enormous props such as a spaceship crashed into a building facade. This aesthetic is borrowed in part from European streets and piazzas but also from the theme park industry, leading an increasing number of theme park designers and fabricators to become active in the retail sector.

Free "street" performances, another form of ambient entertainment, strive to replicate the spontaneity and festivity of the archetypal, if not mythical, marketplace. Because they are dynamic and often interactive, these performances can be highly effective in energizing and engaging crowds. There are several types of common area performances.

Authentic performances are given by street musicians, actors, magicians, jugglers, and so forth who perform solely for tips and are not formally sponsored or invited to the UEC. Almost exclusively, they are found in public spaces like sidewalks and parks in UEC districts. These performers represent the historic archetype upon which all common area performances are based. Yet, because they work independently, their performances can be unpredictable, making them potentially disruptive to both visitors and tenants. Thus, they are not commonly allowed on the private property of UEC complexes.

Sanctioned performances resemble authentic performances yet are explicitly permitted or even contracted for in common areas of UECs. Although sanctioned performers aim to replicate the liveliness of authentic performances, there are several distinctions. They tend to exclude some of the more unusual offerings characteristic of the authentic genre, such as psychics, palm readers, mannequin imitators, and so forth. However, they commonly include performers not typical of au-

thentic performances, like roaming robots and costumed characters. In general, they tend to feature a higher level of presentation in terms of costumes and stage set-ups. In addition, they frequently are scheduled for specific times of the day and week to target particular visitor segments. For example, costumed characters or magicians that appeal to children would be scheduled during the day, while reggae or jazz bands would be scheduled in the evening.

Programmed entertainment like fashion shows, arts and crafts festivals, traveling museum displays, and opportunities to be photographed with Santa Claus can occur in common areas or public spaces at UECs. These programmed and promoted events are arranged by complex managers and district associations for the purpose of drawing crowds to the center and establishing community rapport. Thus, programmed entertainment can become a temporary form of destination entertainment. It may be financed entirely by center owners or through marketing funds to which tenants contribute.

The latest concept in performances features audience participation. At Universal Studios, Florida, a live show, *Hercules & Zena, Wizards of the Screen,* uses a dozen different audience members at each performance.

Universal Studios Florida

33

Impulse Entertainment

Impulse entertainment provides opportunities for guests to pay, on a whim, to engage in spontaneous experiences that fulfill their immediate needs and desires. Attractions like carousels, rock-climbing walls, bungee-trampolines, portrait artists, and human gyroscopes can be located in common areas, giving them the visibility that may lead to impulse sales. They also can serve as an effective form of ambient entertainment for nonparticipants who gather to watch and enjoy the experience vicariously. They be operated by center management or by outside vendors under special arrangement. Other impulse entertainment attractions like motion simulators and virtual reality and video games typically are operated as dedicated attractions or within entertainment venues like indoor theme parks, family entertainment centers, and high-tech game centers (see the feature box on page 44).

There are several similarities among impulse entertainment experiences. One, they are of short duration. Two, there are frequent or continuous entry opportunities. And three, access, for instance through the purchase of tickets, can be obtained on site just prior to entry. Beyond these common characteristics, impulse entertainment attractions can vary in a number of regards. Some, like rock-climbing walls or virtual reality experiences, are interactive—meaning that involvement of the patron is more or less essential for the experience to take place—while others, like motion simulators or carousels, are not. Some, like video games or motion simulators, accept new media or software that ensures their novelty, while others, like carousels, remain unchanged. In addition, some, like simulators and carousels, can accommodate a group of participants at once while others, like bungee-trampolines or portrait artists, can accommodate only one. However, most impulse entertainment experiences are either interactive or accept new media or software, attributes essential to ensuring repeat visits. In fact, even the theme park industry is witnessing a greater demand for these attributes in new attractions.

Impulse entertainment is highly flexible in most regards, allowing new attractions to emerge in response to evolving cultural and technological developments. In many cases they are portable and leased or operated through a revenue split arrangement, allowing "fad" experiences to be added and removed with the ebb and flow of customer interest. For instance, rock-climbing walls, bungee-trampolines, and human gyroscopes fit the extreme sports trend of recent years. The new REI flagship store in Seattle is equipped with a 65-foot climbing pinnacle and other "demonstration stations" that allow customers to test the sports merchandise sold in the store. According to *American Demographics* (June 1997), the U.S. Bungee Association estimated that seven million bungee jumps have occurred since the late 1980s; the U.S. Parachute Association reported that its membership grew 10 percent annually in the prior two years; and membership in the American Mountain Guide Association skyrocketed 3 percent per *month* during the preceding two years.

Destination Entertainment

Destination entertainment venues fulfill a critical role in drawing traffic to a UEC. Examples include

▼ Casinos
▼ Cinema complexes
▼ Dinner theaters
▼ Educational facilities
▼ Family entertainment centers (FECs)
▼ High-tech game centers
▼ Indoor theme parks
▼ Live performance theaters
▼ Nightclubs
▼ Specialty-format film theaters
▼ Sports venues.

All these venues attract large crowds of people at the same time and tend to appeal to a broad demographic range. Worth not-

Caesars Palace Hotel and Casino is a major destination that fulfills the critical role of drawing traffic to the Forum Shops, one of the most successful shopping/entertainment centers in the United States.

ing, however, is that as the brevity, frequency, and accessibility of a destination entertainment experience increase, the more it tends to behave like impulse entertainment. For instance, with megaplex cinemas, patrons are guaranteed that screenings will begin several times an hour, allowing them to catch a movie on impulse rather than having to plan an entire day or evening around a particular showtime, as was customary in the past. Conversely, various impulse entertainment attractions when found in a family entertainment center or indoor theme park often behave in unison as destination entertainment.

Casinos are a form of destination entertainment that can be massively profitable for operators and a lucrative source of tax revenues for local governments. During the last ten years or so, casino gambling has expanded outside of Las Vegas and Atlantic City to become a regional attraction. Casinos

now are operated by Indian tribes in 23 states, on riverboat casinos in six, and in limited land-based casinos in three. In Las Vegas, where entertainment has long coexisted with casinos in the form of live shows, new forms of diversion have appeared in an attempt to broaden the city's appeal to vacationing families.

So far the results have been mixed. Casinos that do not have entertainment reportedly are losing market share to those that do, as the share of revenue from gaming declines and the share from hotels and entertainment increases. Encouragement comes from successes like Caesars Palace, which profitably melded casino gambling with retail, restaurants, and entertainment amenities with the addition of the Forum Shops in 1992. (See case study in Chapter 5). The 250,000-square-foot retail and restaurant complex, which recently was expanded, reportedly has retail

In the new New York–New York Hotel & Casino in Las Vegas, Nevada, a state-of-the-art, fully themed family entertainment center, Coney Island Emporium, sits on the second floor. The evolution and thematic development of this facility is the story of a close working arrangement among Amusement Consultants Ltd. of New Rochelle, New York (the operational partner and owner), the design team of Haverson Architecture and Design of Greenwich, Connecticut, and the hotel itself.

When the New York–New York project was announced, there was no plan to include a family entertainment center. The project already included a Greenwich Village food court, a Park Avenue shopping area, and a theater district for entertainment. Amusement Consultants saw an opportunity—what the New York–themed project needed was a Coney Island!

With operational experience at the real Coney Island in Brooklyn, New York, and a family history in New York City stretching back generations, Amusement Consultants wanted to an create an entertainment center that would evoke the sights, sounds, tastes, and smells of the real Coney Island at the turn of the century at the New York–New York Hotel & Casino.

Development of A Concept

Amusement Consultants called on Haverson Architecture and Design to come up with some sketches based on its preliminary ideas that could be presented to the hotel. The concept had to be profitable for the hotel and for the company, and it had to capture the essence of Coney Island, a place of magic in its heyday.

Steeplechase Park offers bumper cabs, laser patrol, and a prize redemption center. The development strategy concentrated on a midway-style games operation, a form of entertainment that has been successful in a variety of Las Vegas casino venues.

Amusement Consultants presented Haverson's descriptive vignettes to hotel executives. They showed many of the elements needed to create the look and feel of the space: a scenic roller coaster overhead that would run through various parts of the center; a parachute that would be a central feature, reminiscent of the famous parachute drop ride at Coney Island; a variety of facades copied from various Coney Island amusements; and scenes of staff members in classic arcade dress portraying vendors, hawkers, and entertainers. As the hotel was using various time periods in its own theming, a variety of time periods were included.

The decision was made to concentrate on a midway-style games operation, a form of entertainment that had been successful in a variety of casino venues in Las Vegas. Coin-operated equipment as well as a fully stocked redemption center was used to support this part of the operation.

The idea of bumper cars was added, then bumper *cabs*. Next, to make the idea really fly, it was decided to transform the ride area into a facade of New York City, with a sound package duplicating the noises of downtown traffic.

A laser tag arena, called N.Y.N.Y. Laser Patrol, was designed as a New York street, with street lamps, shop fronts, and another sound package. Virtual reality attractions, a multiplayer driving simulator, and an old-time shooting gallery (updated with modern electronics) created almost all the elements necessary for attaining the length of stay

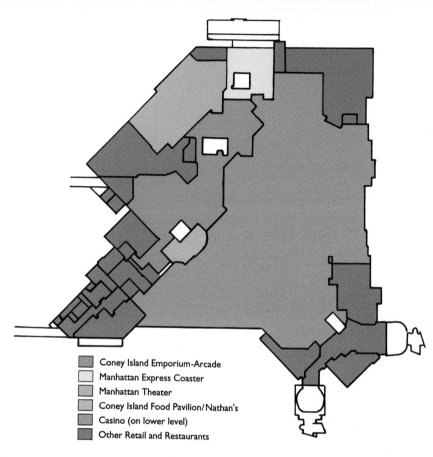

- Coney Island Emporium-Arcade
- Manhattan Express Coaster
- Manhattan Theater
- Coney Island Food Pavilion/Nathan's
- Casino (on lower level)
- Other Retail and Restaurants

Coney Island Emporium is situated on a portion of the second floor of the New York–New York Hotel overlooking Central Park Casino.

needed to make the Coney Island Emporium successful.

Operational Refinements

Serious consideration began of the operational functionality of each attraction and the difficulty inherent in placing each one. The New York–New York hotel designers had designated a portion of the second floor of the hotel for the entertainment center that had originally been a catering hall. There were large structural columns and elevator shafts throughout the site, and space was at a premium. The logistics of the operation

and the need for merchandise storage facilities were a challenge.

Many of the features of the area were both positive and negative. The entertainment center was to serve as both entrance and exit to the $12 million Manhattan Express roller coaster and also as an entrance to the hotel itself, requiring a 24-hour operation with all of the associated challenges. Including an entertainment project within a larger entity such as a hotel or shopping complex demands a financial arrangement that recognizes that the fortunes of the entertainment project rise and fall with those of the larger facility. That is certainly the

Gridlock Alert Bumper Cabs™ occupies one of the major activity zones at Coney Island Emporium.

The systems for cash control and computer tracking, many of them based on proprietary software, are unique to the facility. Many were designed in house by Amusement Consultants, then tested at the company's New Rochelle office and shipped out for installation at Coney Island Emporium.

Periodicals, books, videotapes, and poster images were researched to prepare a history of Coney Island. A plan was developed to organize the space into four distinct areas representing the three original parks that constituted Coney Island: Luna Park, Dreamland, and Steeplechase. A contemporary "New York Fun" area with a subway/industrial theme was added for the laser tag and bumper cab attractions.

Various manufacturers were contacted to create variations on traditional and contemporary games that would be consistent with the facility's overall theme. Selection of merchandise for the midway games and redemption center and the development

case with Coney Island Emporium, which depends on the roller coaster, run by the hotel, to drive business its way.

The financial arrangements were negotiated with this in mind. The deal with the hotel was arranged on a percentage basis, with New York–New York Hotel & Casino benefiting from the success of Coney Island Emporium. This type of arrangement creates the kind of mutual cooperation between landlord and tenant that benefits both parties by ensuring that needed changes will be made to upgrade and update the entertainment offerings at the hotel (or shopping center) as the years go by.

As the deal with the hotel solidified, initial space layouts were prepared to "zone" the location of the coin-operated games, midway games, bumper cars, and the laser tag and administrative areas. Because base

construction was proceeding on the space, the time frame was short. Thematic components were designed for game facades and counters, along with wiring for electronic control systems and computers; all design and operational work proceeded simultaneously.

Coney Island Emporium™ Features

▼ 32,000 square feet of attractions
▼ N.Y.N.Y. Laser Patrol™
▼ Gridlock Alert Bumper Cabs™
▼ Daytona USA deluxe multiplayer driving simulator
▼ Virtual-reality Pac-Man
▼ Coney Island theme electronic shooting gallery
▼ 22 midway games with plush prizes
▼ 180 coin-operated amusement and redemption games
▼ Redemption center with 25 linear feet of showcases
▼ Coney Island Emporium™ serves as an entrance to the New York–New York Hotel & Casino™ and as the entrance and exit to the Manhattan Express™ roller coaster

of the Coney Island Emporium logo and custom merchandise proceeded along the same lines. A complete package with thematically consistent components had to be in place on the day of the hotel's grand opening.

Dreams into Reality

After field surveys were completed, each area of the facility was developed with a specific visual theme in mind. Luna Park has repetitive arched openings with twisted minarets; Steeplechase Park is adorned with large murals of vintage photos depicting Coney Island visitors having fun; and the area that was to be Dreamland was changed to the Tunnel of Love. Each area has a color theme that is distinct from the others.

New York icons were used to create internally illuminated graphics for each midway game, from the humorous Summer in the City with fire hydrants and Dalmatians as prizes, to Wack-A-Mayor with various molded reproductions of the heads of New York mayors, to simple plays on words and sight gags. A traditional peach basket game, for example, became Tunnel Toss; the baskets were transformed into New York City tunnels and labeled Lincoln, Holland, Queens-Midtown, and Brooklyn-Battery.

A lighting scheme was developed to create an outdoor feeling with festive chasing lights, sign lighters, pin spots, and cove horizons to accentuate the scenic architecture and provide color and depth. In Luna Park, the shooting gallery design, which included three dimensional targets set in a beach scene with a backdrop of

The Parachute Jump greets visitors at the entrance of Coney Island Emporium.

painted rides and attractions, was combined with sideshow poster reproductions. All the ideas began to come together, and as construction continued, more details were added. At this point, amusement equipment was being delivered and installed; testing and connection to control equipment followed.

A sound package was installed on the overhead roller coaster that recreated the sound of a Coney Island roller coaster in full four-channel splendor, and a Nathan's restaurant selling hot dogs and French fries was placed in the middle of the facility. With the hot dogs and freshly popped popcorn, the Emporium even smelled like Coney Island—all that was missing was the ocean!

The management staff, all trained and experienced Amusement Consultants cast members, worked with newly hired Las Vegas cast to rehearse the

procedures and skills needed to "create smiles" on the faces of all the guests on opening night.

The grand opening of the New York–New York Hotel & Casino and Coney Island Emporium was a tremendous success. Attendance for the first three days of operation was estimated at 68,000, 85,000, and 55,000 people, respectively. From the beginning, the development team wanted to create something new and exciting. If the guest response is any indication, they accomplished their goal at Coney Island Emporium.

Source: Michael Getlan, Amusement Consultants Ltd., in cooperation with Haverson Architecture and Design.

sales per square foot of more than $1,200, the highest in the nation.

Cinema complexes are, without doubt, the quintessential destination entertainment component of UECs (see feature box on page 42). In fact, it is difficult to find an example of a UEC that does not include a movie theater. Although cinemas have rather modest per-square-foot earnings in comparison with restaurants and retail stores, they have an unequaled ability to attract repeat visitors because they offer a continually refreshed supply of entertainment. In order to exploit cinema complexes' considerable traffic generating abilities, developers now are locating them in prime locations within the shopping center proper rather than on the outskirts of the parking lot, where they once were relegated.

Dinner theaters serve complete table-service meals and usually have defined per-

Marco Lorenzetti: Hedrich-Blessing

The spectacular Sony Theaters at Lincoln Square in New York City, designed by Gensler, provide state-of-the-art movie going, including a 3-D IMAX screen.

formance and seating times, yet their main draw is their unique entertainment value. The types of performance found in dinner theaters can range enormously. Along with the classic form of dinner theater, in which live music or dancing is performed on a stage, multitudes of innovative concepts have emerged. For instance, performance-cooking in open display kitchens or on table-based grills, as popularized by Benihana in the 1970s, allows patrons to observe skilled chefs engage in theatrical knifework. Robotic dinner-theater performances, as found at Chuck E. Cheese, use "audio-animatronic" characters—pioneered by Disney—to enact musical shows at programmed intervals. Action spectaculars like Medieval Times and Buffalo Bill's offer a spectacle of live stunts, costuming, and special effects all based on horse-riding scenarios within a central indoor arena. In these facilities, diners are divided into groups and are encouraged to root for one of several competing teams of performers. Meanwhile, at Caesars Magical Empire at Caesars Palace in Las Vegas, guests witness enchanting effects first hand. Murder-mystery dining experiences are another type of dinner theater, challenging patrons to solve a crime over the course of a meal.

Educational facilities, or "edutainment," have emerged as a unique category of destination entertainment for UECs that likely will become more prevalent as the population ages in coming years. Decades ago, marine, zoological, and botanical parks like the Sea World chain and Busch Gardens Tampa Bay in Florida established the potential for educational leisure ventures. Today, cable television channels like Discovery Channel, A&E (Arts & Entertainment), History Channel, Animal Planet, and so forth illustrate the education boom in another typical entertainment medium.

The possibilities for education-oriented features in UECs go beyond retail tenants like the Museum Co., Nature Company (which is being renamed by its new owners, the Discovery Channel), and Scientific Revolution

DESTINATION ENTERTAINMENT TYPES

Type	Description	Examples
Casinos	Casinos with games of chance and/or skill	Circus Circus; MGM Grand; Luxor; Star Trek Experience; Las Vegas
Cinema complexes	"Category killer" complexes with up to 30+ screens	AMC 30-screen at Ontario Mills, Ontario; Edwards 21-screen cinema at Entertainment Center, Irvine Spectrum, Irvine, California
Dinner theaters	Complete meals accompanied by a live performance	Caesars Magical Empire, Caesars Palace, Las Vegas
Educational facilities	Museums, aquariums, halls of fame, hands-on exhibits, extension classrooms	National Sports Gallery, MCI Center, Washington, D.C.; UCLA Extension, Universal CityWalk, Los Angeles
Family entertainment centers (FECs)	Traditional mix of games and attractions on pay-as-you-go basis, often with concession stands and party rooms	Coney Island Emporium, New York City; Las Vegas
High-tech game centers	Off-the-shelf and proprietary technology-based games in enclosed center, often with café and retail boutique	Dave & Busters; DisneyQuest; GameWorks
Indoor theme parks	Full-sized rides, show, and attractions; food and beverage outlets; souvenir shops	Camp Snoopy, Mall of America, Minneapolis; Galaxyland, West Edmonton Mall, Canada
Live performance theaters	Scheduled live shows with theater seating	Country music theaters of Branson, Missouri; New Amsterdam Theater, 42nd Street, Times Square, New York City
Nightclubs	Alcoholic beverages in conjunction with performances or interactive activities	Billboard Live!, the Venetian, Las Vegas; House of Blues, Wildhorse Saloon, Walt Disney World
Specialty-format film theaters	Large-format, domed, 360-degree, 3-D film presentations; films with computer-controlled seating linked to on-screen action	Sony Theaters 3-D IMAX, Lincoln Center, New York; 3-D IMAX Entertainment Center, Irvine Spectrum, Irvine, California; Iwerks Ultrascreen, Ontario Mills, Ontario
Sports venues	Stadiums, arenas	Candlestick Mills, L.A. Arena Project; MCI Center, Washington, D.C.

Source: Economics Research Associates.

MEGAPLEX CINEMAS

Changes in the nature of theater exhibition in recent years have served to accentuate the benefits of cinema complexes as UEC draws. Between 1980 and 1996 the number of movie screens has more than doubled in the United States, while the number of cinema locations has remained relatively stable. Explaining this phenomenon is the fact that cinemas have been increasing the number of auditoriums per location and reducing their size. At first, large single-screen movie houses were split to form two auditoriums. Then new theaters were designed as multiplexes, as pioneered by AMC in the 1960s. Currently, the vogue is megaplex—or category killer—cinema complexes with up to 20 or 30 screens per facility. For patrons, this means a wider selection of movies, from Hollywood blockbusters to niche art films, and increased frequency of showings at a given site. Theater-going thus has become more convenient for consumers, even allowing movies to serve as impulse entertainment.

Meanwhile, a slew of technical advancements has improved the cinema experience, making it both more thrilling and more comfortable. Larger screens; steep stadium seating, which enhances viewing; and directional digital sound have intensified movies' sensory impact. Wider, more

AMC's 24-screen Grand Theater in Dallas lives up to its name.

plush seats with higher backs and moveable arm rests that allow patrons to sit "love seat" style raise the comfort level. Other modern enhancements include spacious lobby areas with more sophisticated food and beverage options, retail boutiques, and handicapped amenities.

Theater chains also are adding specialty-format film theaters to their multiplexes to broaden their appeal. Edwards Theaters and Regal Cinemas, for instance, each has plans to open IMAX 3-D theaters in upcoming multiplexes. Furthermore, some cinema chains are developing multifaceted, cinema-based entertainment center concepts in house, such as Regal Cine-

ma's Funscape and adult-oriented the Escape locations. Meanwhile, others are coventuring with theme restaurants and entertainment-oriented retailers to form other products. "Planet Movies by AMC," among the first of such endeavors, is a joint venture that will combine Planet Hollywood theme restaurants and AMC cinemas along with additional retail and entertainment offerings at sites worldwide. Similarly, Carmike Cinemas, Wal-Mart, and Ultrazone laser tag are involved in a coventure.

Source: Raymond E. Braun and Jay D. Wheatley, Economics Research Associates (ERA).

and temporary exhibits like the Smithsonian Institution Traveling Exhibitions (SITES), all of which already are found in retail centers. They also have taken the form of permanent educational facilities like the UnderWater World aquarium at the Mall of America, Pier 39 in San Francisco, and the National Sports Gallery at Washington, D.C.'s MCI Center. Another UEC site anchored by education amenities is Yerba Buena Gardens in San Francisco, which is bordered by the Visual Arts Center, Performing Arts Center, and San

Francisco Museum of Art on a adjacent block. Similarly, at Baltimore's Inner Harbor there is a children's museum, marine biology exposition, city life museum, and visionary art museum.

The experiential focus of UECs makes them even more suitable for educational amenities than shopping malls. At Universal CityWalk, for example, a UCLA extension center where classes are held by the University of California, Los Angeles, sits side by side with theme restaurants and cinemas. Rather than being merely a community service, extension classes also are a mode of entertainment, offering students an opportunity to meet people, improve themselves, and explore their hobbies and interests. The Disney Institute at Walt Disney World, which offers educational programs in a resort setting, and the rise of "eco-resorts" worldwide further demonstrate the viability of educational entertainment.

Family entertainment centers, or FECs, which can range from 20,000 square feet to 100,000 square feet, typically comprise a large number of impulse entertainment attractions like video games, redemption games such as Skeeball, virtual reality experiences, motion simulators, rock-climbing walls, and batting cages, which in unison create a destination entertainment venue. Because many of these individual activities are highly participatory, they are highly repeatable, encouraging repeat visitation. Certain traditional FEC components that tend to be the most destination oriented—like miniature golf, bumper boats, soft modular play equipment, and go-karts—are less able to fit within the physical constraints of indoor UEC-based FECs. Nevertheless, FECs have been an increasingly popular tenant at shopping malls, often filling vacancies left by anchor department stores.

High-tech game centers are indoor facilities featuring interactive computer, simulation, and online games. They range from 30,000 square feet, such as Dave & Busters and GameWorks, to 100,000 square feet, such as DisneyQuest. Along with cutting-edge, off-the-shelf and proprietary games, these centers also frequently offer traditional games such as billiards and darts to create broad-based appeal. They are differentiated from FECs by their greater adult and nighttime orientation and the common inclusion of sophisticated food and beverage options, from quick-service cafés à la Cheescake Factory to brand-name microbrewery beer and gourmet coffee counters. In addition, they frequently are developed as brand-name chains by well-funded entertainment companies and they typically are located within UEC complexes and districts. In contrast, FECs have a traditional suburban stand-alone format (see the feature box on page 44).

Indoor theme parks range from 100,000 square feet to 500,000 square feet and can be found in such massive developments as the West Edmonton Mall in Edmonton, Canada; the Mall of America in Bloomington, Minnesota; and the Circus Circus resort casino in Las Vegas. They also are found increasingly throughout Asia. These venues can feature a higher caliber of attractions than FECs, including full-sized rides like roller coasters and log flumes. Yet their size, autonomy, and breadth of amenities—attractions, food and beverage outlets, and souvenir shops—create the potential for their serving as an alternative rather than a complement to the UEC as a whole. In other cases, these venues may occupy younger visitors, to whom they especially appeal, while their parents patronize more adult-oriented amenities like retail, restaurants, casinos, and shows.

Live performance theaters, characterized by scheduled, ticketed stage shows and theater seating, are another increasingly popular form of destination entertainment venue. The success of Branson, Missouri, which draws visitors from hundreds of miles to enjoy big-name country music entertainers in indoor theaters, has been a great inspiration in this regard. Another example is Disney's renovation of the New Amsterdam theater on 42nd Street in New York City's Times Square, which serves as a home for the company's Broadway-style productions.

ACRONYM SOUP

Children's Entertainment Center—CEC

Offers children's games and attractions, with admission charge. Commonly includes soft modular play systems, party rooms, redemption games, art and crafts, edutainment experiences, and concession stands. Operated by a single business entity.

Examples: Club Disney; Discovery Zone; Jeepers

Entertainment-Oriented Retail—EOC

Retail stores with interactive and entertainment-oriented in-store displays and activities, from kiosks to cafés. Often these stores act as brand-building marketing devices for manufacturers and entertainment companies.

Examples: Barnes & Noble Bookseller, Bass Pro Shops Outdoor World, Borders Books & Music, the Disney Store, NikeTown, Planet Reebok, REI Seattle, Warner Bros. Studio Store, Virgin Records Megastore

Family Entertainment Center—FEC

Indoor and/or outdoor facility offering traditional mix of games and attractions on pay-as-you-go basis. Commonly includes video-game arcades, mini-golf, go-karts, batting cages, and concession stands. Operated by a single business entity.

Examples: Exhilarama; Fun Factory; Mountasia; Nickels & Dimes; Putt Putt Golf & Games; Regal Cinemas Funscape; Q-City

Location-Based Entertainment—LBE

(1) Any form of commercial out-of-home entertainment. (2) A facility dedicated to one attraction type in contrast to FECs, which have multiple attraction types, or facilities that do not fit within other categories, like high-tech game centers.

Examples: (1) CECs; FECs; UECs; theme parks. (2) American Wilderness Experience; Dave & Busters; DisneyQuest; GameWorks; IMAX; skating rinks; virtual reality parlors

Urban Entertainment Center—UEC
Urban Entertainment Destination—UED
Leisure Entertainment Destination—LEC
Retail Dining Entertainment—RDE

Offers a synergistic combination of entertainment, food and beverage, and retail. May take the form of a (1) cohesively owned and operated complex with tenants or a (2) downtown district of independent property owners/tenants.

Examples: (1) Universal CityWalk; CocoWalk; Entertainment Center at Irvine Spectrum; Mall of America. (2) Old Pasadena; Santa Monica's Third Street Promenade; Times Square/42nd Street

Source: Economics Research Associates.

Nightclubs include establishments that primarily serve alcoholic beverages in conjunction with performances and interactive activities and provide table seating as well as standing room. These facilities typically revolve around a particular theme, thereby attracting a clientele with specific tastes in alcohol or entertainment. Types of nightclubs include sports bars, country-western bars, "techno" dance clubs, comedy clubs, martini bars, jazz clubs, piano bars, and so forth. Gaylord Entertainment's Wildhorse Saloon, the House of Blues at Walt Disney World's Pleasure Island, and Billboard Live! are high-profile examples.

Specialty-format films, or large-format films, as the most common versions are called, employ variations in screen size, aspect ratio, seating configuration, sound quality, and image definition to create a more immersive and therefore high-impact theater-going experience. Exotic manifestations such as domed screens, 3-D, and 360-degree presentations—in which a ring of screens completely surrounds viewers—illustrate the extent of innovation in this genre. Although specialty-format films have long been incorporated into visitor destinations like theme parks, museums, and world's fairs, they only recently have been integrated into cinema megaplexes and entertainment retail developments (see feature box on page 42).

Sports venues as destinations have proliferated in recent years in response to a number of factors. In some cases, such as Baltimore's Camden Yards, sports venues have been part of municipal planners' efforts to revitalize the downtown district. When new sports venues are built, complementary businesses, including restaurants and retail, often

At GameWorks, the Arena is the heart of its interactive computer, simulation, and online games.

Technological advances during the last few decades have led to the development of captivating new forms of entertainment like motion simulators, specialty-format films, video games, and virtual reality attractions. Similarities among them allow them to be easily confused with one another. Other than the fact that they are all "high tech" and under constant improvement in response to cutting-edge hardware and software developments, they each also offer participants the illusion of being in another world. Further adding to the confusion are new hybrids created by combining the various attributes and technologies of these attractions.

Motion Simulators

Derived from military and commercial pilot training technologies of the 1970s, motion simulators synchronize physical movement and imagery to provide the audience with the realistic sensation that they are moving. Operators' enthusiasm about motion simulators is due both to their ability to offer a thrill-ride-caliber experience in a minimum of space as well as their use of changeable media—in the form of film and motion programming—that allows the attraction to offer new experiences using the same motion base.

Motion simulators are composed of two elements. One is the motion base, which is the mechanism that moves the audience. The other is the film or video presentation, which can either be projected onto a screen or displayed on a monitor. A variety of motion-base platforms exist, from

two-person capsules to cabins seating several dozen people. With some platforms the screen upon which the image is displayed is mounted to, and moves with, the platform; in others the motion base is positioned in front of, yet remains detached from, the screen. In all cases, the motion is supplied by some array of hydraulic, pneumatic, or electromagnetic actuators that follow a programmed sequence that is orchestrated when the film is produced.

The Tour of the Universe at Toronto's CN Tower, which made its debut in 1985, is credited with establishing simulators as a viable attraction. Other high points in simulator development include the opening of the Star Tours attraction at Disneyland in 1987 and the Back to the Future ride at Universal Studios Florida in 1991. The compact size and, in many cases, portability of simulators have facilitated their use in various venues, including theme parks, museums, festivals, shopping centers, and UECs. For instance, Showscan (which was acquired by Iwerks in 1997) operates the Cinemania simulator at Universal City-Walk, while Pier 39 in San Francisco features an Iwerks TurboRide. As with specialty-format films, the availability of new films is critical to the growth of motion simulators. Moreover, the singular emphasis on movement, as with

The compact size of motion simulators, such as the one created and operated by Iwerks, has helped make them popular not only in UECs but also in museums, theme parks, and shopping centers.

other thrill rides, tends to relegate this attraction to being a novelty experience.

Specialty-Format Films

Specialty-format film presentations combine digital surround sound and enormous screen images that surpass the viewer's field of view to give audiences the stunning cinematographic illusion that they are *in* the film. The most common specialty-format films are large-format films, which feature flat screens up to 70 by 100 feet in size. Other types include domed screens; 3-D films, which require viewers to wear polarized glasses; and 360-degree presentations, which surround viewers with a complete ring of screens for a surreal sense of immersion. Technically, specialty-format film types are distinguished by their frame size and perf count (number of perforations per frame along the edges of the film strip). Theater configuration likewise varies among different formats, although most feature steep stadium seating. Films tend to be around 40 minutes long, and they usually feature a documentary-style presentation about nature, space, or history.

Large-format films have existed since the 1920s under such brand names as Cinerama and Vistavision; today, IMAX of Toronto and Iwerks of Burbank, California, are the leading producers. In recent decades, specialty-format films have been more prevalent at entertainment venues like theme parks, museums, and world's fairs than at community facilities. Because these tourist-oriented

IMAX uses the largest film frame in motion picture history—a 70-mm, 15-perforation format. *Destiny in Space* **is on screen.**

entertainment venues commonly feature specially produced films related to the mission or theme of the sponsoring institution, the institution is able to exhibit the same film for months or even years, allowing the venue to amortize the costs associated with producing and exhibiting the film over its lifetime. This is quite unlike regular cinemas, which require a constant stream of new commercial movies each week.

The ability of specialty-format film venues to attract local audiences on a recurring basis—the key to their effectiveness as a UEC draw—relies on the continued production of new films, as for the regular cinema. However, film producers are reluctant to produce expensive specialty-format films until there are enough theaters in which to show them to make it worthwhile; therefore, the specialty-format film sector seems destined to grow incrementally.

Recently, however, specialty-format films have made inroads into community theater and entertainment complexes. Such cinemas as the Sony Theater complex at Lincoln Square in New York City and the Edwards Theaters cinema at the Entertainment Center at Irvine Spectrum have incorporated specialty-format film theaters within their facilities. In fact, leading theater chains like Edwards Theaters, AMC Theaters, and Regal Cinemas recently have announced wide-scale plans to include specialty-format film theaters in forthcoming multiplexes. Eventually, it is expected that Hollywood studios will begin producing narrative films in specialty formats as long as there are a sufficient number of screens on which to show them.

Video Games

Video games have been a popular form of entertainment since 1972, when Nolan Bushnel, founder of Atari, released Pong, creating the first video game sensation. Although primitive by today's standards, the game of pixel paddle-ball became a mainstay of bars and restaurants and gave birth to today's multibillion dollar industry. Although the ensuing growth in computer processing power has led to much more complicated graphics and game play during the past quarter century, in most respects video games have remained the same. Generally, they still come in stand-up and sit-down formats; offer a self-initiated game lasting a few minutes depending on the player's skill; and employ a large monitor and input devices such as joysticks, buttons, and roller balls.

During the 1980s, video games like Pac-Man and Donkey Kong could be found in nearly any business that had a few spare square feet, including retail stores, restaurants, bars, and movie theaters. Dedicated video game arcades—which were modeled after casinos as well as pachinko and

At Virtuality, an interactive virtual reality game at Dave & Busters, images are displayed within the individual headsets.

pinball parlors—proliferated as well. They appeared in shopping centers in the suburbs; in streetfront stores in cities; in amusement and theme parks; and in hotels, casinos, and cruise ships. They became a defining component of family entertainment centers. The increasing size and cost of video games and the rise of the home video game industry have led to a sharp decline in the number of "mom-and-pop" operated neighborhood arcades. Recently, companies such as GameWorks and Dave & Busters have revised the concept of the dedicated arcade for a more mature market by combining additional amenities with the games, including high-quality food and alcoholic beverages, to form high-tech game centers.

In the face of continued competition from console and personal computer games, the future of video games relies on the development of proprietary technologies that are beyond the capacity of home systems. In large part, this will continue to take the form of exotic interface devices, like Sega WaveRunner's jet-ski interface and Namco's Alpine Surfer snowboard interface, which are impossible to mimic at home. Yet by emphasizing elaborate hardware, the units will continue to tend upward in size and cost, ruling out all but the most well-capitalized operators.

Virtual Reality Attractions

It was not until the 1980s, after decades of gestation in government-sponsored research laboratories, that virtual reality appeared. Immediately, "VR" captivated the public and media's attention and inspired the immense enthusiasm and expectations that the technology since has struggled to meet.

In archetypal VR, the exact position of the user's eyes is tracked continually by magnetic sensors so that real-time, computer-generated imagery of a fictitious world that matches the user's point of view can be displayed to the user. The display device typically takes the form of stereoscopic goggles—or head-mounted displays—that use two miniature screens to present a slightly askew view to each eye, thereby creating the immersive quality of depth. Thus, VR can offer the simulated—if not quite realistic—sensation of being in the fictitious world. In modest versions of VR, such as in Virtual World's Battletech games, the image is displayed on a monitor within a cockpit-like capsule; therefore, it does not require point-of-view tracking.

Often, users' computers are linked so that they can inhabit and interact with each other in the same fictional space at the same time. Often, users also are equipped with some sort of motion-tracked input device such as a data-glove, wand, or—in most cases—a gun, which they can use to point or shoot at objects or other users in the imaginary space.

The technologies required today for a typical VR station are prohibitively expensive for operators and consumers. Thus, VR has served largely as the basis for proprietary stand-alone facilities such as the Virtual World chain or in off-the-shelf formats in larger, well-capitalized family entertainment centers, such as at

Enchanted Castle in Lombard, Illinois, and at Dave & Busters locations.

In large part, VR has served as a loss leader, attracting attention to entertainment centers yet failing to earn much of a return. Eventually, as the economic disadvantages of VR became clear and the hype wore off, many VR companies folded, including industry leader Virtuality of the United Kingdom, which reportedly held 80 percent of the market. However, as the cost of computer processing power continues to decline, VR will eventually become financially feasible. VR, like video games, will require a continued supply of new games to thrive, and several fundamental operational hurdles will need to be overcome. These include hygiene issues related to sharing of intimate interfaces like head-mounted displays; eyestrain caused by the fact that each user's interocular distance is different, requiring custom adjustment of stereoscopic displays; the inefficiencies resulting from the time required for users to don, remove, and adjust equipment; and the nausea that can result when the images do not accurately match the user's changing perspective.

Conclusion

To an extent, these entertainment technologies are converging. Motion simulators are being combined with specialty-format film presentations for ultimate impact, and new-breed video games like Sega's Daytona USA combine virtual reality–like three-dimensional graphics and gyrating race car cockpits with force-feedback

In Virtual World's Battletech, images are displayed on a monitor within a cockpit-like capsule.

steering wheel effects. This convergence also is seen in flight simulator games where motion-base technology is combined with virtual reality computer imaging technology to create an experience that is much like the interactive pilot training simulators from which motion simulators evolved. These highly immersive experiences—which can cost consumers in excess of ten times what a typical video game costs—are often combined with pre-show and post-show experiences, lounges, and retail boutiques to form dedicated stand-alone centers like FighterTown in Lake Forest, California; the Speedworld auto-racing attraction at the Sahara Hotel and Casino in Las Vegas; and Silicon Speedway at Mall of America in Bloomington, Minnesota.

Source: Raymond E. Braun and Jay D. Wheatley, Economics Research Associates (ERA).

The planned San Francisco 49ers stadium will be linked to a massive off-price entertainment megamall—Candlestick Mills.

Cesar Rubio

are drawn to the adjacent area to take advantage of the large game-day crowds. This can result in renovation, construction, job creation, and tax revenue generation in otherwise blighted areas.

In other cases, team owners and developers have exploited the traffic-generating abilities of professional sporting events to increase their revenues as well as create amenities to attract off-season users. For example, the MCI Center in Washington, D.C., home to the Wizards NBA and the Washington Capitals NHL franchises, features a 23,000-square-foot Discovery Channel superstore, a 25,000-square-foot National Sports Gallery interactive museum, and a 19,300-square-foot, sports-theme Velocity Grill.

The demand for new stadiums and arenas has come from various trends within the professional sports industry itself. These include the economic obsolescence of existing stadiums because they lack lucrative luxury suites, preferential club seating, and high-

revenue concourse activities; the surging popularity of professional basketball and hockey; the need to spark enthusiasm for baseball with more intimate and nostalgic ballparks; and the evolution of professional sports into a true entertainment industry. This last trend is evident in the celebrity status accorded pro athletes; the explosion of team logo licensing and merchandising; and the increasing ownership of sports franchises by entertainment companies like Disney, Nintendo, Time Warner Inc., and others. As a further example, in 1997, Sony Corporation of America and the National Basketball Association agreed to a sponsorship deal through the year 2000 worth more than $10 million, making Sony an official U.S. sponsor of the NBA. Under the agreement, Sony will be allowed to advertise during broadcasts of NBA games, conduct promotions, provide musical talent for NBA events, and feature the company's recording artists in songs and videos presented at NBA arenas; in addition, Sony will codevelop NBA-based television shows and motion pictures with the sports league.

Dining

Dining plays a critical role in UECs due to two fundamental factors. First is the human biological need for sustenance throughout the day, requiring food service at places where people spend extended periods of time. Second is the fact that eating and drinking are intrinsically pleasurable—although more so with some types of foods and beverages than others—which has led to a long association between dining and entertainment that today has been termed "eatertainment" or "dinnertainment."

Fast-food outlets, food courts, and casual restaurants exist to accommodate UEC visitors' demand for food and beverage when it is motivated more or less by hunger; theme restaurants meet their demand for food coupled with entertainment. Between these extremes are mixed-purpose, "impulse" dining amenities such as portable concession carts, built-in counters, and in-store cafés that serve to satisfy hunger and/or the demand for pleasure.

Functional Dining

Functional dining both promotes and capitalizes on the extended length of visitation associated with entertainment/retail centers. The longer visitors stay, the more likely they are to eat on site. Conversely, on-site dining accommodations allow for longer stays. Since maximizing the time visitors spend at the UEC is key to the success of all the center's amenities, the role of dining is critical.

In a UEC, as in shopping centers, food courts may be an effective format for meeting some visitors' dining needs. The rise in popularity of ethnic as well as specialized foods—like fruit smoothies, gourmet coffee, and "flavored" pretzels—has led to multitudes of brand-name chains with tightly focused product lines. Baja Fresh, Auntie Anne's Pretzels, Boardwalk Fries, and Hot Dog on a Stick are a few examples. Food courts are uniquely suited to offer the variety and comprehensiveness that attract a diverse market. An added advantage is that the physical proximity of the food court outlets allows for efficient use of shared resources like seating areas and trays.

While some brand-name casual restaurants, like Red Robin, Bennigan's, T.G.I. Friday's, and California Pizza Kitchen, sometimes can be found inside shopping malls, historically most have been found in freestanding "pad" units on outparcels. The reasons that casual restaurants typically have elected sites outside the mall are numerous. They may have a signature building style that is critical to their identity; their hours may differ from those of the center (for instance, they may have a bar that gets most of its business at nighttime after the mall has closed); they may require an allotment or configuration of space that is not compatible with the mall's structure; and mall traffic may not be enough to support the restaurant, making an in-mall location a liability. However, as UECs tend to have more leisure-oriented evening business centered around dining, they generally are more suitable than a mall as a site for a casual restaurant.

As at Planet Hollywood on Pennsylvania Avenue in Washington, D.C, you can't always tell what's on the inside by what's on the outside.

Impulse Dining

Impulse dining operations often are compact, taking the form of portable carts, built-in counters, and in-store cafés. Because human eating behavior is dramatically affected by context, the types of food they offer tend to exhibit two key attributes. One, in keeping with the leisure nature of UECs, the food items available generally are of the pleasure or indulgence variety—hot dogs, gourmet coffee, popcorn, soda, ice cream, pretzels, and so forth. Two, they are immediately available and portable, making them suitable for impulse purchase and ambulatory consumption. Impulse dining amenities can often be found within various retail and entertainment venues. The French fry counters in the Game-Works centers and the in-store cafés serving espresso drinks and pastries in Barnes & Noble bookstores are examples.

Entertainment Dining

The link between dining and entertainment stretches back to the feasts of ancient times. Today, this combination is represented best by the theme restaurant, whose origins most observers trace to the founding in 1971 of the rock-and-roll-based Hard Rock Cafe in London. This landmark eatery established many precepts that are followed today. First, the restaurant features a theme—a unifying motif derived from a pop-cultural genre, medium, industry, or intellectual property. Examples that have emerged in recent years include Planet Hollywood, Harley Davidson Cafe, Fashion Cafe, Rainforest Cafe, NASCAR Cafe, Official All-Star Cafe, Motown Cafe, Dive!, and Marvel Mania, among many others. Second, the theme is expressed through elaborate interior design features, including exotic finishes, props, museum-style displays of theme-related artifacts, theatrical lighting, audio effects, and video presentations. Third, the development expense—from $5 million to $15 million for a typical theme restaurant, depending on size and location—generally has relegated these eateries to densely populated, urban, or tourist locations. Fourth, their affiliation with cherished pop-cultural themes with which many people identify, along with their tourist appeal (each city's version of a particular chain is slightly unique) allows theme restaurants to sell large quantities of logo merchandise at on-site boutiques. Fifth—demonstrating theme restaurants' emphasis on the entertainment experience instead of cuisine and their efforts to appeal to as broad a market as possible—nearly every one serves the same American fare: hamburgers, chicken sandwiches, pasta, French fries, and so forth.

Retail

Unlike traditional retail centers, which attract more dedicated shoppers (49 percent of whom have a specific store or purchase in mind, according to the International Conference of Shopping Center's *1996 Mall Customer Shopping Patterns Report*), UECs attract more leisurely patrons. Stores found at UECs generally fall within the category of entertainment-oriented retail. This retail type is characterized by functional leisure-oriented goods such as books, recorded music, and sporting goods as well as by nonessential gifts, novelties, or collectibles. In either case, merchandise and stores tend to be highly branded.

Many of these stores are operated by large, vertically integrated entertainment or manufacturing companies. Due to the financial resources of these companies and their use of the stores as a strategic tool for building their

---

THEME RESTAURANT CONCEPTS

Sports

2nd & Goal Sports Cafe
ESPN Club
Front Row Sports Grill
Michael Jordan's
NASCAR Cafe
Official All-Star Cafe
Race Rock
Rookies Restaurant & Sports Bar
Sports City Cafe & Brewery
Velocity Grill
Winning Streak
X Treme Sports Cafe

Computers

Apple Cafe
Cafe@Play
Cybars
Cybersmith
Virtua Cage
Web Cafe

Americana

Airsteam Roadside Cafe
Alan Jackson Showcar Cafe
Daily Planet
Easyriders
Ed Debevic's
Harley Davidson Cafe
USA Cafe
Vegas!

Adventure

Club Kokomo
Copperfield's Magic Underground
Crash Cafe
Dive!
Elroy's
Encounter
Jekyll & Hyde
Margarittaville
Planet Ocean
Rainforest Cafe
The Sci-Fi Cafe

Entertainment

B.B. King's Blues Club
BET SoundStage
Bubba Gump Shrimp Co.
Caroline's Comedy Nation
Country Star
Dick Clark's American Bandstand Grill
Elvis Presley's Memphis
Fashion Cafe
Hard Rock Cafe
Marvel Mania
Mickey Gilley's Texas Cafe
Motown Cafe
Nashville Country Club Restaurant
National Lampoon
Planet Hollywood
The Amazing Randolph's Restaurant

Other

Cafe Tu Tu Tango
Chefs of the World

Source: Economics Research Associates.

THEMED EATING

A Brief History of Themed Eating

Year Opened	Eatery	Units in 1997
1971	Hard Rock Cafe	67
1991	Planet Hollywood	48
1992	House of Blues	4
1993	Harley Davidson Cafe	1
1994	Country Star	4
	Dive!	3
	Rainforest Cafe	8
1995	Fashion Cafe	1
	Jekyll & Hyde Club	1
	Motown Cafe	1
	Official All Star Cafe	1
1996	Billboard Live!	1
	ESPN Club	1
	Marvel Mania	1
	MTV R'n'B	1
	NASCAR Cafe	1
	Race Rock	1
	Television City	1
1997/98	Chefs of the World	
	Comedy Nation	
	Laugh Factory	
	Funhouse	
	Magic Underground	
	New Planet Hollywood Concept	
	Hotel Discovery	

Average 1995 Revenues

	Per Unit ($ millions)	Per Square Foot ($)
Country Star	5.2	288
Dive!	10.0	909
Hard Rock Cafe	10.8	–
House of Blues	10.0	–
Motown Cafe	17.0	–
Planet Hollywood	14.3	840
Rainforest Cafe	10.4	732
National Restaurant Association Median	–	204

Source: Andrew Zarnet, managing director of Ladenburg Thalman & Co., *EZone* (Urban Land Institute, January 1998).

brand and supporting other corporate divisions, the level of store design and visual merchandising is among the best there is.

Along with an emphasis on unique environmental designs, these retailers often offer added amenities like "play-before-you-pay" or "try-before-you-buy" opportunities, in-store cafés, and entertainment in the form of live music, D.J.'s, and video projection screens. These features allow the retailers to link the *goods* to a pleasurable and memorable *experience*.

Brand-Name Souvenir Boutiques

The rise of branding has inspired a new, aggressive breed of souvenir retailing. Nearly every brand-name eatery or entertainment venue with any degree of exclusivity, from Rainforest Cafe restaurants to Virtual World virtual reality parlors, offers a line of brand merchandise including such items as logo-emblazoned t-shirts, leather bomber jackets, hats, sweatshirts, and keychains. By purchasing these items, patrons are able to affiliate with the place's cultural cachet: hipness, sophistication, exoticism, and elitism.

When successful, boutiques selling brand merchandise may have impressive sales by any standard. It has been estimated, for instance, that a boutique at a theme restaurant like Planet Hollywood, which may be only 500 square feet in size, can account for as much as 20 percent to 30 percent of the establishment's profits. Contributing to this is the fact that the mark-up on merchandise can be upward of 200 percent. Logo wear also can act as an effective form of advertising, partially explaining why Planet Hollywood is such a highly recognized property even though it spends virtually nothing on advertising while McDonald's, for example, reportedly spends about a half a billion dollars annually.

Specialty Stores

Independent and chain specialty stores like Glow at Universal CityWalk (which sells glow-in-the-dark novelties in an ultraviolet-lighted environment), Dapy, the Museum Co., and

Brookstone are common to UEC complexes and districts. These retailers, which tend to focus on an explicit theme, product category, or lifestyle profile, usually occupy 3,000 square feet to 4,000 square feet of moderately designed space, with more elaborate decors found in stores at high-profile locations.

What makes these retailers especially suited to the UEC environment is the "browse-ability" of the goods they sell. Because they offer a large number of small, unique items, a visit to such stores is akin to a treasure hunt. It also becomes a social experience when shopping companions excitedly show each other the interesting items they discover. Rather than being out-of-reach behind glass, within boxes, or in shrink-wrap packaging, the merchandise is completely accessible, allowing patrons to experience the items first hand. Often these goods in fact *do* something or create a sensory effect that can be experienced immediately within the store.

Brand Extension Stores

Brand extension stores are operated by vertically integrated entertainment and media companies that possess well-known intellectual or creative properties, primarily characters and logos. These retailers include the Disney Stores and Warner Bros. Studio Stores and the upstart Viacom Entertainment Store, which sells MTV, Nickelodeon, and Star Trek–related items. The businesses behind these stores are seeking to exploit their ephemeral assets to the fullest by selling brand goods directly to the public. ESPN–The Store and the chain of outlets opened by Discovery Communications Inc., which operates the educational Discovery Channel, illustrate how the niche focus of cable channels can translate to niche specialty retail concepts. In the future, with the oft-promised 500 channels, the number of cable-to-retail brand extensions is likely to grow.

Brand License Stores

Due to the popularity of brand extension stores and the enormous demand for goods

The Warner Bros. Store is an example of a brand extension store that exploits its ephemeral assets to the fullest by selling its name-brand goods directly to the public.

featuring characters and logos in general, a number of specialty stores have emerged that are operated by retailers who have licensed, well-known creative or intellectual properties. NASCAR- and NFL-based stores are recent examples of this genre, as well as a chain of shops developed by Store of Knowledge, Inc., in partnership with local PBS affiliates nationwide, which sell items related to PBS programming. The drawback of brand license stores is the inefficiency of the licensor and licensee relationship, which prevents the degree of synergy that brand extension stores enjoy. For instance, with brand license stores, the licensor does not have control over the stores that represent the public exposition of its valuable properties and the licensee has little sway over the development of creative or intellectual properties as it relates to merchandising.

Product Showcase Stores

Product showcase stores are glamorous retail outlets operated by manufacturers of brand-name goods that serve as much as brand-building devices as they do as revenue generators. The NikeTown stores, with their bold environmental design and dynamic merchandise presentation techniques, best exemplify this type. Planet Reebok, Sony's the Entertainment Store at Yerba Buena Gardens, and Everything Coca-Cola at the Showcase on the Las Vegas Strip are additional examples. As at world's fair pavilions, the selling of the *brand image* at these stores is as important as the selling of *merchandise*. With the growth of alternative retail distribution channels like on-line shopping, which make middleman retailers less essential, these types of flashy product showcases are likely to proliferate. Shoppers in the near future may visit a product showcase store to try on various athletic shoes or peruse housewares and then order the items directly from the factory over the Internet for next-day delivery.

Leisure-Oriented Category Killers

Leisure-oriented category-killer retail stores offer a wide selection of brand-name leisure-oriented goods like books, recorded music, and sporting goods in a big-box format. Often, these stores are referred to as "big books" or "big music" stores and so forth, as well as "megastores" or "superstores." These large retailers frequently offer innovative visit-extending and intimacy-inducing in-store experiences for patrons, exemplifying the current vogue of lifestyle retailing. At Barnes & Noble and Borders Books & Music, amenities such as in-store cafés and coffee bars serving espresso drinks, "sitting room" lounge areas with comfortable reading chairs, and live jazz music are employed. Similarly, music listening stations, multimedia audio and video presentations, and in-store D.J.'s perform the same role in Virgin Records Megastores.

Sporting and outdoor gear retailers also offer new experiential elements. The 170,000-square-foot Bass Pro Shops Outdoor World in Springfield, Missouri, offers myriad "play-before-you-pay" activity areas, including a

NikeTown, the apotheosis of a product showcase store, is designed as much for brand-building as for revenue generation.

The Disney Store on Fifth Avenue in New York City is the flagship store in Disney's worldwide network of stores selling goods that feature its characters and logos.

trout pond for testing fishing flies as well as rifle and bow ranges. Likewise, the 80,000-square-foot REI (Recreation Equipment Inc.) flagship store in Seattle features a mountain-bike test track outside and a rock-climbing pinnacle within, along with a room for testing rainproof gear and a simulated hiking trail. Meanwhile, Oshman's Super Sports USA stores let customers shoot hoops and practice their putting. The link among these retailers is that the merchandise that they sell is for leisure use and customers have almost as much fun giving these goods a trial run in the store as they do going to an entertainment center.

CHAPTER 3

STRATEGIC DEVELOPMENT
Positioning, Programming, Financing and Execution

This chapter addresses the unique challenges of developing retail/ entertainment destinations with respect to strategic positioning, programming, financing, and execution. These projects represent a new form of retailing as dramatic in potential impact as were the grand department stores at the turn of the century and the regional malls some 50 years later. As described in the introductory chapter, a number of powerful forces are reshaping the very nature of the places where consumers go to dine, shop, and be entertained. A handful of developers, along with cutting-edge retailers and restaurateurs, a number of entertainment companies, and innovative local governments, have led this revolution, introducing an array of exciting projects, from Miami's CocoWalk to the Forum Shops in Las Vegas. The first wave of entertainment-enhanced development varies widely in terms of scale, merchandise mix, configuration, and anchoring features. In fact, efforts to categorize these projects have resulted in nearly as many categories as there are developments today.

Nevertheless, the first developments share a common characteristic —the introduction of environments and entertainment features designed to distinguish these projects as *destinations*. The difference between traditional retail developments and entertainment-enhanced developments is in essence a difference in the scope and impact of the projects

The Jerde Partnership

Canal City Hakata in Fukuoka, Japan, is the largest retail entertainment center in Japan. (Preceding page: The Hollywood Entertainment Museum.)

—in short, their ability to perform as destinations. The performance goal sought in the next wave of projects is to attract patrons from a geographic range two to three times that of a regional mall who will stay on average two to three times longer.

This chapter does not dwell on specific types of entertainment-enhanced developments: urban entertainment centers, suburban entertainment destinations, sports-linked retail entertainment developments, evening entertainment destinations, "mills" projects, or "signature entertainment" developments. Rather, the focus is on the unique requirements involved in positioning, programming, financing, and executing an array of projects that are intended to perform as destinations.

Throughout the chapter "destination developments" refers to a mix of urban and suburban projects that employ entertainment-enhanced strategies to draw patrons from a broad regional market. More than other retail centers or even mixed-use developments, destination developments require significant innovation in programs, tenant mix, tenant configuration, venue creation, siting decisions, anchoring components, vertical linkages, and execution. The need for novelty is only partly related to the destination development's new place in the real estate landscape. Even after destination developments have widely taken root and a group of experienced developers has emerged, the very nature of the projects will continue to require a level of innovation that exceeds that of other forms of retail and mixed-use development.

Offsetting the extra effort required to develop destination projects is their potential performance. Destination developments can significantly exceed the sales and rents generated by top urban and suburban malls.

This chapter examines the benefits and risks associated with destination developments by discussing the four key stages of a strategic positioning and development process. A number of examples are provided to illustrate the factors that contribute to successful development.

STRATEGIC POSITIONING: EVALUATION OF MARKET OPPORTUNITIES AND DEVELOPMENT CHALLENGES

Successful development of a retail/entertainment project begins with a strategic evaluation of the opportunities to *position* the project to compete as a destination. Assessing the performance potential of a destination involves more than the market analysis and modeling typically used to evaluate retail opportunities. Destination developments, after all, are intended to outperform these projects across five dimensions that will be referred to as the five Ds. They include

▼ Distinctiveness of the product
▼ Drawing power
▼ Depth of penetration
▼ Duration of visit
▼ Demand periods.

Strategically positioning a destination development involves an assessment of each of these dimensions as it relates to

▼ Market dynamics
▼ Competitive developments and leisure attractions
▼ Consumer psychographics
▼ Location and access factors
▼ Complementary developments and attractions
▼ Timing of the development.

While rigorous market evaluation is at the core of strategic positioning, the novelty of these developments also requires strategic insight on the part of the developer in configuring a project to take advantage of competitive opportunities and gaps in the regional market.

Distinctiveness of the Product

Strategic positioning of a destination development begins with an assessment of its potential distinctiveness within a market region. Direct competition from other offerings within the same region will directly constrain performance, as it does that of a regional mall. But the retail/entertainment destination also is intended to be a regional centerpoint for a variety of activities including family entertainment, evening entertainment, shopping, and dining. There are therefore a broader array of potential competitors that need to be considered in evaluating the opportunities to achieve *distinctiveness*.

Universal CityWalk is intended to be a regional centerpoint for a variety of activities including family entertainment, evening entertainment, shopping, and dining.

The Jerde Partnership

61

The area in and around Yerba Buena Gardens, south of Market Street, is being revitalized. Today, cultural institutions (the Yerba Buena Center for the Arts and the San Francisco Museum of Modern Art), the Moscone Convention Center, retail establishments (the San Francisco Center, anchored by Nordstrom), and restaurants (Chevy's, Max's Diner) attract visitors and residents alike to the neighborhood. In the past, however, "south of Market Street" was considered an isolated location where commercial development was infeasible.

Against this backdrop, Sony Retail Entertainment (SRE) has begun work on Metreon, a Sony Entertainment Center, overlooking Yerba Buena Gardens Esplanade. In so doing, the company hopes to create a model for future successful urban entertainment development.

What distinguishes Metreon is that Sony Retail Entertainment has chosen to approach it as a retail business venture, rather than as a more traditional real estate project. It has partnered with Millennium Partners of New York and WDG Ventures of San Francisco, which will develop the physical site. SRE will assume the role of master tenant and lease the entire building from the San Francisco Redevelopment Agency. This approach allows Sony to focus on its primary concern—ensuring that each component of the center operates as a profitable business. An SRE division, Sony Development,

Metreon Gateway forms the entrance to the 350,000-square-foot urban entertainment project underway in San Francisco's Yerba Buena Gardens cultural and entertainment district.

Additional sources of competition may include an array of regional leisure attractions, concentrated clusters of restaurants that act as evening destinations, cinema megaplexes, and existing retail destinations. Strategic positioning sometimes involves turning potential competitors into complementary features. For example, Metreon, Sony's entertainment retail complex in San Francisco, was strategically positioned in the Yerba Buena Gardens district to take advantage of the existing museums, restaurants, shops, hotels, and convention facilities that make this area distinctive as a destination for tourists, conventioneers, and locals.

Distinctiveness also requires achieving dominance within a region. While there may be a variety of retail centers within a region that are enhanced by entertainment features, there are a limited number of true destination projects that a market can support. Distinctiveness involves creating a regional identity and product mix that differentiate the destination from other offerings that compete for the leisure time and expenditures of the region's consumer base.

Third Street Promenade in Santa Monica is an example of a development that has achieved a level of distinctiveness in a market with a variety of malls, seaside attractions, and nearby entertainment destinations. The distinctiveness of Third Street was built on the creation of a street-oriented retail envi-

Sony Retail Entertainment is working with famed children's author and illustrator Maurice Sendak to create a large family area featuring the characters and storyline of his books, including *Where the Wild Things Are.*

has worked with designers and marketing specialists to refine the center's look, feel, and mix of offerings.

The four-story, 350,000-square-foot project will include a 15-screen Sony Theaters complex, a Sony IMAX theater, theme attractions, new restaurants, and retail shopping, all of which will be reached through a central area called the Metreon Gateway. Technology-based entertainment will feature an interactive 3-D show and presentation of the book "The Way Things Work" by David Macaulay, as well as a PC-based electronic game and virtual reality experience called "Airtight Garage" created by the French graphic-novelist Möebius. The Sony retail entertainment team also is working with author and illustrator Maurice Sendak on a large family attraction featuring the characters and story lines from Sendak's well-loved books, including *Where The Wild Things Are.*

According to Sony Retail Entertainment, the Yerba Buena development could serve as a useful prototype for future location-based entertainment projects. This business model enables Sony to focus on what it does best—providing state-of-the-art technology and high-quality entertainment.

Source: Daniel C. Scheffey.

ronment and an aggressive tenant subsidy program that attracted a rich mix of restaurants, theaters, and unique-to-the-market retailers. In the case of Third Street, sustaining distinctiveness as a competitive advantage involves maintaining the project's one-of-a-kind restaurants and shops and its vibrant street environment, while adding signature dining, icon retailers and new entertainment offerings. (See the case study in Chapter 5.)

Achieving dominance also requires evaluating a variety of factors that *support* a development's distinctiveness, including access, location, and the ability to shape consumer perceptions regarding the identity of the destination. All factors must work together in order to avoid the developer's greatest concern: the possibility of being intercepted or outmaneuvered by another project with an advantageous location, program, or anchoring elements.

The critical point of evaluation is to determine whether an opportunity exists to achieve a *sustainable competitive advantage* through the creation of a distinctive destination that acts as a regional centerpoint for entertainment, dining, and shopping. The timing of a development in relation to the presence or entry of targeted tenants is of great significance in achieving distinctiveness. Icon and showcase stores, signature restaurants, and entertainment venues limit

Centro Oberhausen in Oberhausen, Germany, is an entertainment megamall that combines indoor and outdoor shopping, entertainment, and leisure activities. Due to its enormous size and distinctive offerings, its depth of penetration of the primary market far exceeds that of most other retail projects.

RTKL Associates

RTKL Associates

their presence in any region so that losing key tenants to other developments has far more impact on a destination development than on a regional mall with its more traditional tenant mix.

Drawing Power

A destination development is designed to attract consumers from a geographic range at least twice that of a regional mall. Typical regional centers rely heavily on the population in close proximity to the mall. According to a Stillerman Jones 1997 survey, 56 percent of mall visitors traveled less than 15 miles and 87 percent of visitors came from within a 30-minute radius. Most malls report that only 5 percent of their business is generated by tourists. In contrast, destination projects are regional attractions, attracting patrons from across a metropolitan statistical area (MSA) and acting as a must-see for tourists. Universal CityWalk, for example, draws more than 40 percent of its visitors from residential areas that are more than 30 minutes from the project. While the range varies according to the region of the country (e.g., larger in the Midwest, tighter in the Northeast) the median draw of a destination development is about 35 miles, compared with the 15- to 18-mile drawing range of a regional mall. That extended drawing power is related both to unique features and offerings provided by the destination development (i.e., supply) and to various factors that affect consumer leisure-time decisions (i.e., demand).

From the supply perspective, the destination development needs to provide an itinerary of experiences that are unique to the region and justify commute times that may extend up to 90 minutes. From the demand perspective, assessing the development's potential to draw consumers requires a solid analysis of current leisure-time and expenditure patterns. These patterns vary significantly by region, so the analysis must be market-specific to account for regional competitors, regional demographics and psychographics, tourism, and locational factors. A

destination development should not proceed without the confidence that it can capture the extended regional market.

Depth of Penetration

Destination developments also require a depth of penetration of the primary market that far exceeds that of most other retail projects. Penetration is the percentage of market captured within a primary zone surrounding the site, typically five to ten miles depending on the density of the metropolitan area. Capture rates of more than 100 percent and up to 700 percent have been achieved when a development combines broad-based appeal across a variety of market segments and very high repeat visitation from a number of specially targeted segments.

For example, although more than 67 percent of visitors to traditional malls in 1996 were women, destination projects must offer a mix that draws a higher percentage of both men and women and strong family participation. Universal CityWalk's visitor mix, 51 percent female and 49 percent male, represents the balance sought by a destination development. CocoWalk is noted for its success in achieving a very high level of repeat visitation from local residents. Mall of America, which draws a substantial number of consumers from a vast 300-mile range, also achieves a penetration of between 600 percent to 700 percent of the 20-mile regional market.

The new wave of destination developments—including projects such as Pacific Place in Seattle, Sunset Place in Miami, Penn's Landing in Philadelphia, and Hollywood and Highland in Los Angeles—are being programmed to take this critically important performance factor into account. Programmable entertainment venues (e.g., megaplexes, ice skating rinks, live performance venues, sports venues, cultural attractions, events) are being designed in attractive public environments to renew demand and achieve high rates of repeat visitation. Successfully increasing repeat visitation also requires customized research on the psychographics and leisure-time expenditures of consumer segments, as well as their location relative to the project and the competitive developments that may intercept them. Market penetration also requires that destination developments draw on more market segments than do traditional retail projects by offering entertainment, dining, and shopping choices that appeal to a variety of consumers.

Appealing to an array of market segments is important in two respects. First, a destination development needs to appeal to a mix of families, young adults, and older adults (e.g., empty-nesters) in order to achieve a reasonable penetration of the regional market. This has been a challenge for projects designed as evening destinations, which often have limited appeal to families and therefore must rely on very deep penetration of adult market segments.

Second, decisions to visit a destination involve trade-offs with other leisure-time attractions. These choices often are made by a group—whether a family of five or two adult couples—and therefore must satisfy the interests of a number of people. To the degree that a project accommodates a mix of preferences, its depth of penetration will be elevated. Serving the interests and tastes of diverse groups is no easy task. The development team must consider consumer psychographics and leisure-time expenditure patterns as it determines the program components and special features that may enhance the project's appeal.

Duration of Visit

Leisure expenditures are correlated with the length of time a patron spends at a location. The duration of a visit is in turn related to the variety of choices and number of linked activities provided as part of the guest experience—referred to here as the visitor itinerary. Maximum spending generally is thought

The inclusion of stores and attractions that appeal to families and encourage browsing and extended indoor play are being introduced in projects such as Simon DeBartolo's Shops at Sunset Place.

to occur with a length of stay of three to four hours. A destination development therefore should be designed to provide a number of daytime and evening itineraries that create three- to four-hour visitation patterns. For example, the inclusion of stores that appeal to families and encourage extended browsing and in-store play are being introduced in projects such as Metreon, the Shops at Sunset Place, and the Point in Orlando. Cultural attractions, large-format theaters with discovery films (e.g., IMAX), and theme restaurants in these developments serve to extend a family itinerary with entertainment and dining. At night, the movies play the primary role in drawing patrons, with pre-show shopping and post-show dining and entertainment acting to extend the visitor itinerary. The Entertainment Center at Irvine Spectrum in Irvine, California, illustrates this potential with its piazza of five signature restaurants located opposite the entrance to a 22-screen Edwards cinema and IMAX theater.

Demand Periods

Evaluating a destination development's market also involves considering a variety of distinct demand periods. Demand at all retail projects varies according to the availability and motivations of various market segments, and very distinct changes in consumer profiles occur throughout the week. A potential advantage of entertainment-enhanced destinations is their ability to integrate components that attract particular consumer segments during times that are nonproductive in traditional retail settings.

This dimension of performance is the most challenging to assess and to address strategically. In a strong tourist market, for example, a destination project may be able to elevate the typically low productivity of mornings and mid-afternoons by attracting the overnight visitor with daytime entertainment venues or events. In a market with a large base of university students, the productivity of weekday evenings might be similarly

enhanced. Multiplex theaters now are seeking to capitalize on their stadium seating and enhanced multimedia capabilities to attract local school children, business groups, and conventioneers during the day with special film programs and satellite broadcasting of events and conferences. With destination developments, strong performance depends on identifying the programmatic fit between available consumer segments and key demand periods. Insight into daily and weekly patterns can significantly elevate performance, allowing the developer to introduce a mix of tenants and venues that match the motivations of key consumer segments.

In summary, capitalizing on the five Ds (distinctiveness, drawing range, depth of penetration, duration of visit, and demand periods) can significantly increase the performance potential of the destination development over that of traditional retail developments. Achieving that potential involves recognizing market patterns that are unique to destination developments and using them to shape a distinctive offering.

DEFINING THE PRODUCT: MULTI-ANCHORING, MIX, SCALE, AND PLACE MAKING

Destination developments are far less formula-driven than are other forms of retail development. The typical mix of super regional malls is 80 percent retail, 10 percent dining, 5 percent entertainment, and 5 percent other services and uses. Pacific Place in Seattle and Sunset Place in Miami (see the feature box on page 74) are distinct from traditional retail developments in terms of tenant mix, positioning of anchors, approach to verticality, and scale of retail executions and also in terms of overall configuration and design. This variation in approach is driven by the urgency of creating destinations that act as centerpoints within very different urban contexts and regional markets.

Entertainment desti-
nations such as the
Westside, at Disney
World's Downtown
Disney, employs
multi-anchoring
to create a com-
bined pull on the
market that extends
the project's geo-
graphic reach and
penetration.

While destination developments vary far more dramatically than other retail centers, the process of defining the product does not. Seven common considerations are integral to the creation of a distinctive destination development:

1. *Multi-anchoring* the development
2. Enhancing *tenant identity*
3. Creating *itinerary-based configurations*
4. Gauging scale in relation to a *critical mix*
5. Building the project around *people places*
6. Leveraging the distinctiveness of the place through *contextual links*
7. Integrating these factors to create a *sense of identity* for the development as a regional destination.

Multi-Anchoring

Destination developments are distinguished from other forms of retail development in the way that anchor tenants are defined. Traditionally, large department stores have anchored retail developments, generating the base of consumer traffic that supports a mix of retailers. Entertainment-enhanced destinations involve a very different approach to anchoring based on the creation of nighttime and daytime activity patterns. The anchors in these projects, which take three forms, are designed to create a *combined pull* on the market that extends the project's geographic reach and penetration. This blend of anchoring elements is referred to as *multi-anchoring*.

Entertainment as Activity Generator

The first type of anchor in an entertainment-enhanced destination is the *entertainment anchor*. The typical super regional mall includes only 5 percent of its gross leasable area (GLA) as entertainment. In contrast, destination projects program from 30 percent to 50 percent of the GLA for entertainment uses. Multiplex cinemas, consisting of 20 to 30 screens, with stadium seating, torus screens, and digital sound systems, have become the most significant traffic generators for evening activity. Supported by a well-established software development company (i.e., Hollywood) whose new releases allow weekly changes to the marquee, the multiplex is the foundation for drawing repeat customers. When reinforced by large-format theaters (notably IMAX and Iwerks) that provide a unique double attraction, some theater exhibitors have tripled their drawing radius. This drawing power gives a significant boost to retail and dining sales within destination projects. At CocoWalk, for example, while retail uses account for only 34 percent of GLA, retail sales account for 55 percent of total sales, with sales of more than $700 per square foot. By comparison, in traditional malls retail space accounts for 80 percent of GLA and 82 percent of sales, with the top 10 percent of super regional malls averaging sales of $284 per square foot.

Other types of entertainment anchors also have become important to the success of destination developments. Games-based and sports-oriented entertainment venues currently are being introduced with the goal of drawing families and adults at different times of the day and evening. At the same time, a number of media companies and entrepreneurs are introducing unique entertainment venues that provide for regionally distinct anchors. These products are just beginning to enter the market, with efforts underway by Disney, Universal, Sony, Paramount, and Ogden Entertainment. Sony Retail Entertainment (SRE) is pioneering a number of customized venues in its Metreon project in San Francisco. Disney is introducing a variety of large new venues into the market, including the ESPN Sports Cafe in Baltimore, DisneyQuest in Orlando and Chicago, and Club Disney in Los Angeles. There also has been a great deal of interest in coupling live entertainment with destination developments, most notably as part of the redevelopment of 42nd Street in New York and in Toronto's theater district, adjacent to the Sky Dome. The common denominator among entertainment-based anchors is that they are *activity generators*,

drawing a broad array of patrons to the destination development.

Restaurants as Activity Extenders

The second form of anchoring involves dining—or more particularly, the clustering of a number of signature restaurants—to create a second draw. Whereas traditional malls allocate an average of 10 percent of GLA to dining, leading destination projects include 20 to 30 percent for restaurants, cafés, and food halls. Dining can be an effective way to generate traffic, but its primary function as an anchor is to extend the length of stay or visitor itinerary and to increase repeat visitation. The types of restaurant most effective as activity extenders vary by market, but in all cases the key to using dining as an anchor lies in clustering a number of offerings. Cluster-

Forest City

The multiplex theater is an important foundation for drawing repeat customers to boost retail and dining sales within destination projects such as Forest City's UEC on 42nd Street in New York City.

MULTI-ANCHORING THE URBAN ENTERTAINMENT CENTER

Type of Anchor	Function	Example

Activity Generator
Mainly entertainment-based venues
	▼ Draw broad segment of consumer market
	▼ Extend geographic range
	▼ Enhance penetration
		▼ Cineplex/megaplex
		▼ Large-format theaters
		▼ Games-based attractions
		   GameWorks
		▼ Sports-based attractions
		   ESPN Club
		▼ Location-based entertainment (LBE) attractions
		   American Wilderness Experience
		▼ Live performance venues

Activity Extender
Mainly dining venues
	▼ Enhance length of stay
	▼ Elevate repeat visitation (penetration)
	▼ Extend multisegment appeal
	▼ Support daytime and evening itineraries
		▼ Signature restaurants
		   Il Fornaio; Cheesecake Factory
		▼ Theme restaurants
		   Planet Hollywood; Rainforest Cafe
		▼ Entertainment restaurants and clubs
		   Wildhorse Saloon; House of Blues

Activity Inducer
Mainly icon retailers
	▼ Extend geographic range for unique shopping experience
	▼ Create shopping itinerary
		▼ Icon retailers
		   Barnes & Noble; Williams Sonoma; Crate & Barrel
		▼ Brand Retailers
		   Sony Style Store; NikeTown; Virgin Records; Viacom Brands Store

Source: MRA International.

ing provides the consumer with a range of choices and (in much the same way the multiplex cinema does) minimizes the likelihood of long waits or the need for a great deal of preplanning. Projects such as Third Street Promenade and Old Town Pasadena illustrate the significance of clustering restaurants to create a regional draw. The power of clustering is clearly evident in sales performance. Isolated restaurants on pads adjacent to super regional malls have median sales of $268 per square foot; in contrast, the clustered dining offerings at CocoWalk have sales of $622 per square foot. Sales in individual theme and signature restaurants in destination projects often exceed $1,000 per square foot (see table on page 87).

Icon Retailing as Activity Inducers.
The third type of anchor involves a select set of "icon" or "brand" retailers that draw a broad mix of consumers and create a shopping itinerary. A number of recent entertainment-enhanced projects have overlooked the importance of mixing retail anchors with supportive retail, focusing instead only on entertainment (i.e., movie theaters) as the anchor. But multiplexes and other entertainment venues do not provide direct support to daytime shopping itineraries. Rather, they support an evening itinerary that includes dining out, other recreational or leisure activities, pre-show shopping, and post-event browsing. Icon retailers create a second daytime and evening itinerary focused on shopping.

They act as *activity inducers*, drawing customers to the development for a unique shopping experience.

Tenant Identity

Just as innovative developers are driving change in entertainment-enhanced retail development, so too are innovative tenants. Indeed, a revolution in retailing is now underway. Retailers increasingly have turned away from ubiquitous, predictable mall stalls. Now in demand are street-oriented, high-ceilinged, multilevel presentations enhanced by facade treatments, interior architecture, and multimedia displays. The motivations behind this trend include an effort to re-engage the customer, a concern over product identity and consumer brand affiliation, and increased competition from the full spectrum of retail distribution outlets from catalogs to off-price centers.

In the context of changing tenant orientations, the challenge for the developer in creating a successful destination development is to provide the level of customized expression that tenants seek within an environment that must have the integrated character required

KMD Architects

The primary function of restaurants as an anchor is to extend the length of stay or visitor itinerary and to increase repeat visitation, as at One Colorado in Pasadena, California.

to convey a strong sense of place. Traditional elements of cityscapes—great streets, piazzas, and public stairways—also are the foundation for creating this character in the destination development. At the Shops at Sunset Place in Miami, a curving street and Spanish Steps were carved into the development block; at Pacific Place in Seattle, the city street grid connects to the development.

The balance between tenant identity and overall development character is critically important in creating a regional *centerpoint*. The uniqueness of particular store executions piques consumer interest, while the quality of the environment reinforces the distinctiveness of the development as a destination. To achieve this balance, developers sometimes establish criteria to govern to store facade designs and provide financial support (i.e., tenant allowances) for considerable levels of individual expression in store interiors.

Itinerary-Based Configurations

Tenant identity also is linked closely with the layout and adjacency of stores. Unlike the straightforward tenant configurations of traditional shopping centers—with department stores anchoring the ends of shopping corridors—configurations for destination developments involve considerable planning and customization. Factors contributing to this complexity include multilevel tenant executions, the distribution of multiple anchors, street-oriented retail and dining executions, and the differences between daytime and evening activity patterns.

Successful programming within this context involves creating tenant configurations that directly support a variety of distinct visitor itineraries. The primary itineraries are day-trip visits by families on the weekend, evening visits, shopping itineraries, and tourist-oriented itineraries. Itineraries provide the framework for addressing anchor tenant locations, tenant adjacencies, vertical linkages, and various place-making decisions.

While there are no specific rules for accommodating a mix of itineraries, six basic characteristics of successful configurations can be identified. First, daytime shopping is reinforced by streets or street-like spaces that

The proposed Seoul Entertainment Center in Seoul, Korea, will have an itinerary-based configuration that includes multilevel tenant executions, a distribution of anchors, street-oriented retail and dining executions, and different daytime and evening activity patterns.

KMD Architects

72

organize a sequence of exciting stores with distinct identities. Second, the stores are designed to contribute to the streetscape while at the same time introducing an experiential space that draws the patron off the street and into the upper levels of the development. Third, unlike at the mall, the patron is not pulled by anchor department stores on either end of a shopping corridor but is drawn by a sequence of icon and brand stores at various points along the length of the shopping street.

Fourth, dining tends to be clustered around public spaces such as piazzas or squares or, in the case of a streetscape, at corner locations or "crossroads." Dining often serves to extend all four of the predominant itineraries—shopping, family excursions, evenings out, and tourist visits.

The fifth point concerns the location of entertainment venues. Accommodating weekend and evening itineraries often is a programming challenge. Such itineraries may require some degree of isolation to accommodate the peak-period crowding and long lines that accompany these activities. Yet, these venues also provide an opportunity to enhance retail sales through spillover activity. In vertical projects, one response has been to locate theaters and location-based entertainment venues on upper levels, closely adjacent to upper-level dining. Patrons thus must pass through the retail areas as part of their itinerary. In Pacific Place, express escalators speed entertainment and dining patrons to the third level, where there are four signature restaurants and the lobby of a multiscreen theater. On descent, patrons move floor by floor through the retail core along scissors escalators that encourage browsing.

Sixth, in street-oriented destination developments the pattern has been to "district" entertainment venues to balance the need to segregate evening activities with the economic imperative of integrating entertainment itineraries with retail activity. At Broadway at the Beach in Myrtle Beach, South Carolina, a cineplex and IMAX theater are located at one end

The entertainment attractions in Times Square already have achieved both critical mix and critical mass, and the diversity of attractions continues to expand.

of the main shopping street with restaurants concentrated at the other end, creating a flow of activity that provides for spillover shopping. However, a mix of nightclubs and bars, anchored by a Hard Rock Cafe, is separated from the main promenade by a footbridge. This configuration allows dining patrons to easily extend their stay to include late-night activities, while nightclub patrons can also gain access to the club district through a separate entry adjacent to the Hard Rock.

Scale: Critical Mix versus Critical Mass

Destination development projects tend to encompass between 250,000 to 650,000 square feet. The scale is driven by three interrelated factors: First, retail, dining, and entertainment offerings have increased significantly in scale relative to tradition mall presentations. A Barnes & Noble bookstore or Virgin Megastore can range from 30,000 to 70,000 square feet; restaurants as varied as Cheesecake Factory and Rainforest Cafe range between 15,000 and 30,000 square feet; and multiplexes range between 70,000 square feet and 120,000 square feet.

Sunset Place is a 550,000-square-foot entertainment-anchored retail destination under development in South Miami by the Simon DeBartolo Group (SDG) in association with the Comras Company. The project, scheduled to open October 1998, is representative of a new type of development being pursued by SDG across the United States that is designed to perform as a regional destination through the application of multi-anchoring; branding; and the creation of distinctive, people-oriented environments. SDG recently created a $1 billion venture fund with investment bankers Donaldson, Lufkin, Jenrette (DLJ) to develop such entertainment-enhanced destination projects.

Multi-anchoring at Sunset Place comprises a variety of entertainment venues, including a 24-screen AMC theater, a 450-seat IMAX theater, and a 40,000-square-foot, two-level GameWorks entertainment center; a number of brand and icon retailers, including a Virgin Megastore, Nike-Town, FAO Schwartz, Barnes & Noble, and Z-Gallerie; and signature restaurants that are new to Miami, such as New York's Coco Pazza and China Grill, the Santa Fe Beer Factory from Mexico City, and new dining concepts such as the Country Store Restaurant and Swampy's Wilderness Grill.

In addition to employing a multi-anchoring strategy, SDG has emphasized the importance of creating a distinctive sense of place to distinguish Sunset Place as a destination in the context of competitive projects such as the Bayside Festival Market Place, CocoWalk, and a recently announced retail complex in Coral Gables.

Context, Choreography, Back Story, and Brand Identity

Stan Eckstut of Ehrenkrantz Eckstut & Kuhn Architects was charged with developing a plan that complied with South Miami's Hometown Plan—which requires integration of the project within the existing urban fabric—while creating a one-of-a-kind experience. Miami's Wolfberg, Alvarez and Partners executed the architectural design and oversaw the integration of scenographics and landscape. McBride & Company created the environmental treatments and special effects used throughout the project's public spaces.

Context

The street plan developed for Sunset Place connects both with the surrounding grid of streets and subtly introduces a more romantic, curvilinear system of internal streets. The internal streets open onto a Grand Plaza and a Grand Stair, suggestive of the colonial cities of the Caribbean in which the grid plan is juxtaposed with streets that curve to address the challenges of a hill, the tropical sun, or the entrepreneurial verve of local merchants.

The internal streets have been planned to allow for penetration by cars into the block of the project for both valet parking and garage access. The automobile, which is very much part of Miami's urban culture, is meant to be part of this environment. Pedestrian streets are an extension of these vehicular entryways into the project, with lush plantings and colorful sidewalk mosaics signaling the transition.

The plan also addresses the significant challenges of vertical circulation by treating stairways, escalators, and elevators within the context of a city center. There is a bit of the feeling of a great colonial fortresses that over time became integrated within an expanding city fabric. The most dramatic example of this is the Grand Stair, which is carved into the block of the project as the central feature. It provides both seating for "people watching" and street performances and access to the second and third levels of shops and entertainment.

Choreography

Considerable effort has been directed at creating a "guest experience" at Sunset Place by paying attention to visitor itineraries. The curvilinear streets invite exploration, rewarding patrons with surprises as they round a corner to discover a piazza, a lush tropical water garden, a special effects show, or the drama of the Grand Stair.

The designers have in effect *choreographed* the visitor experience from the multiple entries into the block to the sequence of experiences that lead through the project. For example, at the Sunset Entry, visitors enter the project through the organic lattice of a banyan tree. This transition from the heat of the city streets is reinforced by natural tropical sounds and Caribbean music, along with flowering ground cover and water features. After emerging from the banyan tree, visitors find themselves in a large rotunda with two levels of

The back story at Sunset Place is based on the notion of a festive Latin city within a city to be discovered behind an ancient banyan grove and the stone walls of a triangular stone fortress.

shops, shaded by a second higher canopy modeled on a grove of banyan trees and designed to provide a mix of shade and filtered light by day and a chiaroscuro of colored light and dappled shadows by night.

Several times a day, special effects are used to create a storm in the rotunda, complete with thunder and lighting but without the downpour that accompanies Mother Nature's version.

Back Story

No literal story serves as the theme for Sunset Place, but a back story informs design decisions. The back story is based on the notion of a festive Latin city within the city, to be discovered behind an ancient banyan grove and the stone walls of a triangular colonial fortress. The back story allows for a mix of images, a kind of temporal collage in which Sunset Place has evolved from Colonial fortress, to Caribbean village, to a vibrant Latin city center. Images of colonial arches are juxtaposed with the graceful angles of Caribbean village architecture with its pastel hues and steel roofs. A fanciful red steel bridge is symbolic of the Flagler Overseas Railroad, which once connected Miami to Key West.

Brand Identity

Sunset Place also is designed to evoke a powerful brand identity by creating a distinctive sense of place and a unique experience. The term "sunset" is meant to be more than a place name, connoting the moment of transition in which the memories of the day fade in anticipation of the evening. The architecture, graphics, and lighting effects are meant to reinforce this image both subtly and directly. The entry along heavily traveled U.S. Highway 1 features the abstract image of a sailboat gliding past a setting sun. The 120-foot elevator tower looks like a grand ruin overrun by tropical plants by day, which transforms into a beacon of lighting and laser effects by night.

The positioning of Sunset Place as a destination has as much to do with its distinctiveness as a place and as an experience as with its critical mix of tenants and multiple anchors. Sunset Place's brand identity is intended to convey the project's appeal as a destination for both daytime and evening excursions.

Source: Michael S. Rubin, MRA International, Philadelphia, Pennsylvania.

The distinctiveness of destination developments like Two Rodeo Center in Beverly Hills, California, depends on the creation of a sense of place. Streets, piazzas, esplanades, and variations in facade are the sine qua non of great cities.

The second factor is the need for *tenant diversity,* which is achieved through including a sufficient number and variety of core tenants and through infilling with smaller specialty tenants that are often unique to a particular region. Core tenants may comprise as much as 85 percent of net leasable space, but smaller tenants can play a special role in enhancing the visitor experience by adding a more intimate scale and a sense of local authenticity. In larger destination developments, specialty tenants may expand to as much as 25 percent of the program with a mix of boutiques, specialty stores, small cafés, and concessions. The larger the development, the more infill is typically included in the mix.

The third, closely related, factor is critical mass. Critical mass is a strategic concern because a key source of competitive differentiation is providing an array of retailers and restaurants that dominate the competition within a region. However, domination depends more on assembling a particular *group* of retailers and restaurants than on the overall number of offerings. The term *critical mix* is preferable because it more accurately communicates the importance of securing a base of key retail, restaurant, and entertainment tenants designed for a particular market.

Emphasis on Place Making

In large part, the distinctiveness of a destination development derives from the design of environments that create a sense of place for patrons and a strong presence for tenants. Rather than the predictable interior courts and shopping corridors that characterize malls and retail centers, destination developments have reintroduced the streets, piazzas, esplanades, and variations in facade that are the sine qua non of great cities. A variety of retail environments that successfully employ street-oriented presentations and emphasize the vitality of public spaces have, of course, preceded these developments. The festival marketplaces created by Jim Rouse and village-style shopping centers such as Sturbridge Village are examples, as are developments such as Mizner Square in Boca Raton, Country Club Plaza in Kansas City, and Two Rodeo Drive in Beverly Hills. But these environments have been the exceptions in the mall-dominated retail world of the past four decades.

There is greater complexity in shaping the distinctive environments that define destinations. Developers must address the individual demands of retail and restaurant tenants for a wide variety of presentations that permit streetfront access, strong brand identity, and multilevel spaces. Creating engaging public places and an overall identity and sense of cohesiveness while trying to meet competing tenant demands not only requires a skillful development team but a whole new approach to design.

Developers of destination projects engage in an interactive design process, adjusting and readjusting plans throughout the predevelopment stage to address the various requirements of tenants, perceived consumer preferences, the particular demands of the site, and often the standards set by public codes.

The soft costs associated with creating the sense of place that contributes to a project's distinctiveness are considerably higher than those for the formula-like configurations of malls and shopping centers. In addition to the design costs related to an iterative process, the design team often is expanded to include scenographic artists, landscape architects, special effects designers, festival planners, graphic artists, and branding consultants.

The hard costs associated with common spaces, tenant facades, and store interiors also are higher than those for other forms of retail development. A central challenge in making these projects economically feasible therefore becomes the assignment of costs among the developer, the tenants, the public sector, and in some cases even the corporate sponsors. Most of the forerunners in creating destination projects have seen these costs pay off in increased rents and sales.

Trocadero, a UEC in London, is a distinctive, complex, and highly engaging place that has a strong identity.

Contextual Links

Part of the art of creating a destination involves the recognition of existing activities, attractions, and amenities that can be leveraged by the development. A significant part of what makes a project successful actually may exist outside the development itself.

When SRE's development group selected the Yerba Buena Gardens district in San Francisco as the site for its prototype destination development, the importance of existing activities figured prominently in the decision. San Francisco is a destination city with a wide variety of cultural, recreational, shopping, and dining districts, including Fisherman's Wharf/ Pier 39, Ghirardelli Square, Chinatown, and Union Square. For SRE, the potential advantages of San Francisco as a market had to be weighed against the disadvantages, such as significant existing competition, seasonal visitation patterns, and the uncertainties associated with a prototype project.

Sony's response was to position its Metreon entertainment center adjacent to the Moscone Convention Center, the San Francisco Museum of Modern Art, two planned museums, a block of gardens above the Convention Center, and a strong existing base of destination restaurants. Its decision was based on a deep appreciation of visitor motivations. Yerba Buena, with its base of cultural attractions, was seen as a potential draw for families; regional visitors seeking unique dining experiences; conventioneers (who also represent a potential follow-on leisure trip to the city); and tourists staying in nearby hotels. Metreon's 350,000-square-foot development fits within the existing set of assets while introducing missing elements designed to increase nighttime visits (cinemas, unique dining experiences), family visits (signature entertainment experiences, IMAX), shopping excursions (unique-to-the-market retail), and cultural excursions (music and film-based dining cafés and showcase retailing).

In a destination development, success is intimately linked to leveraging and bolstering an existing base of assets, which increases the attractiveness of both the project and its surroundings. Developments designed as stand-alone destinations are at a distinct disadvantage in achieving and sustaining competitive advantage.

Another example of a strategic fit between a development and its surroundings is Simon DeBartolo Group's (SDG) planned development at Penn's Landing in Philadelphia, which is located at a waterfront site long isolated from the city street grid by a major interstate highway. SDG and the city of Philadelphia sought to establish a number of strong physical and programmatic links between the project and Philadelphia's famous historic district, an adjacent restaurant district, an emerging nightlife district, attractions on the opposite side of the waterfront, and the needs of the surrounding residential community.

Taking advantage of bridges and elevated platforms that link the project to the city grid, SDG's architect, Stan Eckstut, designed a rooftop amphitheater, ice rink, and park on the palisade overlooking the waterfront. Recognizing the site's potential as an extension of and enhancement to the established visitor itinerary within Independence National Historic Park, the city and SDG are collaborating to create a unique entertainment venue designed to make the history of the United States come alive.

The project also allows for the potential inclusion of a dramatic aerial tram that will span the Delaware River, linking the 550,000-square-foot development with a variety of entertainment venues in Camden, New Jersey, including the state aquarium and the 25,000-seat Waterfront Entertainment Center.

Creating a Destination with Identity

The success of a destination development depends, finally, on creating a place that provides a shared identity for a larger region—what downtowns once provided. Indeed, a large part of the appeal of destination projects to local governments is their potential

TrizecHahn's redevelopment of Hollywood Boulevard integrates recreations of historic icons and the great movie sets of the 1930s to establish the centerpoint destination that has eluded generations of tourists in their frustrated efforts to find "Hollywood."

to reestablish residents' and visitors' affinity for a downtown or regional center.

Crafting this identity involves researching a variety of sources regarding the culture, history, events, characters, and stories that typify the region. The entrance to the cinemas at Pacific Place, for example, is a two-and-a-half-story space framed in heavy native timber with stone fireplaces reminiscent of the great lodges of the Northwest and the traditional wood crafts of the region's Native American Tribes.

TrizecHahn's redevelopment of Hollywood Boulevard integrates recreations of historic icons and the great movie sets of the 1930s to establish the centerpoint destination that eluded generations of tourists in their frustrated efforts to find "Hollywood."

A technique borrowed from the entertainment industry recently has been used to craft an identity for destination projects. Called a "back story," this technique involves

the creation of a distinctive context for a project drawn from local history and culture or from a fictional concept. Walt Disney Company historically has used back stories to provide a consistent identity for its theme parks and attractions, as well as for its more recent retail, dining, and entertainment projects outside the parks.

Pleasure Island, Disney's gated nightlife district, first was formulated around a back story based on a kind of Brigadoon that appeared at twilight and vanished by morning. Efforts to increase the performance of Pleasure Island's mix of nightclubs and evening entertainment were shaped partly by a new back story in which every night was New Year's Eve and the party was taken outside the individual clubs and music venues onto the street.

Other approaches to crafting a distinct identity include using the existing historical, cultural, or physical context of a place. The

The Walt Disney Company

Pleasure Island, Disney's gated night-life district at Disney World, Florida, has employed a back-story in which every night is New Year's Eve and the party is taken outside the individual clubs and music venues onto the street.

plans for the destination development at Penn's Landing on the waterfront in Philadelphia use historical images, the cultural significance of the landing as a festival site, and the physical proximity of Philadelphia's historic district to create a rich, multifaceted identity. The project's waterfront promenade, elevated esplanade, and amphitheater are designed to reinforce Penn's Landing as a regional destination.

Evaluating and Enhancing Financial Performance

The financial performance of a destination development is distinct from that of other retail-based developments in four important respects. First, the costs associated with differentiating the development as a regional destination can be significantly higher than those for comparably scaled regional malls.

Second, the calculus of tenant leases is far more complicated than in other retail developments due to multi-anchoring, the scale and requirements of core tenants, and the risks associated with new tenant concepts. Third, financing presents special challenges due to the actual and perceived risks associated with novel projects and the lack of comparable developments with performance histories. These factors—development cost, lease structure, and financial risk—shape the formulation of project pro formas.

The fourth and most significant factor from a strategic perspective involves the enhancement of performance through strategic adjustments to programs, anchors, operations, and ownership. The developer of a destination development has considerably more freedom to enhance performance than does the developer of a comparably scaled retail development by strategically positioning the development to take advantage of *destination economics*. Destination economics refers to the ability of a project to exceed the performance of a traditional retail center by drawing from a much larger market region, broadening market penetration through multisegment appeal and higher repeat visitation, and increasing consumers' expenditures by extending their length of stay. Each of these potential competitive advantages needs to be pursued in the context of the iterative process through which a destination development is progressively designed, programmed, and tenanted.

Destination Development Costs

Destination developments involve a variety of costs that exceed those of traditional malls, particularly costs related to public spaces and common areas, facade treatments, and tenant fit-outs.

The central problem faced by developers in budgeting costs against performance assumptions is the lack of comparables with performance histories. Instead, a variety of retail projects with comparable features or similar tenants are used as surrogates to estimate project performance. Until a range of destination projects are operating in a variety of markets this situation is unlikely to change.

As a result, performance expectations are based on developments that do not exhibit "destination economics," creating a set of conservative assumptions that place constraints on development budgets. The dilemma here is that creating a destination project requires a level of execution that is more costly than that of the retail projects used as a performance model. The developer therefore has four possible responses:

▼ To prioritize and fund those features most critical to positioning the project as a destination
▼ To pretest rental assumptions with likely tenants and ideally prelease the majority of the project prior to seeking financing
▼ To seek creative ways to subsidize development costs
▼ To partner with public bodies or strategic partners capable of making investments to benefit the development.

CityPlace, to be developed in downtown West Palm Beach, Florida, by the Palladium Company, will create a destination with a strong regional identity. Crafting identity involves researching a variety of sources regarding the culture, history, events, characters, and stories that typify the region.

Prioritizing development features begins with the first cost estimates. Of the many features that contribute to the project's distinctiveness, the most prominent and memorable are the public spaces that create a distinctive sense of place. Creating such places within the constraints of the development pro forma may ultimately involve a number of cost-sharing strategies. In developments that involve public sector participation, some of the costs associated with streets, promenades, piazzas, public stairs, and street amenities may be partially defrayed through grants, subsidies, direct investment, or various abatement programs.

Government participation typically focuses on the infrastructure and redevelopment costs that otherwise would render a project commercially infeasible. (Structured parking, access improvements, demolition, and site improvements can constitute as much as 40 percent of total development costs.) However, given the public nature of a destination development's streets and piazzas, local governments also have demonstrated a willingness to either share or help defray these costs. For governments, the decision to invest often is tied to broader economic development goals or to an effort to enhance public access and amenities. The public spaces in a destination development may operate as commercial common space or as city streets, depending on the particular development. The Palladium Company's 750,000-square-foot entertainment retail complex under development in West Palm Beach is organized around a six-block public promenade that will be owned by the city and maintained privately.

Another approach to cost sharing is to establish design guidelines for tenant facades, signage, and street furniture. Since retail and restaurant tenants in these projects are interested in strong streetfront identities, the distinctiveness of the project's public spaces may be reinforced through individual store executions.

The retail and restaurant executions sought for destination developments also involve higher levels of investment on the part of tenants, which in turn translates into expectations of higher tenant improvement allowances. Again, recovery of these costs through rental rates and terms is part of the balancing act that a developer must perform. Often developers will establish a hierarchy of tenant improvements allowances based on the relative significance of various tenants to the development (see discussion of weighted leases on page 84).

The primary entertainment anchor is the most challenging tenant. To date, the principal activity generator for all forms of entertainment-enhanced development (outside of Las Vegas and the theme parks) has been the megaplex with 24 to 30 screens and a footprint ranging from 70,000 to 120,000 square feet (which can account for 15 percent to as much as 50 percent of GLA). The lease terms for these anchors vary widely by project, tenant allowance, and geographic area (in 1996 ranging from $7.00 to about $22.00 per square foot), but typically they involve occupancy costs of no more than half of the average cost for retail tenants. The lower rents have led to a number of cost management steps on the part of developers, principally to locate theaters on the upper levels to reduce the amount of valuable street-level space given over to this use. This approach has the added benefit of creating a vertical flow of consumers, which provides the opportunity to lease upper-level spaces to restaurant and retail tenants at better rates. Developers also have worked with exhibitors to create two-level theater operations and at times to contain the overall size of the theaters.

There also is a growing concern that megaplexes lack the brand loyalty associated with department stores and therefore are more vulnerable to competitive offerings. Frenetic expansion activity by exhibitors seeking regional dominance, along with consolidation in the exhibition industry, has exacerbated these concerns. Regardless, from a financing perspective, the megaplex—with its demonstrated drawing power—is consid-

The recently opened Westside in Walt Disney World's Downtown Disney has a 24-screen AMC cinema, a 70,000-square-foot Cirque de Soleil pavilion, and a 100,000-square-foot family entertainment–oriented DisneyQuest.

ered essential to the success of entertainment-enhanced retail. To date no other entertainment venue has demonstrated such broad appeal or the ability to generate an equivalent number of annual visits.

Within this context the interest among developers for alternative forms of location-based entertainment is very high. Recent product introductions by major entertainment companies and entrepreneurs, such as DisneyQuest, Ogden's American Wilderness Experience, and David Copperfield's Magic Underground, may come to represent new entertainment anchors with greater brand identity. In addition, exhibitors have launched efforts to create brand-differentiated products by integrating the theater with dining and complementary entertainment offerings. AMC theaters has forged a joint venture relationship with Planet Hollywood to create "Planet Movies" brand theaters and has created a new subsidiary, AMC Centertainment, to develop integrated entertainment anchors with a variety of pre- and post-show dining and entertainment options. Regal Theaters, Virgin Entertainment, Loews/Sony theaters, and General Cinema Corporation also have embarked on branding strategies.

From the developer's perspective, clustering a number of venues may allow greater latitude in assembling entertainment anchors. The recently opened Westside in Walt Disney World's Downtown Disney area exemplifies clustering's potential. Here, in addition to a 24-screen AMC theater, signature entertainment venues have been introduced, including a 70,000-square-foot Cirque de Soleil pavilion and a 100,000-square-foot family entertainment–oriented DisneyQuest.

Despite the prospect of brand-name venues increasing project performance, developers have been working with development budgets gauged to more traditional retail projects. This has required considerable inventiveness in the design, leasing, and operation of these projects and has led to creative partnering arrangements with public entities. The financial community recently has begun to recognize the potential of destination projects to support a higher cost structure than

Dave & Buster's functions as a major entertainment anchor. The Grand Dining Room is pictured above.

Loer Pearce & Associates

comparably scaled retail developments. In 1997, three projects alone raised more than $2.3 billion through traditional institutional financing. Development of destination projects has required considerable equity from developers, which has been pooled with investment equity from traditional lending sources including pension funds and investment banks. Pooled equity has in turn been used to attract debt, which has been both available and relatively inexpensive in the current market.

Lease Structures in Multi-Anchored Development

The complexities of this highly customized form of development are reflected in the valuing of tenant rents and lease terms. Rather than a mix of anchor and infill tenants, the destination development includes a range of tenants, from established icon retailers to new entertainment venues. The greatest leasing challenge with a multi-anchored project is to properly structure leases to optimize project performance.

One approach has been to weight leases to achieve a desirable mix of anchors, core tenants, and supportive uses. Weighting involves balancing seven interrelated criteria:

▼ Location within the project
▼ Value of the tenancy
▼ Expectations of tenant performance
▼ Tenant space requirements
▼ Regional uniqueness or exclusivity
▼ Tenant credit
▼ Product life-cycle expectations.

This approach is consistent with that taken in other retail developments in its emphasis on leases as the principal source of income. However, weighting leases in a destination development is distinctively linked to its unique structure.

For example, the value of specific locations within a destination development varies significantly from that in retail malls where anchors, entry courts, and food courts generate a formula-like configuration. In destination developments the value of tenant location varies according to

▼ Distribution of entertainment venues, both on street and upper levels
▼ Design and location of public spaces
▼ Location of icon retailers
▼ Clustering of signature restaurants.

Maximizing the perceived value of leasable space by using these points of leverage is critical to successful destination development and serves as the foundation for lease negotiations. Equally significant is the degree to which performance is optimized through a well-conceived merchandise mix. Thus, the second aspect of weighting involves an analysis of the relative value of tenants, which varies according to the competition in the marketplace, the scale of the project, and the demographics and psychographics of the consumer base. For example, in a market saturated with Barnes & Noble and Borders book stores, the value of a signature bookstore is diminished relative to that of other types of tenants. The bookstore still may be considered an important part of the mix, but it does not contribute significantly to differentiating the project as a destination. The types of tenant selected to draw visitors also vary relative to lifestyles and buying power in a given region—identical tenant rosters in two locations will yield different tenant values. For the developer these values form part of the calculus of lease terms, from improvement allowances to location and space allocations.

Other considerations include estimating tenant performance, which relates closely to life-cycle expectations. For example, a hot theme restaurant may contribute significantly to project performance during the early years, only to run its course as the development stabilizes. Decisions regarding lease terms and developer participation require considerable judgment and a level of familiarity with the full range of tenant concepts and operating teams.

Space requirements for core tenants have become particularly tricky in configuring destination developments and achieving effective lease-ups. Icon stores, brand showcases, concept stores, and theme restaurants have

expanded to presentations that often are ten times as large as those traditional in-line stores and restaurants. Retail executions of 30,000 to 70,000 square feet and restaurants of 10,000 to 30,000 square feet can present a variety of challenges. While the larger formats assist the developer in reaching pre-leasing requirements with fewer commitments, fitting these stores into projects in which streetfront access is a priority requires an unusual level of innovation in creating sufficient "address points" and designing a variety of multilevel presentations. The challenges for the developer include positioning larger tenants to optimize the value of key locations and to enhance the value of secondary locations effectively.

The final consideration in weighting tenant value is uniqueness, either in terms of regional exclusivity or one-of-a-kind presentation. In the case of regional exclusivity, a strategic advantage can be gained by attracting a major tenant committed to either a limited presence or a single location within a market. A variety of brand stores and retail showcases are moving in this direction, with rollout plans often based on single stores in priority markets. Nike, for example, has limited

REI's flagship store in Seattle is the type of one-of-a-kind store that could be particularly valuable in sustaining an entertainment project's distinctiveness.

the rollout of NikeTown to six to ten markets domestically, while Virgin limits its mega-stores to destinations offering high synergy and leverage for its brand.

One-of-a-kind presentations can be even more valuable in sustaining a project's distinctiveness. Coca Cola's showcase in Atlanta, Warner Brothers' nine-story studio store in New York, REI's flagship store in Seattle, and Discovery Channel's store in the MCI Center in Washington, D.C., fall into this category. Customized entertainment venues, such as Simon DeBartolo Group's proposed American Experience in Philadelphia and Sony's *Where the Wild Things Are* children's attraction at Metreon in San Francisco also represent one-of-a-kind experiences that can reinforce the destination status of a project. The value of these venues in drawing visitors and encouraging repeat visits needs to be weighed against a variety of other tenant decisions and component costs.

Tenant credit also is critical to securing financing for a project. Once again, the developer must balance a desire to differentiate the project through unique and innovative tenants with a need to ensure that a significant percentage of leases are secured by strong credit. A more aggressive strategy currently being pursued by a number of developers is to mitigate some of the risks of customizing entertainment development through partial or full ownership in entertainment anchors or restaurants and novel dining venues. REIT spinoffs represent a new vehicle for such investments.

DESTINATION DEVELOPMENT RISK PROFILE

Risk Profile	Current Response	Alternative Response
New, untested product type	Emphasize entertainment as a substitute anchor.	Differentiate unproven features from other components; identify specific risk mitigation of these features.
Location-specific customization	Emphasize a UEC "formula": cinema anchor, similar tenant rosters, similar scale.	Identify cost-sharing approaches with public sector, tenants, sponsors.
No comparables to use as basis for evaluation	Use urban malls, regional malls, and selected other projects as comparables.	Use benchmarking on a component basis; aggressively prelease projects.
Added hard and soft development costs	Limit costs within parameters of a retail pro forma.	Identify cost-sharing measures for key features and components.
Unproven entertainment anchors that lack sustainable differentiation	Emphasize anchors as activity generators; de-emphasize mechanics of multi-anchoring.	Emphasize multi-anchoring.
Unproven "destination economics"	Emphasize five- and ten-mile proximate and primary markets.	Identify components within project with demonstrated regional drawing power.

Source: MRA International.

ILLUSTRATIVE ENTERTAINMENT RESTAURANT SALES FIGURES

	Average Sales PSF[1]	Percent of Mall-Based Average	Top-Performing Unit Sales PSF	Percent of Mall-Based Average
Top 10% Mall-Based Restaurants[1]	$429	100	N/A	N/A
Cheesecake Factory	$833	194	$861	201
Planet Hollywood	$841	196	$1,799	419
Rainforest Cafe	$774	180	$1,100	256

1. Mall-based figure is for average sales per square foot for the top 10% of national restaurants serving liquor in U.S. super regional malls. Figures reflect owned and operated units only.

Sources: Company financial disclosures; *Dollars & Cents of Shopping Centers.*

Risk Profiles of Entertainment-Based Developments

As previously discussed, the developers of UEC's and other entertainment-based developments face a number of challenges in meeting financial investment criteria. These challenges include the novel character of the developments; the customization required to position projects as destinations; the lack of true comparables with relevant performance histories; additional development costs associated with differentiating the projects; risks related to entertainment-based anchoring; and concerns over the difficulty of achieving destination status.

To a large extent, the financial sources interested in funding destination projects have a *real estate* rather than a *new venture* orientation and therefore have based financial commitments on comparable real estate transactions. Destination economics is understandably held in suspicion given that the limited number of projects that *have* achieved destination status are still anomalies (e.g., the Forum Shops in Las Vegas with its $1,200-per-square-foot sales in 1996). Accordingly, in presenting these projects developers have emphasized the features that are most similar to those of recognized retail models and have suggested that these developments follow an entertainment retail formula of sorts. The resulting paradox is that developers have been pressed into creating developments that appear to perform like retail malls, while they work to craft destination projects with far more robust performance. This is a critical issue in that it constrains the ability of entertainment-enhanced retail developments to achieve destination-level performance. The way out of this dilemma may be found through alternative sources of financing, through the successful operation of a number of threshold projects, and through the mitigation of several perceived risks. The matrix on the facing page identifies six key aspects of the risk profile of the destination development, the common responses to these risks, and a set of alternative responses that developers might pursue.

Financial institutions' primary concern about destination developments is that they are new and untested. The typical response from developers has been to assert that this form of development is similar in most respects to familiar forms of retail development, with the substitution of entertainment anchors for traditional department stores. Given the rapid expansion and redesign of theaters, that response has been accepted, albeit with some reservations about the sustainability of the multiplex as an anchor. The problem, as discussed earlier, is that this approach places constraints on the strategic positioning of destination projects.

A more strategic response to this issue is to focus on a multi-anchor structure, emphasizing the component features that increase performance. Within this mix of activity generators, activity inducers, and activity extenders there is a strong body of proven and demonstrable concepts. The table on page 87, for example, lists a set of top-performing destination restaurants, relative to industry standards. Similar performance records for icon retailers can be demonstrated. While entertainment venues, other than the megaplex, do not have sufficient operating history to provide demonstrable levels of performance, within the broader matrix of multi-anchoring the tolerance for risk may be extended.

Another financial concern relates to customization of destination developments to achieve distinctiveness. The strategic response is to emphasize the significance of place mak-

The Fremont Street Experience was created by the city of Las Vegas in 1995 in an effort to restore lost glitter to its downtown. The Jerde Partnership wrapped Fremont Street in light, sound, and motion, creating a dynamic stage for urban theater.

The Jerde Partnership

ing in differentiating the destination development. The positive role of place making can be demonstrated across a variety of developments including Third Street Promenade, Universal CityWalk, Reston Town Center, CocoWalk, the Forum Shops, and others (see case studies in Chapter 5).

Equally important from a financial perspective is to identify ways to share the costs of customization of public spaces and facade treatments. As noted earlier, the public sector can be an important ally in creating public spaces that exhibit a higher level of amenities and design quality than would be feasible otherwise. The public spaces of a destination development can contribute to the character and identity of a downtown in an important and lasting way. From a local government perspective, sharing these costs can represent an investment in the city that has both tangible and intangible benefits.

The third issue involves the lack of comparable projects with relevant performance histories. The response has been to use traditional retail projects as the performance model with the previously noted dilemma that this constrains the projected performance of the destination project. The alternative is to develop a program that captures the vision for creating a destination project, calculating the rents that are necessary to provide the hurdle returns and testing these assumptions with likely tenants. The "pitch" to the tenants needs to be based on a detailed understanding of their respective business models, conveying how the destination project will increase their sales and brand recognition in the market region.

In addition to the costs associated with public spaces, costly store facade treatments and tenant improvements can increase hard costs. The interactive process involved in addressing the customized requirements of key tenants also adds to soft costs. The strategic response is to work with tenants to arrange for equitable allocation of these costs and to apply the same weighting criteria to allowances that were applied to the project's lease

ENHANCING PERFORMANCE TO ACHIEVE DESTINATION ECONOMICS

Seven features of destination projects have the potential to increase project performance:

▼ Multiple anchors whose combined "pull" draws visitors from a broad region
▼ Programmable venues and enhanced consumer choices that encourage repeat visitation
▼ Regionally exclusive offerings that help achieve market dominance
▼ Broad appeal across a spectrum of consumers based on providing a variety of consumer itineraries and choices.
▼ Extended length of visit and increased consumer expenditures per visit
▼ Entertainment and cultural and recreational activities that increase productivity during low-demand periods
▼ A base of overnight and day-trip tourists drawn by a distinctive mix of offerings and links with established attractions.

Source: MRA International.

structure. Clearly, the track record of the development team in successfully executing similar projects will be a key issue for financing sources.

Of all the perceived risks the most significant from the perspective of financial sources is the lack of performance data demonstrating the ability of destination developments to manifest destination economics. The response here is to identify a number of components within the project that have demonstrated an ability either to draw patrons from broad geographic distances or achieve very high market penetration. These components typically would include the activity generators (megaplexes), activity extenders (theme and signature restaurants), and activity inducers (brand and icon retailers) that anchor the project. As noted earlier, tenant confidence reflected in rental rates achieved during preleasing also can be important in elevating performance assessments by financial institutions.

In the end, the acceptance of more robust performance parameters for these projects will depend upon the existence of an array of successful developments that have achieved these results in a number of markets over time. The next four to five years will be a critical period in which a variety

of developments including Metreon, Sunset Place, Pacific Place, Hollywood and Highland, Penn's Landing, and others establish a record of performance.

These features of a destination development (see feature box above) have considerably greater potential than those of other forms of retailing to increase project performance. As the table on the next page illustrates, the difference in performance expectations of a regional mall and those of a destination project is considerable. Realizing those expectations requires considerable skill and strategic insight on the part of the development team. To create the combined pull from entertainment, dining, and retail components required to achieve the status of a regional centerpoint requires a deep understanding of consumer segments and competitive offerings within the market; the ability to secure key tenants (and often push them to create unique executions of their products); and the ability to effectively array anchoring components in a configuration that supports a variety of visitor itineraries. Similarly, using clustered dining to draw a broad spectrum of patrons and to extend visit duration requires an intimate understanding of how specific restaurants can be effectively combined to increase consumer choices and attract specific visitor segments.

COMPARISON OF PERFORMANCE EXPECTATIONS

Performance Parameters	Super Regional Mall	Destination Development
Scale	800,000 to 1.7 million square feet	250,000 to 600,000 square feet
Sales/square foot	$300 to $330/square foot	$700 to $1,200/square foot
Drawing Radius	Approximately 20 miles	Estimated 35/40 miles
Repeat Visitation	Average of three times per month; penetration of 80–200 percent	Average of two to four times per month; penetration of 100–400 percent
Regional Dominance	Achieved through department store anchors/scale/mix	Achieved through unique-to-region offerings
Multisegment Appeal	Tends to be focused on shopping trips	Broadened via entertainment and dining offerings
Visit Duration	Approximately 1.24 hours	Estimated 3.5 hours
Demand Period Productivity	Concentrated across number of periods; affected by seasonality	Concentrated over evening and day-time periods; enhancement of low periods via tourist and leisure activities
Tourist Draw	Limited	Potentially 20 percent to 40 percent of visitor base depending on location

Source: MRA International.

This attention to detail begins with the strategic positioning of the destination development, when assessments of the market, demographic and psychographic patterns, competitive offerings, and locational attributes are made. The same level of scrutiny is required in defining the program, anchoring features, and other components.

EXECUTING A DESTINATION DEVELOPMENT

Successfully defining and executing a development that can perform as a regional destination requires a development team with unique capabilities that often cannot be found in a single development company. Therefore a development team that brings together the requisite skills must be assembled.

Working with Local Governments

The costs associated with executing destination developments typically require the participation of the public sector. Generally speaking, UEC and SED (signature entertainment development) projects involve infrastructure support in the form of access improvements, structured parking, and other enhancements to site capacity. As discussed earlier, public spaces and amenities also may require various levels of support from local governments or quasi-public organizations.

Working effectively with local governments in the 1990s involves skills that exceed those required by the public/private ventures of the 1970s and 1980s, which were largely supported by federal programs such as urban development action grants (UDAGs) and community development block grants (CDBGs). Funding today is derived primarily from local resources and programs such as tax increment financing (TIF), community improvement grants, and creative financing instruments (such as sale-leasebacks). Local governments have therefore become far more rigorous in their evaluation and expectations of project investments.

Returns on investment from the local government perspective are judged on the basis of both share in project performance and potential impact of the development on broader economic development priorities. For a majority of cities, the tourism and leisure industry has risen to the status of an economic generator, equivalent in economic importance to the service and manufacturing sectors. In large part, this reflects the competitive advantage of cities in serving as centers

of regional and overnight tourism through unique sports, cultural, and entertainment offerings. Investments in convention centers, performing arts centers, museums, sports facilities, waterfronts, and parks in the past decade have been designed to enhance the performance of cities as visitor centers. Within this context, destination developments also are being viewed as important strategic investments.

For the development team, working collaboratively with a local government (often in a development partnership) requires understanding public sector goals, capacities, and constraints. Specific areas of collaboration may include incorporating public amenities within the development; accommodating cultural facilities or events; participating in community goal setting and dialogues on issues; participating in a master-planning effort to integrate the development within a broader context; structuring development financing to effectively use both public and private investment; and working together to achieve destination status for the project.

The principal skill required of the development team in a public/private collaboration is the ability to create and manage a process

Sony's Metreon is a UEC that is under construction in San Francisco's city-sponsored cultural and entertainment district at Yerba Buena Gardens, south of Market Street. It is close to the city's convention center, museum of modern art, and public esplanade.

Sony Retail Entertainment

that effectively deploys the resources of both parties, assigns roles and responsibilities, maintains a schedule of joint and separate tasks, and supports a working relationship over the course of predevelopment and development. The greatest challenge often occurs in making the transition from bidding or negotiating for the project (in which the parties are on opposite sides of the table) to collaborating on its execution. While a successful partnership requires the best efforts of both parties, the developer's familiarity with project planning and execution may require taking the lead in forging a working relationship.

Collaborating with Core Tenants

Meeting the unique demands of core entertainment, retail, and restaurant tenants in destination developments also requires collaborative skills on the part of the development team. However, the scope and focus of the collaboration are different. Working with tenants involves continuous negotiations on venue location, tenant improvements, lease terms, timing, and related issues that need to be effectively managed while pushing to achieve mutually successful results. Tenants focus on the optimal performance of their product more than on the project's overall performance.

The development team must reconfigure tenant locations, spatial configurations, and store presentations to satisfy tenant objectives while optimizing the overall potential of the development to perform as a regional destination. The team needs to have a good understanding of core tenants' target markets, presentation concepts, and operations in order to address and balance individual expectations while pushing tenants toward commitments that support the distinctiveness of the project as a whole.

Unlike traditional retail developments, destination projects cannot rely on a leasing plan early in the predevelopment process as the template for tenanting. Changes and adjustments are made well into predevelopment to accommodate customized presentations and to craft a development that optimally addresses the overall guest experience.

Master Plan and Urban Development Skills

The context of a destination project is of equal importance to the developer and the local government. From the developer's perspective, supportive activities, amenities, and infrastructure are instrumental to positioning the project as a destination. To the public sector, the destination development often is a means of leveraging cultural and commercial assets near the project or increasing the competitive position of public facilities such as a convention facility or sports arena.

To address this issue effectively, the development team often needs to become involved in a master-planning effort that extends well beyond the boundaries of the destination development itself. This has been the case in developments such as Hollywood and Highland, Penn's Landing, and CityPlace in West Palm Beach. In the recently announced waterfront development in Long Beach, California, the developer, Oliver McMillan, is working with the city of Long Beach not only to master plan the extensive waterfront but to create a codevelopment plan for the city's existing restaurant district on Pine Avenue, nearly one-half mile north of the project.

While regional centers and mixed-use developments also often require developers to get involved in broader master-planning issues, destination developments may require a more effort given the integral link between these projects and a city's strategic goals as a visitor center.

Community Relations

Closely related to the development team's role in master planning is its role in interacting with surrounding communities. Community concerns may be centered on traffic, view

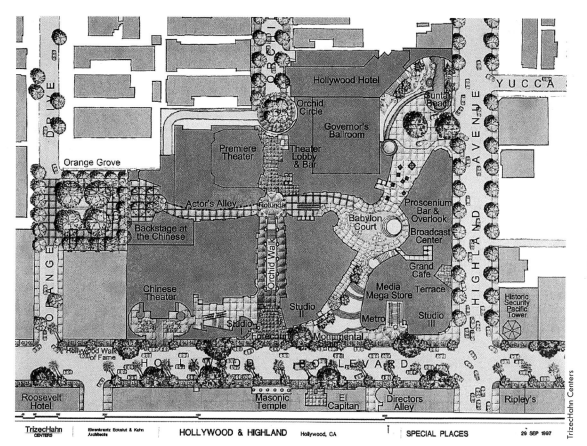

Orange Grove · Orchid Circle · Hollywood Hotel · YUCCA · Sunken Garden · Governor's Ballroom · Premiere Theater · Theater Lobby & Bar · Actor's Alley · Rotunda · Proscenium Bar & Overlook · Babylon Court · Broadcast Center · Backstage at the Chinese · Orchid Walk · Grand Cafe · Media Mega Store · Terrace · Chinese Theater · Studio II · Studio · Forecourt · Studio III · Metro · Monumental Stair · Historic Security Pacific Tower · Hollywood Walk of Fame · HOLLYWOOD BOULEVARD · Roosevelt Hotel · Masonic Temple · El Capitan · Directors Alley · Ripley's · HIGHLAND AVENUE · ORANGE DRIVE · ORANGE

TrizecHahn CENTERS · Ehrenkrantz Eckstut & Kuhn Architects · HOLLYWOOD & HIGHLAND · Hollywood, CA · SPECIAL PLACES · 29 SEP 1997 · TrizecHahn Centers

TrizecHahn's Hollywood and Highland project required the development team to work closely with Mann Theaters to recreate the majestic theaters of Hollywood's golden age by renovating the historic Chinese Theater and creating the opulent 1,000-seat Babylon Theater.

corridors, impacts on existing businesses, public sector investments, environmental issues, noise, crime, and a host of other issues. Destination projects can have a significant impact on surrounding areas, attracting more visits per year than the convention and sports facilities of a major city.

The development team needs to incorporate professionals who have broad experience in similar projects involving community relations as well as a number of specific skills that range from managing transportation to ensuring security.

In working together with the community, the development team and local government representatives should assume roles that reflect their responsibilities. Like other aspects of the predevelopment process, working with the community involves a series of meetings to identify community concerns, prioritize issues, assess means of addressing concerns, provide credible analysis and alternatives for dialogue, and often negotiate with community representatives to achieve project support. In

some cases the local government will take primary responsibility for working with the community and the development team's role will be limited to a series of community presentations.

Community residents often are concerned about developments that serve an outside day-visitor or tourist market and their impact on the local environment and quality of life. However, a well-conceived destination development can add a significant dimension to surrounding neighborhoods as well as boost local real estate values and business performance. A key feature of the development team's interaction with the local community is to identify these potential community enhancements and develop a program, plan, and execution strategy to incorporate them as part of the destination. The Penn's Landing project in Philadelphia involved an extensive series of community meetings that resulted in a plan that nearly doubled the scale of public amenities over the existing waterfront facilities.

Forum Shops at Caesars Palace

Integration of Entertainment, Retail and Dining Products

The development team will be involved in integrating entertainment venues within the project and may need to work with core tenants to create customized presentations. TrizecHahn's Hollywood and Highland project required the development team to work closely with Mann Theaters to recreate the majestic theaters of Hollywood's golden age by renovating the historic Chinese Theater and creating the opulent 1,000-seat Babylon Theater.

Similar attention to the details of location, presentation, and operations also is required for core dining and retail tenants. In the end, the development team is responsible for orchestrating a *guest experience*, based on the combined effect of between ten to 20 entertainment, dining, and retail tenants.

The Guest Experience

Destination development requires skills more akin to those associated with resort development than with typical retail projects. The guest experience must be thought through for each major visitor segment, with a focus on the sequence of activities needed to create a satisfying itinerary. Generally, achieving destination-level performance requires that visitors stay three to four hours.

The Forum Shops in Las Vegas serves as an example of a project in which the guest experience takes precedence in configuring tenant locations and public spaces. The challenge undertaken by the developers, the Simon DeBartolo Group and the Gordon Company, was to create a *centerpoint* in a city of extraordinary but often ephemeral attractions. Organized around three public spaces, two enlivened by animatronic statues and special-effects fountains and the third by a re-creation of the sculptural waterworks at Rome's Piazza Navonna, the Forum creates a sequence of programmed and unprogrammed experiences. The Forum succeeds not only as a must-see attraction but also as the city's centerpoint, attracting both first-time visitors and return guests.

Developments such as Sunset Place, Penn's Landing, Hollywood and Highland and CityPlace in West Palm Beach also are being developed around the guest experience. The challenge for the development team is to recognize the diverse mix of patrons to be accommodated and configure the project to address multiple visitor itineraries.

Brand Development and Identity

The final skill required in executing a destination development is creating a unique identity related to a particular city, town, or context. Given a similar roster of tenants, similar development parameters, and similar performance requirements, this is no mean task. Indeed, the complexities in programming, financing, and executing these projects might favor a more formulaic approach, but the success of a destination depends in large part on the perception that it offers a unique experience and identity.

The elements involved in creating such an identity include the design of public spaces; architecture and scenographics; the use of back stories or contextual associations; and at times the application of brand development techniques. In a variety of developments, branding consultants are being used to apply the techniques used in creating identities for consumer products. Branding has been applied to destination development in the past, as is evident in the strong brand associations consumers have for theme parks and resorts. However, the application of branding to retail environments is new and represents an important skill to be acquired and exercised by the development team.

Interestingly, the cities which often act as partners in developing destinations also have been turning to branding consultants to define and differentiate themselves as destinations for conventioneers and overnight tourists. These efforts have focused on blending the authenticity of a particular place with a sense of fantasy or romance to appeal to the potential visitor.

TOWARD THE DESTINATION DEVELOPMENT

Entertainment-enhanced development is taking a wide variety of forms, ranging from megaplex additions to existing malls to major destination developments. Nevertheless, these projects share a central defining feature: the use of entertainment in combination with dining and retail venues to increase the capacity of the development to draw patrons from a broader market, more frequently, and for longer durations.

The evolution of entertainment-enhanced projects in the 1990s clearly favors developments that perform at the level of destinations, acting as the centerpoint for an entire city or region. The challenges in achieving this status are considerable, for these projects represent nothing less than a new product as dramatic in its impact as were the grand department stores at the turn of the century. The skills required of the developer are not dissimilar from those of the merchant princes who created Macy's and Wanamaker's, which were theaters and museums as much as they were emporiums. Those skills must include the ability to draw diverse consumers from a broad market by integrating entertainment, dining, and shopping in an environment that delights the senses. The developer has a collaborator in that endeavor in the cities and towns searching for ways to distinguish themselves as a regional center and tourism destination.

The prospect offered by the next wave of developments, from Metreon to Penn's Landing, is to achieve a geographic draw three times greater and a length of stay four times longer than that of the top-performing regional centers. Achieving this level of performance is the threshold for a new generation of destination developments.

CHAPTER 4

PLANNING AND DESIGN

PLANNING CONTEXT

The goal of urban entertainment center planning and design should be to create a destination that, in addition to including entertainment and retail uses, is in itself entertaining, because what draws customers is the desire for personal enjoyment and stimulation as much as the opportunity to purchase specific goods. To achieve this result, successful developments—and the architecture that shapes, defines, and houses them—must offer variety and create a sense of discovery and excitement in visitors. To be successful, urban entertainment centers must provide, through their design, an experience that feels continually "new" to the repeat visitor and do so in a way that is both intimate and energized.

While the design of most shopping environments has moved toward standardization, particularly that of the large-scale multilevel shopping mall, the daily life of the shopper has moved toward greater variety. Television and films create extraordinary special effects; moderately priced leisure travel is taking more people to more exotic locations; and restaurant dining has become more frequent and more entertaining. All of this means that consumers increasingly demand wider variety in their daily life, and they are most attracted to new visual, intellectual, and emotional experiences that surprise, entertain, and offer engaging activities and spaces.

Americans also have become "plugged in" at home to large-screen televisions, VCRs, laser disks, surround-sound speakers, Nintendos, laptops, fax machines, and the Internet. The result is that experiences outside the home must provide an even greater level of stimulation through the introduction of light, color, sound, smell, movement, variety, and detail in spaces designed not so much for circulation as for interaction.

Along with heightened expectations for entertaining experiences in entertaining places, people also want and need social and verbal contact with others—something that is not available at home. Creating "people spaces" that are activated, comfortable, safe, and engaging is therefore a critical element of entertainment centers. Shopping mall food courts were the first attempt to create people places, but the UEC takes this effort much further by emphasizing contact between people throughout the center and recreating the essential public experience.

Another factor influencing entertainment center design is that people are willing to spend more time in a center than in other retail environments. They do not plan to buy a few items and rush home. Rather, they come to engage in multiple activities: to dine, see a movie, browse, and shop or perhaps just to hang out, to see and be seen. Developers of entertainment centers seek to attract this type of consumer, the recreational shopper who will spend discretionary time at the center, rather than the target shopper, who will come and go quickly. To accomplish this requires designing spaces that encourage strolling and browsing while at the same time setting the stage for multiple activities, impulse decision making, and spontaneous interaction.

The architecture of entertainment centers must respond to all of these needs. This does not mean that the architecture need be extreme. It does mean that it should have variety, complexity, drama, and texture and be readily changeable. The visitor should be able to notice new things on repeat visits. It also means that there should be a feeling of ele-gance, of being in an upscale and special place. The design should encourage visitors to dress up a bit and be an actor on the urban entertainment stage. A sense of local heritage and historical continuity also is important, since the energy of change is enhanced and supported by a distinct cultural framework.

The basic elements of the tenant mix are discussed in Chapter 2; however, even if the mix is good, the overall design must provide activated, attractive public spaces—from alleys to piazzas. It must provide energy, excitement, and a sense of adventure and novelty, but, at the same time, familiarity and security. How and where can this be done? The design strategies depend on the setting.

DESIGN SETTINGS

Entertainment centers can exist in a wide variety of settings: urban entertainment districts, shopping malls; large-scale, mixed-use projects; and stand-alone entertainment centers, including those collocated with stadiums, arenas, convention centers, and casinos. Each of these venues has specific planning and design requirements that are addressed in the following sections.

Integration of Uses

The mix of experiences and attractions in UECs augments and strengthens surrounding land uses as it attracts more people. Many communities are courting entertainment development to encourage urban revitalization and generate retail jobs as well as to increase property and sales taxes. The urban entertainment center can be a regional draw, attracting dollars from other communities within a trade area that can extend as far as 20 to 30 miles. Large centers also are tourist attractions that draw out-of-town visitors who otherwise might not visit.

Perhaps most important, entertainment centers are a source of community pride and

interaction because they project an exciting new image of the city to the outside world—an important key to successful urban revitalization. This is particularly true when the project is sited in the older or historic part of the city where cultural facilities are concentrated and where the city's unique essence is most powerful.

The integration of public facilities adds a local flavor and cultural context to a project, a key to long-term project success. Community facilities such as libraries, university branches, museums, performing arts venues, and even civic offices strengthen the mix of activities at entertainment centers and help differentiate them from similar projects in other cities or at other locations in the metropolitan area. Universal CityWalk, in Universal City, California, for example, includes a UCLA extension on the upper levels above the stores and restaurants. In New York City, numerous performing arts theaters—includ-

ing one devoted to children's theater, the New Victory Theater—are near the two major entertainment centers now under construction on 42nd Street in Manhattan.

Many college campuses do not have entertaining places to gather, but the pent-up demand for retail/entertainment uses is evident. At the University of California, San Diego, the student union, the Price Center, has a classroom/lecture hall that serves as a commercial cinema in the evening. The campus bookstore faces the cinema across an active piazza bordered by a variety of food and small-scale retail enterprises. The center has been well received by campus users, with the bookstore and food service operations posting some of the highest profits per square foot of any similar operation, on or off campus. Reported sales are in the $900 per square foot range—even though school is in session for only eight months a year and there is no Christmas buying season.

The Price Center at the University of California, San Diego, has a classroom/lecture hall that serves as a commercial cinema in the evening.

Urban Entertainment Districts

Entertainment centers act as anchors within larger historic or cultural districts much as department stores act as anchors in traditional shopping centers, and they can generate spin-off developments that over time can create or revitalize entire districts. The evolution of these districts usually involves multiple property owners and some level of public involvement in their planning, design, and creation. In this section, the creation and evolution of several different types of urban entertainment district are described in relation to the degree of local government planning required to achieve success.

One Colorado in Old Town Pasadena, California, a small, cineplex-anchored entertainment center in the heart of a thriving urban entertainment district, required limited government support.

KMD Architects

Limited government planning

The success of One Colorado, a small, cineplex-anchored entertainment center in the Old Town section of Pasadena, California, demonstrates what a vital part of an urban renewal strategy entertainment centers can be and how they can sometimes be created with relatively minor government support. In the 12 blocks around One Colorado, retail taxes tripled in the last three years. The pace of new development has been extraordinary. Retail uses came first, followed by apartments, and much of the construction is attributable to the success of One Colorado. Furthermore, it was not necessary to invoke local government powers to develop the project, and many of the costs of traditional city-funded redevelopment were avoided. One Colorado was privately financed, and municipal aid was limited to bond financing of parking garages that also serve local office buildings. Occupying a little less than a city block, the project has energized an entire neighborhood.

The design of public spaces within the project is very much a factor in the success of One Colorado. So too are the cinemas, convenient parking, and large floor plates in the remodeled buildings that accommodate sizeable anchor tenants, including Gordon Biersch and Il Fornaio. But it is the mix of public spaces—from narrow walkways to a generous piazza activated by the two anchor restaurants—that has made the difference. It has lifted the performance of the nearby small retail stores that were struggling on Colorado Boulevard—a wonderfully ample street that is perfect for the annual Rose Bowl Parade, but much too wide for the intimate and activated scene that shoppers prefer.

Moderate government planning

While One Colorado is perhaps the most dramatic example of successful urban district rejuvenation with minimal government intervention, Santa Monica's Third Street Promenade represents a higher level of government support. Its experience is revealing in a variety of ways. While the promenade is anchored

Sundance Square, a mixed-use residential and entertainment-oriented project in downtown Ft. Worth, Texas, has succeeded despite a difficult development environment.

by a large and prosperous Rouse-owned shopping mall with successful tenants, in the 1980s the merchants of Third Street were not doing well. The first step toward revitalization was made in 1989, when the street was closed to traffic; however, the closing had little positive impact on retail performance. The city, recognizing the vitality of cinemas as a retail draw, then enacted an ordinance dictating that no cinema construction would be allowed in Santa Monica except in the Third Street district. Three new privately financed cineplexes and publicly financed parking garages were then built there, causing an immediate upsurge in business and an influx of new restaurant and retail tenants. That in turn created strong demand for offices and hotel rooms in the district, and Santa Monica has since become one of Southern California's premiere places to shop, visit, and work.

What made Third Street succeed? It was not the closing of the street or its redesigned landscaping; they were relatively minor elements. The city government's clever redevelopment planning, which brought in the cineplex anchors and convenient parking, made the real difference, drawing a supporting cast of entertainment-oriented restaurants and shops.

It is also important to note that the West Side of Los Angeles, where Santa Monica is located, has been the beneficiary of an extraordinary economic boom that that undoubtedly speeded up the redevelopment process. (See the case study of Third Street Promenade in Chapter 5).

Why do some entertainment districts succeed and others struggle? Westwood, California, provides an instructive example. This very pleasant suburban downtown adjoins the southern edge of the sprawling UCLA campus and would seem to have every advantage as an entertainment center. It has a low-rise profile, a history of retail success, major office employment, wealthy residential neighborhoods, and even a department store. Yet it has not flourished as One Colorado and Third Street Promenade have. The answer seems to be that the city has not been able to implement a coordinated public plan to create activated public spaces with strong security, adequate parking, a critical mass of cinemas, and the large floor plates demanded by anchor entertainment tenants. With such a strategy, Westwood could become a vital and successful entertainment center.

Sundance Square, a mixed-use residential and entertainment-oriented project anchored by a cineplex in downtown Ft. Worth, Texas, demonstrates the benefits of these efforts in a much more difficult development environment. This project has become a popular place to go to the movies, clubs, and shops even though the neighborhood being revitalized around it lacks many of the basic design features that most successful urban entertainment districts have, particularly a neighborhood scale and a strong sense of place.

Massive local government planning

The rejuvenation of Times Square in New York City represents a massive government effort that in a remarkably short time has completely changed what had become a dangerous and sleazy neighborhood into what once again is the world's entertainment center. Public/private organizations, including a redevelopment authority and a business improvement district, were established to oversee the transformation. Some of the major public efforts successfully restoring the glitter to Times Square include the city's closing of the majority of the sex-related businesses and its use of its powers of condemnation to permit property assembly for redevelopment; public subsidies for major projects, starting with Disney's spectacular restoration of the New Amsterdam Theater; public infrastructure improvements such as the ongoing rebuilding of the massive 42nd Street subway station; elaborate new zoning regulations; and dazzling signage requirements and building design. Several major entertainment anchors are under construction on 42nd Street, including E-Walk, developed by Tishman Urban Development Corporation on the street's north side at Eighth Avenue, and Forest City Ratner's major cineplex and entertainment center anchored by Madame Tussaud's on the south side.

Shopping Malls with Entertainment

The introduction of entertainment can enliven a traditional shopping mall only if it is physically connected to the center in a way that creates a synergy of activities. Until recently, the traditional design strategy has been to place a few entertainment components—usually cinemas and restaurants—on outpads, either on individual sites or loosely interlinked, but without using a comprehensive design to create a compelling destination. Shopping center developers employed this strategy for decades because they were not interested in leasing prime space to low-rent-paying tenants like cinemas. However, that does not bring the cinema customer into the mall itself or the mall customer into the cinema, and it certainly does not create the synergy that bundled entertainment attractions can.

A second strategy is to use land adjacent to an existing shopping center and create a complete entertainment center—with streets, piazzas, and a mix of tenants—that is functionally connected to the original center so that pedestrians can move effortlessly from one part to the other. Third Street Promenade, for example, was created adjacent to an enclosed shopping mall, Santa Monica Place, which was reconfigured to encourage customers to move between the two. However, few malls have the necessary amount of land, ten to 40 acres, to do so. In some cases structured parking can be created, reclaiming the necessary land from surface parking; however, this adds a significant cost that may render the project infeasible without financial assistance, such as public funding at Third Street Promenade.

The third strategy involves integrating entertainment into a shopping center, as was done at Mall of America in Bloomington, Minnesota, where patrons have taken the escalator to the third floor to a multiplex and a collection of clubs since the late 1980s, and at CocoWalk in Florida. (See case studies of Mall of America and CocoWalk in Chapter 5). Mall of America and West Edmonton Mall in Edmonton, Alberta, both have large-scale entertainment attractions in interior atriums that are surrounded by traditional

Centro Oberhausen is a massive retail/entertainment mega-mall that features enclosed and open-air sections as well as leisure activities designed around elaborate water features.

shopping venues. Some of the entertainment attractions at Mall of America are the LEGO Imagination Center, UnderWater World, and Camp Snoopy, an amusement park with a roller coaster; West Edmonton Mall has a wave pool and submarine. These places convey a strong sense of vitality because visitors can view others enjoying the entertainment attractions from numerous vantage points on all levels of the shopping center and because there are many opportunities to wander and wonder.

A variation of this design strategy is to add a separate wing to the shopping center at the end of which is a cineplex and food court that act as the anchor rather than a department store. Entertainment retail and theme attractions line the corridor to the cinema. One of the nation's premier regional centers, Tysons Corner Center in suburban Washington, D.C., plans to pursue this strategy in 1998.

Integrating entertainment with shopping in a traditional mall poses several design challenges. Operating hours for cinemas and other entertainment attractions often are longer than store hours. Access during these hours can be provided by installing escalators that can be shut off from the main mall. Care also must be taken to ensure that pedestrian traffic is not impeded by the lines that may form at major entertainment venues. At the same time, access between shopping and entertainment areas must remain easy, open, and visually connected, encouraging natural movement between the two. Finally, food and beverage service, a major adjunct to the entertainment attractions, should be located next to these attractions or readily accessible to take advantage of the obvious opportunity for synergy.

Entertainment in Mixed-Use Centers

Entertainment/retail uses can be a vital factor in energizing a large mixed-use development. Shopping, dining, and entertainment can help energize the entire development and make it a vibrant part of the larger community. Major examples include Rockefeller Center in New York and Embarcadero Center in San Francisco.

Embarcadero Center demonstrates clearly how appropriate retail and entertainment attractions can dramatically enhance the market appeal of a mixed-use development and become a profit center in themselves. When built, the center was in what was considered a slightly out-of-the-way location. However, the three-story retail component made the center individual, varied, and interesting from the start, and it was a key factor in ensuring that the center's office towers commanded top rents. In 1995, when the center consisted of six office buildings and two hotels on an eight-block site, an eight-screen cinema was added to the second level of retail shops in an attempt to reenergize the space and draw people to the upper levels to shop and dine. The effort has been dramatically successful. Pedestrian traffic has increased, sales

A proposed mixed-use development in Japan will contain major retail/ entertainment components.

KMD Architects

have increased, and the entire center vibrates with ever-increasing activity.

What design lessons can be learned from this? First, food service and shops on the upper levels of a large-scale urban project are much energized by a cinema. Prior to the introduction of the cinema, the fast food outlets and restaurants were doing a reasonable lunchtime business due to their generally high quality and the presence of a large number of on-site office workers. At dinner, however, it was a very different story.

Second, it is critical that the entertainment/retail segment of a dense, high-rise project be designed on an intimate scale—not an easy task. Attention to detail, drama, and diversity should be observed. In the case of a very large center, some separation between the dominant tower forms, particularly those of office buildings, and the entertainment retail section allows a "village" to be formed on a more intimate scale than is possible when large–floor-plate towers are clustered together above the retail component, dominating it with their enormous size.

Third, a large-scale, mixed-use project with an entertainment/retail component is a better neighbor to adjoining residential developments than office towers that are abandoned in the evening.

Fourth, the Embarcadero Center's basic layout is instructive. It is long and narrow, with one tight pedestrian circulation path winding eventfully down the middle of its length, providing interesting pedestrian-scaled places for retail activity. Some criticize the bridges between blocks as awkward, but when they are well activated and used for seating, pedestrian traffic is strong. When seating is not present and the bridges become too narrow and long, traffic and vitality vanish.

Stand-Alone Urban Entertainment Centers

Developers still are trying to determine precisely which components, in what combinations, and in what amounts of space are op-

Dive! is an underwater-theme restaurant created by Steven Spielberg with a readily identifiable design.

timal for different locations and situations. Once a track record has been established for various types of entertainment centers, the range of physical requirements and size guidelines will undoubtedly be clearer. But today only the broadest and most general conclusions can be drawn.

The maximum size for an urban entertainment center has not yet been determined. Expansion of the Forum Shops and the planned expansion of the Entertainment Center at Irvine Spectrum demonstrate a trend toward increasing size that is being driven in part by the entertainment tenants themselves as standard sizes for cineplexes, restaurants, and other retailers grow.

Cinema complexes with more than 24 screens increasingly are being proposed and built in suburban shopping centers as well as downtown locations. Ontario Mills in Ontario, California, currently has 54 screens in two separately owned and operated megaplexes. Theme restaurants such as Dive! and Nascar Cafe, which typically occupy between 18,000 and 30,000 square feet, are booming with larger and more dramatic themes and floor-plate sizes. Entertainment attractions increasingly are combining multiple functions that require 60,000 to more than 100,000 square feet of space within a single environment; examples are Dave & Busters and Game-Works, which combine various types of participatory virtual reality games and other entertainment features along with food and drink operations. Supporting entertainment retailers also are joining the rush to increase individual store sizes. Finally, educational, cultural, and civic uses that increasingly are being added to the entertainment mix also can require wide-ranging amounts of space.

The primary issue may well be how small an urban entertainment center can be and still be successful. Based on the limited number of operational centers, a minimum size may include 3,500 cinema seats occupying roughly 140,000 square feet; 400 restaurant seats in about 22,000 square feet; and between 16,000 and 60,000 square feet of general entertainment/retail space, for a total rough minimum of 175,000 to 200,000 square feet. This figure is preliminary and may change over time as more market examples become available. Smaller entertainment center prototypes are likely to be successful in smaller communities. A wide range of parking ratios will be the norm. In an urban area with existing street and office parking the need could be as low as four per 1,000 square feet of retail space. In isolated suburban projects, particularly those with a large proportion of cinema space, the need can be as high as 17 per 1,000 square feet.

SITE PLANNING

Successful urban entertainment centers provide spaces for people to come together to see and enjoy themselves in ways that rarely have been found in the United States. The

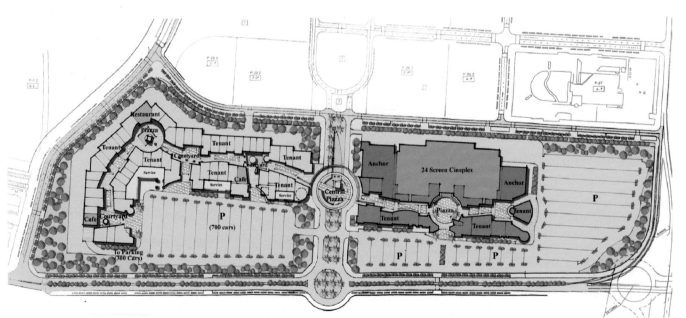

The site plan for the planned Las Rozas retail/entertainment center in Madrid, Spain, shows a deliberately meandering pedestrian spine that has an intriguing variety of widths and scales and includes piazzas where people can gather.

traditional American main street, idealized today, was usually so wide and the retail that opened onto it of such low density that relatively little social interaction was associated with it. The American town square, actually a park, was even less social. Successful entertainment centers, on the other hand, often have spaces and scenes, whether indoor or outdoor, that are similar to those of the ideal small European village with intricate but active streets and the energized square or piazza whose size, sense of enclosure, and high level of activity developers seek to emulate and improve upon.

Village Design and Scale

To date, many entertainment centers have been designed in a traditional village style and scale. Some, like Third Street Promenade and One Colorado, are largely renovations in which new construction has been designed to fit into the historic context. This is particularly noticeable at One Colorado, where the one large new building that houses restaurants and cinemas is a close match of the existing red-brick industrial buildings that form most of the streetscape. This technique gives the complex, like a village or city, the appearance of having evolved over time.

The village style reinforces a sense of heritage and continuity within a strong cultural framework that enhances and supports the energy of change. As in Universal City-Walk's Jerde-designed Phase I and in the KMD plan for Phase II with its idealized design references to Los Angeles in the 1930s, the design context should be recognizable but heighten the sense of activity, energy, and detail. Exterior style is critical. Every storefront should be unique, and in order to achieve the desired scale, one store may occupy two or even three storefronts.

The configuration of the land needed for a stand-alone entertainment center is quite flexible. The most important factor is that there be enough room to allow for at least 300 feet of pedestrian walkways of various

KMD Architects

widths and scales to connect the features of the center, providing a "yellow brick road" along which customers can stroll and enjoy the attractions. Some form of piazza or town square also is a key ingredient. Indoors or outdoors, a piazza provides a gathering place where people can congregate to enjoy the passing scene and prolong their stay.

The importance of public spaces and their design cannot be overstated. In many ways the character and design of entertainment centers, even more than the tenant mix, differentiate them from a traditional shopping mall. Usually, the only mall space that even remotely resembles a town square is the food court, and the resemblance is remote. Entertainment centers function best when their town square is augmented by a variety of pedestrian "streets" for strolling. These can

Two Rodeo Center in Beverly Hills, while not an urban entertainment center, demonstrates the drama of grand staircases and curving pedestrian walkways in new-generation retail projects.

be indoor or outdoor, depending on climate and market preferences. Universal CityWalk; the Forum Shops; CocoWalk; Reston Town Center; and One Colorado are some of the best examples of entertainment centers with central gathering places and streets for strolling (see case studies in Chapter 5).

In laying out the configuration of streets and gathering places, care must be taken to ensure that the desired mix of large and small tenant spaces can be accommodated without introducing blank walls, inactive spaces, and other design gaps that interrupt the continuous stimulus provided by shop windows, marquees, lights, signs, and action. In multilevel entertainment centers, continuous vantage points should be maintained so that customers can connect visually with other parts of the center and are continuously stimulated by the buzz of other people's activities.

Pedestrian Streets

Pedestrian streets in entertainment centers, whether indoor or outdoor, are ideally rich in detail and used only by pedestrians. Broad avenues and boulevards can indeed be retail successes—the Champs Elysees in Paris and North Michigan Avenue in Chicago are notable examples. However, experience at existing entertainment centers strongly indicates that the ideal street for the desired sense of discovery and novelty is one that curves, is 30 to 55 feet wide, and has no cars. In addition, its width should vary if it is longer than 100 feet in order to avoid visual monotony.

The failure of the strategy of closing traditional retail streets to auto traffic, a popular revitalization strategy in the 1960s, is well known. The antidotes, which have had varied success, have been to introduce buses, as at Nicollet Mall in Minneapolis, or to allow limited automobile traffic, as at Third Street Promenade in Santa Monica. However, the strategic failure of closing traditional retail streets does not necessarily apply to UECs. Narrow pedestrian-only streets work well at

One Colorado, Universal CityWalk, and the Entertainment Center at Irvine Spectrum.

Curved streets seem to enhance pedestrians' experience by increasing their curiosity about what lies beyond the bend. The power of the curve and of the accompanying detail perhaps is demonstrated best at Two Rodeo Center, a small and extraordinarily successful specialty shopping center on Rodeo Drive in Beverly Hills. A new pedestrian street, Via Rodeo, was created as its focal space. This popular gathering and strolling place is curved and even slopes upward from the main point of access with the street in order to create two levels of streetfront retail. The shops facing Rodeo Drive itself are located under Via Rodeo. The project has emerged as a major retail and community center.

The Central Gathering Place

What does the wonderfully evocative word, "piazza," mean in terms of an urban entertainment center? Are there specific techniques for achieving a successful, interactive, central gathering place? The answer, perhaps surprisingly, is "yes." The following are some of the major design principles recommended by a KMD research study of the architectural qualities that make piazzas work well:

▼ Provide ample public seating in a variety of forms and configurations.
▼ Provide a clear sense of enclosure. This is particularly important for an outdoor space. Buildings with multistory facades can provide it, but if they are not located on all sides, berming and dense landscaping can substitute.
▼ Illuminate the space with varied levels of natural and artificial lighting.
▼ Animate the space with moving water, which provides a focal point, a sense of activity, and soothing background noise.
▼ Enliven the edges of the space with visible activity on more than one level if possible.
▼ Use soft geometric forms. Asymmetrical, irregular, and curving forms seem to in-

David Whitcomb

David Whitcomb

Beautifully illuminated spaces, moving water, a sense of enclosure, soft geometric forms, varied walking surfaces, and bold graphics are some notable design features at the Entertainment Center at Irvine Spectrum.

David Whitcomb

David Whitcomb

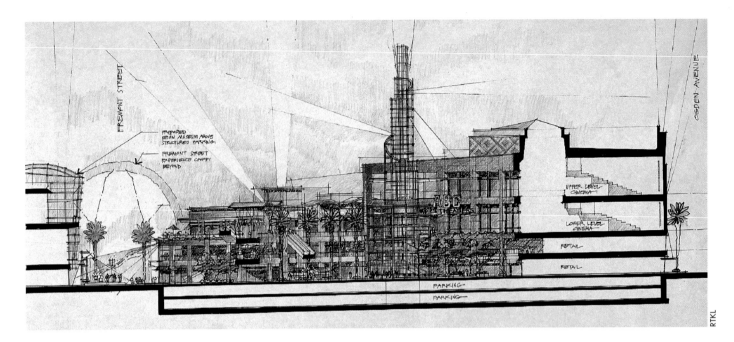

Neonopolis is being designed to extend and deepen the excitement of the Fremont Street Experience in downtown Las Vegas.

crease the chances for successfully animating the gathering place.

▼ Provide walking surfaces that are varied in level and finish. These variations can be relatively subtle.

▼ Enliven the space by using bright colors and bold graphics.

▼ Provide facilities for organized, scheduled entertainment and, perhaps even more important, for spontaneous interaction by visitors themselves.

Parking and Access

As with any other type of retail development, parking must be sited to permit convenient, quick, and safe access. Depending on location, configuration, and project economics, parking may be provided in surface lots or in structures. At Universal CityWalk, structured parking is provided; at the Entertainment Center at Irvine Spectrum, parking is provided in surface lots. In some dense urban locations, parking is not provided at all—for example, at 42nd Street in New York City.

Parking and spillover of traffic into adjoining residential neighborhoods are potential problems that should be carefully mitigated. Much of the traffic at entertainment centers is generated in the evening and on week-

ends, when residents are at home. As with other types of commercial development, there will be less opposition from surrounding residents if developers show a willingness to work with the community from the beginning to provide adequate access and parking before they become problems.

Without adequate parking, customers will not return to the center and neighbors will be plagued with overflow cars. The Urban Land Institute and the International Council of Shopping Centers currently are conducting a survey of shopping centers, including entertainment centers, to update their joint publication *Parking Requirements for Shopping Centers.* This more definitive compilation of parking data will be available in 1999.

In some urban settings, parking needs are mitigated and sometimes eliminated by the availability of alternative modes of transportation and parking garages. Sharing parking often is possible because the timing of demand is different. Offices and college campuses, for example, require parking during hours that complement those during which retail/entertainment centers need it. In addition, office workers create a built-in customer base for restaurants and entertainment and students a base for such things as books, records, and movies.

The new 20,000-seat MCI Center with associated entertainment center that opened in December 1997 in downtown Washington, D.C., has no parking for ordinary customers —a major cost saving for the developer. Half the customers use mass transit; the center has a station on the lower concourse that is served by three lines. The remaining customers use garages in the neighborhood or walk from where they work.

If new parking garages are required, they should be designed with a high degree of detail since they frequently are the largest, most bulky, and most visible part of an entertainment complex. They also should have an open feel; be well lighted, with higher intensity lighting at elevator lobbies; and be well patrolled, so that customers feel secure. In this regard, above-grade facilities with large openings are more desirable than below-grade facilities. It is preferable for garages to be located away from residential neighborhoods because they need to be well lighted until the last movie is over and the restaurants are closed. Glare can be a problem.

Some urban entertainment centers— including Universal CityWalk, One Colorado, and Third Street Promenade—charge parking fees, and they generate enough income to bring the cost per parking space into a range that is competitive with that of many suburban sites. However, where there is a parking charge, customers and employees often will try to park on local streets to avoid paying, leading to neighborhood conflict.

Some general rules for providing parking include the following:

▼ Choose an appropriate site that does not negatively affect surrounding residential neighborhoods.
▼ Use siting and landscaping to shield adjacent neighborhoods from parking and potential glare.
▼ Direct traffic away from residential neighborhoods through careful placement of entrances and exits on arterials that are wide enough to handle the traffic load.

▼ Perhaps most important, provide enough parking spaces so that demand does not spill over into surrounding neighborhoods.

Physical Expansion

With the first generation of entertainment centers, demand was the great unknown. With only slight overstatement, it can be said that the prevailing wisdom held that "if we build it they will come." In fact, in most cases the developers underestimated demand. As a result, within a few years of opening expansions were planned at the Forum Shops (Phase II opened in fall 1997), Universal CityWalk, Reston Town Center, and

KMD Architects

Taichung, a proposed mixed-use development in Taichung, Taiwan, is designed with a serpentine pedestrian way that will be lined with low-rise retail/entertainment venues and stores in the midst of a dense, high-rise environment.

the Entertainment Center at Irvine Spectrum, among others. All four of these examples had allocated space for expansion, and their initial phases were designed in such a way as to make expansion seamless. While not all entertainment centers will be successful enough to justify future expansion, the possibility should be considered during initial project planning.

Designing for expansion must take into account the need for continuity while not repeating the same features. New pedestrian streets should be fully activated with all of the variety and interest built into the first phase without creating the feeling that the expansion is either a separate component or a clone.

ARCHITECTURE

Project Design: Drama, Diversity, and Detail

The 3 Ds—drama, diversity, and detail—should be the guiding principles of entertainment center architecture and design no matter what the setting. The extent to which they are creatively interpreted will be a key factor in the project's long-term success. The architecture, signage, and shop windows should all feature a lively diversity, as do the various facades of a classic shopping street that has evolved over the years. Similarly, interior layout, finish, and decor should be diverse, ideally to the point that they seem to have been built separately over time.

Detail presents itself principally in the development of the storefronts. These also should be varied and richer in nuance than the usual planned retail environment, which often suppresses detail in the interest of both economy and uniformity. Graphics, landscaping, lighting, and merchandise presentation also contribute significantly to the overall impact of the design.

The end result of a well-designed entertainment center focused on drama, diversity, and detail is that the shopper is an active participant, not only as an actor in the scene but also as a consumer who spends time and money enjoying the attractions provided. Active participants want distinct and varied experiences, and they want to wander safely through a friendly environment; at well-designed centers, they can do both. As an example, the average income per square foot at an entertainment retail center such as Universal CityWalk is reported to be in the range of $1,000 per square foot per year, roughly

The Louisville Slugger Museum in Louisville, Kentucky, created an enormous illuminated baseball bat to clearly mark the destination.

four times the average for a traditional shopping center. It is a tribute to its attractiveness and special quality that the visitor usually goes with only a vaguely defined shopping objective. For instance, most of its cinema patrons have not selected a particular movie or starting time before they go, nor have they selected a restaurant. They go, planning to spend more than two hours, confident that they will find a film, food, merchandise, people, and events that will make the outing pleasurable.

Styles

The architectural style of urban entertainment centers is varied. The Entertainment Center at Irvine Spectrum is Mediterranean; Universal CityWalk is a pastiche of 20th-century Los Angeles icons with a few over-scaled facades, signs, and symbols.

One Colorado in Pasadena, which is primarily a rehabilitation of existing structures on the National Register of Historic Places, offers less drama and fantasy but presents a strong architectural image through its historic facades and the complementary facades of the one large new building complex that houses restaurants and movie theaters. The new building, however, is much more vital and energetic than the rehabilitated buildings. It lends a sense of action and vigor to the new piazza, the centerpiece of the development.

Landmarking

Identifying—or landmarking—an entertainment center so that it is visible and identifiable from a distance is vital. A strong entrance dramatized by towers or other prominent architectural features as well as special lighting and graphics heightens the attraction and beckons the customer. In most cases, there are multiple entrances: from surrounding streets and perhaps from a transit station in an urban setting and from parking lots and garages in a suburban setting. Ideally, all of these entrances should have a definite char-

The proposed Samsung Entertainment Center in Seoul, Korea, uses limited but dramatic signage and graphics to achieve a powerful visual effect.

acter—whether provided by architecture or graphics—in order to capture the attention, the imagination, and the heart of the consumer. To do this successfully requires more than just making the center conspicuous. It requires integrating the components, themes, and design elements in a way that will seem fresh and new.

Care should be taken to present enticing facades to the surrounding parking lots as well as to the streets. The bleak, blank look that characterizes the exterior facades of too many shopping centers should be avoided. Rather, there must be regular openings from the main pedestrian passage to the parking area, and they should be enlivened by varied storefronts and signature graphics.

Horizontal or Vertical Configuration?

In a suburban setting, an entertainment center generally will be limited to one or two stories because project economics do not justified a higher density and it may not be allowed by zoning. In a North American urban setting and in most other parts of the world, an entertainment center usually will have multiple stories. Regardless of the number of floors, new features should be revealed gradually throughout the center, and facades should be high enough to provide room for ample detail and enhance the sense of enclosure of the street, piazzas, and other public spaces. This can be done by means of false fronts, but real second floors are preferable.

Due to their height, cinemas create a second-floor facade, and even more so if they are positioned on top of a parking structure or some other use (which is an emerging trend). However, their facades tend to be blank and box-like. Extra care must be taken in the design process to ensure that their upper-level bulk is disguised effectively by arranging active uses around them.

Some nonanchor retailers that depend on high volume, such as bookstores and large-scale entertainment restaurants, sometimes prefer to occupy two floors. Cinemas and some nightclubs also are willing to locate on upper floors. Nonretail upper-story uses that complement retail/entertainment uses can contribute to both activity level and rental income when upper-level retail is not workable. Often a modest demand exists for upper-floor retail services such as insurance and travel agencies. A few centers currently are marketing upper-floor space for outpatient medical use. These are particularly logical choices since their parking demand hours complement those of retail establishments. Educational institutions are another highly desirable second-floor tenant (UCLA at Universal CityWalk), as are offices (Third Street Promenade has become a hot office location).

Stairs to the second floor can be designed as a sculpture for people to climb or to descend to make a grand entrance. Stairs should be wide, inviting, and attractive so as not to seem like too much work for the shopper to use, and they should arouse visitors' curiosity about what lies around the bend. The staircase at Two Rodeo Center includes a fountain and is designed so that the user turns at each landing, which is only six feet higher than the previous one and is the only one that can be seen. Alternatives to stairs, including escalators, elevators, or ramps, still need to be provided to upper levels.

Enclosed versus Open Design

Many stand-alone entertainment centers that are completed, under construction, or planned in warm climates such as those in Florida and California are designed in an open-air configuration. Developers feel that enclosure is climatically unnecessary in those areas and that it would make them seem too "mall-like" and involve an unnecessary expense. However, in climates that are more seasonal, many entertainment centers and entertainment components of shopping centers such as the Forum Shops and Mall of America are being designed as enclosed spaces. An exception is Reston Town Center's open-air retail and entertainment space, which has proven to be a popular attraction even in winter.

Since the basic geometry of public spaces in entertainment centers is apt to be less regular than that of the usual linear shopping mall, designing an enclosure is a bit more complex. In order to provide the necessary spacious feel, the ceiling should be at least 20 feet above the basic walking surface and it should be at least 20 percent glazed to allow natural lighting to infuse the space. In addition, the interior roof lines, if longer than 100 feet, should be varied in design. At Ontario Mills the roof design is dramatically altered every 150 feet.

Graphics and Signage

Graphics and signage must be designed with caution. While they transform a building into a marketing tool for the center and its tenants and add pizzazz to the scene, a very basic question exists concerning how much pizzazz a repeat customer, usually the main source of demand, will tolerate. An informal survey taken by KMD indicates that use of rich architectural detail combined with limited use

SIGNAGE OF THE TIMES

For the 15 years that the city/state re-development project in Times Square has been in progress, government investment and master planning have been the overarching factors, unlike at Fifth Avenue or lower Broadway, where retail growth has been driven by market forces. That effort, backed by at least $1 billion in tax subsidies to developers over the next quarter century, finally has put the Crossroads of the World on the road to recovery, making it a must-see for millions of domestic and international tourists.

Now, the one-time pornography pariah has become so fabulous a location that Condé Nast, the publisher of *Vanity Fair, Glamour,* and *GQ,* is putting its new headquarters there. Big, bold signs overwhelm the eye from every angle, and the rents that supersignage generates have made it a key factor in any new construction being contemplated.

It has become clear, says Gretchen Dykstra, executive director of the Times Square Business Improvement District, that there is now "truly a critical mass in Times Square." The reasons for this success, she says, are as various as the bright lights that catch the eye from 42nd to 51st Streets along Broadway and Seventh Avenue. "When the three legs of the stool—city, state, and community interests—are the same height and have the same vision and same degree of political will, the cynics are put to rest."

Dykstra's soulmate in the redemption of Times Square is Rebecca Robertson, who until early this year headed New York State's redevelopment effort along 42nd Street,

Times Square is a billboard park for retail and entertainment attractions.

where it condemned many properties that were then turned over to a state-selected development group. Robertson echoes Dykstra's emphasis on the collaborative nature of the Times Square project. "It was a totally master-planned trip," she says, "and it stretches the hours one spends coming to eat, buy, see, and recreate."

What drove the effort forward when the market collapsed was a 1992 interim plan designed by a team led by architect Robert A.M. Stern that included entertainment architect David Rockwell and designer Tibor Kalman. At the core of their scheme was a planned anarchy of signage.

But the Stern plan caused havoc among the development team that controlled the four large office-tower development sites, which included George Klein of Park Tower Realty and Prudential Insurance Company.

Klein had a distinctly different aesthetic in mind—the sleek and dignified, if nonetheless festive, office milieu of Rockefeller Center. That ran counter to the signage proposal, and few outside Stern's circle believed that, as one observer put it, "signage could get as crazy and wild—and as lucrative—as it has."

Robertson, Stern, and others eventually succeeded in overcoming —and in some cases simply overriding—those objections, often by making compliance with signage guidelines "the price of entry, because it only works if everybody plays ball," says Robertson. Now, she says, "We've created a signage market. Times Square is a billboard park."

Source: Peter Slatin. "Signage of the Times," *Urban Land* (October 1997), p. 90.

Inside and outside, lighting levels are linked to retailing, entertainment, and potential sales. The right lighting creates a mood, encourages safety, and can boost sales. A poorly-lit store renders the merchandise dull and will not encourage lingering. Lighting outside stores can, and does, play a big part in whether shoppers visit at all, as well as enhance the shopping mood.

Car parking facilities are now perceived, often rightly so, as dark, dingy places that are a veritable haven for muggers. This has kept shoppers away and sent them elsewhere. Sarah Palliser, retail lighting expert at the Design Solution, offers some observations: "Perceived brightness plays a major role in car park lighting, as brightness is linked to the feeling of safety. This is particularly relevant to the female consumer.

"The problem is not really the [sodium] lighting. This light source is cost effective and that is why it is used, but it has considerable failings. Sodium renders green, blue and yellow very badly, so it is often difficult to locate your car in a full car park because you cannot tell one car from another. Also, and more importantly, flesh tones are rendered badly. With the low level of lighting and shadows, anyone walking toward you can look menacing."

Palliser goes on to offer a solution for car parks: "It is now possible to light car parks with white light using compact fluorescent and even mercury discharge lamps. These light sources are fast becoming very cost effective and have all the advantages of good color rendition and providing the consumer with a feeling of safety. It is important to note that if an environment is lit with a white light, everyone can be seen, and that is bad news for criminals."

Floodlighting a building exterior attracts attention and creates a favorable impression with passers-by. For store fronts, floodlighting is often a subtle and dignified yet highly effective form of advertising that has the power to attract tourists, especially in major cities, and new retail businesses. Floodlighting old or distinctive buildings also has great potential —not only because they have great architectural features, but also because it helps reinforce the image of an area as one of exciting retail streets and parks, even when the shops are closed. In Paris, where buildings in the city center are illuminated using only white light, floodlighting has worked well.

Lighting can be used to link areas, guiding the shopper around with a kind of subliminal signage, and to create mood. Lower floors can be gently dappled with light and have higher ambient light levels than floors above, creating visual interest.

Palliser explains the lighting principles in some of Europe's shopping malls: "In Europe, particularly in Spain, Italy, and France, you have greater use of white light partly because people there are more nocturnal and this is a way of providing 'daylight'."

Perhaps the era of interactive video imaging on the fronts and sides of stores will not be far behind. In the meantime, let us just have fewer sodium-lit retail car parks and a better view of our retail entertainment centers.

Excerpted and adopted from Steve Thomas Emberson, "Light Entertainment," *Retail Week* (November 14, 1997), p. 15.

RTKL Associates

The right lighting scheme, such as the one shown here at the Entertainment Center at Irvine Spectrum, creates mood, encourages safety, and can boost sales.

of dramatic graphics may be the optimal solution for most centers. In specialized locations that rely primarily on tourists rather than repeat customers, such as 42nd Street and Times Square in New York City, signage and graphics will play a more dramatic part.

Billboard Architecture

A percentage of the building facades on New York's 42nd Street now are required by ordinance to be masked by massive signage in the tradition of "the Great White Way." Although extreme signage is compelling, this level of billboard architecture is designed to suit a very special case, a special tradition, and a special market. Undoubtedly, some other specialized urban locations, such as Hollywood Boulevard or the Las Vegas Strip, will employ billboard architecture as an important design element. However, it seems unlikely to form a major design element in most entertainment centers, except perhaps in a scaled-down version in centers that cater primarily to tourists.

Lighting

Exterior and interior lighting is a vital element in designing the stage for visitors and in creating a recognizable identity for the center. Lighting should display a hierarchy of intensity, with the brightest lights identifying focal points such as project entrances, central circulation areas, water features, major landscape elements, and significant architectural elements. The overall intensity of the ground lighting should be secondary to that defining the architectural surfaces that form the boundaries of the open spaces. By illuminating them, the perimeter boundaries are defined and a comfortable, dramatic sense of enclosure is established.

Security

Personal security is critical. The most important factor in establishing this feeling is visi-

Universal City Studios

The computer-controlled interactive fountain at Universal CityWalk is one of its most popular attractions.

bility, especially of other people. No matter how well lighted the center is or how many security monitors are provided, visitors' sense of security depends on the feeling that they are visible to others and that they can see clearly into all parts of any space where they might venture. It may be tempting to create cul-de-sacs and small, intimate or out-of-the-way spaces, but the hazards of doing so are clear. Byways and pathways that will be little used should be avoided not only for safety reasons but also because they do not add to the social energy and interaction that are so vital to all entertainment centers.

ACTIVITY GENERATORS

Architecture and design set the stage, but animating the stage requires activity generators. As at any retail development, the tenants themselves and their customers are the major activity generators. The theme retailers, entertainment restaurants, and specialized entertainment attractions that generate the most activity are presented in Chapter 2, and a discussion of how they are bundled to create a synergistic mix of activity is presented in Chapter 3. But there are other generators that set entertainment centers apart from traditional retail development, and they may spell the difference between project success and failure. They include interactive features, events, and education, which increasingly will be added to traditional shopping centers, continuing to blur the distinction between the two forms of development. Cinema anchors are described in this chapter as well because of their unique physical requirements and the need to integrate them carefully into the overall design.

Drama, diversity, and detail set the stage for success, but to attract the repeat shopper an entertainment center should also provide a range of new experiences and activities with each visit. It needs to be designed to include a carefully crafted variety of zones, themes, and environments that together transform each shopping trip into a subtly different event. Experiences in a typical retail entertainment environment generally are defined by seven factors—food, interactive design features, merchandise, events, retail-related education, films, and the ever-changing assortment of people. Continuous changes in each factor provide the new experiences that visitors are looking for: different people are present on each visit; menus change; merchandise varies with the season; new features are added; events are regularly reprogrammed; new educational experiences, offerings, and courses are offered; and new films are shown.

Food

Food is one of the greatest activators of retail environments. But the one-dimensional experience of a typical shopping mall food court is supplanted at an entertainment center by the distinct experiences afforded by a variety of restaurants providing a range of cuisines, often in a highly themed environment. It is absolutely critical that the restaurant design feature strong interaction between the interior and the street and sidewalk. For instance,

entertainment restaurants such as Planet Hollywood, the Hard Rock Cafe, and Dive! are dramatic and attractive. Their prototypical designs should and sometimes do emphasize interaction not only among diners inside the restaurant but also with the people on the street or piazza just outside the door. If they do not, they should be modified. They are described in detail in Chapter 2.

Interactive Features

Interactive features, like the popular computer-controlled fountain at Universal CityWalk, are a great means for generating activity. The fountain is so popular that a successful concession has evolved based on taking photographs of both children and adults while they cavort among its irregularly changing spurts of water. The fountain was designed to encourage such play.

Interactive stores and storefronts are a second major activity generator. Store interiors must be visible so that customers can visually shop before they enter the stores. Window displays need to be intriguing, colorful, educational, whimsical, provocative, and constantly changing. For the retailer, interiors must be dramatic environments that present a strong theme and point of view with their merchandise displays, shopping spaces, materials, and interior finishes. Where possible, multilevel spaces with intriguing places to explore should be created. The variety and presentation of merchandise should provide an ever-changing visual display. The optimal tenant mix includes local, specialized merchants who sell different and even exotic products as well as the national chains that offer the predictable but nevertheless up-to-the-minute, high-quality goods that have become staples of modern life.

Events

Events constitute the third major activity generator. Seasonal holidays—especially Christmas, but increasingly others such as

The introduction of multiscreen cinema complexes into shopping centers is proving to be a win-win situation. Mall owners gain an additional anchor that increases customer traffic to their center and expands their trade area beyond the reach of the other retailers. They also gain a flexible tenant: cinema complexes can activate areas unsuitable for retail or replace anchor stores that have gone dark. What is more, cinemas change their offerings weekly, generating repeat visits. Theater operators reap bottom-line benefits too. By securing a deal with a mall, a cinema chain immediately is associated with an established destination. Shared parking reduces the theater operator's site costs, and automatic ticketing machines (both inside and outside the mall) increase the cinema's prominence, while adding convenience. Key design issues, however, must be mastered for the movie/mall marriage to be successful.

Site Planning Issues

Not long ago, developers feared that movie patrons would clog mall parking spaces, retarding shopper turnover. Consequently, cinemas were placed as far as possible from the mall entrances. Now that consumers have less time, what used to be viewed as two separate trips to the mall is combined into one.

Parking surveys conducted over the past year have shown that demand for mall and theater parking is complementary. Most visits to a mall occur during daylight hours, while most visits to the cinema occur in the evening. Parking conflicts, if they do occur, happen on Saturday afternoons between 5:00 and 7:00 p.m., when weekly mall and cinema peaks coincide briefly. Special peaks are widely separated: mall traffic peaks between Thanksgiving and New Year and cinema traffic peaks in the summer. As a consequence, mall parking does not need to fulfill zoning requirements for both uses. However, the following parking questions must be answered for each site:

▼ Can the mall accommodate the theater operator's desired parking/seat ratio?
▼ How much parking is required by zoning? Can a zoning variance

At the recently opened Brass Mill Center in Waterbury, Connecticut, a stadium 12-plex was positioned on top of the mall with its lobby visible from the parking lot.

be obtained if required parking exceeds what is needed?

▼ Will a parking deck be required?

Concepts for placing the cinema vary from site to site, and each concept comes with its own set of challenges. At the recently opened Brass Mill Center in Waterbury, Connecticut, a stadium 12-plex was positioned on top of the mall. Kathleen Shields, development director for General Growth Properties (GGP) says, "The cinema functions like an additional anchor. We wanted the cinema placed in a dramatic central location where the greatest number of customers would circulate. It is conveniently accessed from the parking deck and the mall's feature entry for after-hours operation. The creation of a third level enhanced the center's visibility from nearby Interstate 84." At Greece Ridge Center in Greece Ridge, New York, an at-grade stadium 12-plex, with access from the mall and the exterior, replaces a failed big-box anchor at one end of the retail spine.

Also, at Solomon Pond Mall in Marlborough, Massachusetts, the addition of a stadium 15-plex cinema at grade filled an underused parking field at the rear of the mall. Joe Koechel, vice president and director of properties of the Wells Park Group, states, "The cinema has benefited the mall in two ways. The overall business has seen an improvement and an increase in traffic, and since the Solomon Pond Mall is not located on a busy street, the cinema has helped make the mall an entertainment destination. We now offer the three tried-and-true elements that draw customers: shopping, dining, and the movies. It's been a successful marriage so far."

Cinema Planning Issues

Planning issues within the mall itself are paramount in the creation of an entertainment complex at a retail mall. Strategic issues to resolve while planning a cinema complex in a mall include

▼ What location will generate the greatest traffic flow through the mall?

▼ What location provides the best opportunities for physical and visual connections between the cinema and the mall?

▼ What location will increase the excitement of the shopping and movie-going experience?

▼ What should the relationship be between the cinema, the food court, other eating and entertainment establishments, and synergistic cotenants such as book and music stores?

The most significant relationship between a cinema complex and a retail mall is circulation and egress, especially when the cinema complex is not located at grade. Locating a cinema complex above or below grade helps encourage people to circulate vertically in a mall. However, unusually large stairs are required to exit both the seated and waiting populations from the cinema complex.

Most codes allow a portion of the cinema population to exit into a mall. In new construction, this additional traffic must be included when deter-

Halloween—offer seemingly endless opportunities to create tie-ins through costuming, displays, ongoing activities, and scheduled events. Events and promotions based on local traditions and cultural attractions are even better because they are, by definition, different from events in other cities. Joint promotions with local performing arts groups and temporary museum shows also can be a great source of entertainment center events.

Small-scale activities and events can take place in niches along the pedestrian streets.

Mid-sized events such as festivals, fairs, and outdoor concerts can be held in the piazza. If possible, spaces large enough for a crowd of 1,000 people should be provided for grander occasions. However, it is difficult to do this in the primary public areas because it tends to make them oversized in terms of day-to-day scale and use. One possibility is to use adjacent open space, such as a parking lot, provided with special lighting and sound facilities.

Entertainment centers need to schedule special events on all scales and at all times.

mining the mall's exit capacity. When a cinema marries into existing mall and exit systems are not sized to handle the additional exit load, additional space will need to be carved out for exit corridors and stairs. This will be a negotiating point in the deal. The square footage of above-grade exit corridors and stairs seldom is included in the typical cinema's lease. Most mall owners are willing to accept this condition to secure a deal for a cinema multiplex in an above- or below-grade configuration.

When a cinema complex is placed in the footprint of a defunct anchor store, the location often is far from the food court, which may weaken the synergy with dining. This can be countered by creating an entire entertainment/recreation area around the cinema with restaurants, cafés, games, and related retail. One of the most interesting examples of this concept is the Shoppingtown Mall in DeWitt, New York.

At Shoppingtown, Wilmorite, the owner of the mall, and Hoyts Cinemas completed a deal whereby Hoyts constructed a sloped-floor ten-plex

cinema in an underused below-grade wing. The structural challenges faced by the design team were great: structural loads were transferred, footings were lowered, and all columns were extended to accommodate the volume of a theater underneath the mall. All the while, the mall above was open for business. With the fit-out work completed and the cinema open to the public, Wilmorite used the newly-established cinema destination to anchor a new entertainment zone, which includes a restaurant/pub, pushcart marketing, a laser tag game area, and a comedy club.

Special zoning, structural, and security issues occur when integrating movies into the mall:

▼ Is a cinema complex allowed by zoning, or is a special permit required?

▼ Is a height variance required? (stadium-seating cinemas require anywhere from 30 to 40 feet in building height).

▼ Is a signage variance required for the cinema's pylon and marquee signs?

▼ Can an existing structure be adapted for the spacing and volume of cinema?

▼ Are additional mall security available if cinema patrons have to exit through the mall after hours? Is after-hour parking lot lighting accounted for in the mall's operating budget?

These challenges notwithstanding, cinema complexes increase mall sales overall. In an October 1997 *Shopping Center Business* article titled "New Entertainment Centers Broaden Appeal," John Bucksbaum, executive vice president of General Growth Properties, Inc., reports that "since opening a 75,000-square-foot AMC Theater in GGP's Deerbrook Mall in Houston, the in-line stores have shown a 15 to 16 percent sales increase every month, with food court tenants increasing sales by as much as 50 percent per month."

Source: Robert S. Holt, AIA, and Dennis B. Carlberg, AIA, Arrowstreet Inc.

It also should be recognized that many of the tenants themselves are, in essence, in the special events business. This is certainly true of theme restaurants and retailers such as the Hard Rock Cafe, on a national level, or a romantic and casual restaurant like Gladstones in Los Angeles, on a local level.

While some special events can be costly, the cost of others is negligible. Watching colorfully clad waiters and vendors on the street or gawking at a radio station announcer and listening to him on the street outside, as at

Universal CityWalk, are free activities. At New York City's Rockefeller Center the skating rink and the television shows being filmed there live, such as the *Today Show,* are wonderful daily events, and they too are free.

Education

This is a knowledge and information-based society, and learning is an important part of people's lives. It also can be an activity generator in an urban entertainment center.

Cinemas such as the Warner Bros. theater in Centro Oberhausen are blessed because Hollywood pumps out more than 200 movies a year, keeping them constantly supplied with new "software."

Teaching customers about the hottest fashion trends; demonstrating hands-on interactive computer techniques; hosting bookstore discussion groups on a best-selling author; offering sewing lessons at a fabric store; and offering evening photography classes at a camera shop all are good examples of how education is being used to stimulate retail activity and make it more entertaining.

Whether an interactive display on the roots of jazz will translate into immediate sales of jazz CDs is debatable, but the fact is that people are interested in gaining knowledge, they feel good about it, and they will remember where they gained it—on their trip to the center. They linger longer when they are entertained and educated, they are more prone to come back, and their interest and appreciation may well be piqued enough to stimulate a sale—not a bad deal!

Movies

Cinemas are blessed because Hollywood pumps out more than 200 movies a year, keeping them continuously supplied with new "software." There always is something new, and as a result, always another reason to return to an entertainment center.

The design of the spectacular new generation of cinemas, the anchor in many entertainment centers, is a major reason for their success. The new 20- to 30-screen behemoths have little in common with the little cinema "boxes" that typically are found in a neighborhood shopping center. The designs are grand, with large screens, comfortable stadium seats, dramatic lobbies and marquees, and sophisticated sound and projection systems.

The issue of the cinema's location within an entertainment center has become more important as the number of screens and the use of stadium seating have increased the height and bulk of the building. The issue becomes even more important when a large-format screen, such as in an IMAX or Iwerks format, is part of the project. Generally, cinemas should not be freestanding because of their bulk and the desirability of integrating them with other center activities. Except for their entrances and marquee, they should be hidden behind other active uses; otherwise their size and the blankness of their walls can be overwhelming and deadening. Cinemas also can be successfully placed on upper levels because they are such a powerful draw that patrons will not hesitate to go to the top of the center to see a movie, and then filter down to the lower levels afterward, stopping at the stores and restaurants along the way. This spin-off activity may justify the higher construction and operating costs of putting cinemas on the upper levels, where other uses may not be appropriate.

In all cases, the relationship of the cinema entrance to the town square or main pedestrian street is critical. The cinema lobby should be designed to enhance the public place but ideally not to dominate it visually. It is difficult to enliven a cinema facade during the day, when it is not usually thronged with people.

Merchandise

Merchandise in entertainment centers is sold not only in stores but also in the theme restaurants and entertainment attractions described in detail in Chapter 2. Most of the merchandise represents discretionary purchases, including brand products, impulse goods, and other types of specialty items. As a result, it needs to be displayed in a way that creates curiosity and draws strollers into the selling space. More so than at a traditional shopping center, interiors and merchandise need to be visible from pedestrian streets because the themed environment and the customers within are themselves part of the merchandising. Merchandise displays ideally should be changed more frequently and be more interactive than at traditional retail centers in order to encourage repeat visits.

People

People are the last and perhaps most important energizing element in a successful entertainment center. People generate activity simply by interacting with one another and their surroundings, and creative design should ensure that this takes place. The other activity generators in an entertainment center draw and energize people, but it is the people themselves who create the buzz of activity that spells magic.

People watching is a continuously changing activity and can be the major reason why people go to an entertainment center repeatedly. They stroll and saunter for enjoyment, rather than rush frantically to purchase a targeted item. Excursion or recreational shopping is seen by customers as much more of an occasion than target shopping, and they frequently are more dressed up when they go and more apt to become a contributing

Santana, a proposed retail entertainment center in São Paulo, Brazil, is designed to allow people to generate activity simply by interacting with one another and their surroundings.

element in a rich and constantly changing scene.

One way to accommodate this is by ensuring that restaurant seating is placed so that it not only is visible from the street but also intrudes into the street without blocking it. It should not be secluded or hidden as it is so often at a traditional shopping mall.

CHELSEA PIERS SPORTS AND ENTERTAINMENT COMPLEX
New York, New York

In 1912, when the Titanic made its first—and last—voyage, its destination was Chelsea Piers in New York City. There, in a classical headhouse of reinforced concrete and pink granite designed by Warren and Wetmore, friends and relatives awaited the survivors of one of the most famous maritime disasters. In the early part of this century, the piers, which are 825 feet in length, served as the starting and ending point for many happy and (not so happy) events.

Unfortunately, shortly after the piers opened they became obsolete when in the 1930s new ships were built to 1,000 feet in length. The piers went through many ups and downs over the next 50 years. During World War II, they were a departure point for ships. In the late 1950s and early 1960s, they served as a cargo terminal. During the 1960s, the piers were turned into rather homely, functional buildings instead of the graceful, elegant buildings they once had been.

In the 1980s, as part of the plan to construct the Westway Highway, Chelsea Piers were slated for demolition. When that plan was quashed, new uses were sought for the piers, and in 1984, the piers' headhouse was first used for television production, which continues today at the Chelsea Piers Sports and Entertainment Complex, a 30-acre sports and television production center located between 17th and 23rd Streets on the Hudson River. The complex is a commercial enterprise developed on public land as part of a strategy to redevelop the riverfront in lower Manhattan with private money and public cooperation. It is located on four finger piers that reach more than 840 feet into the Hudson River. Piers 60 and 61 are covered, and Piers 59 and 62 are open; each offers a different sports activity. An ambitious plan also is being implemented to create a continuous five-mile trail along the river, dotted with parks and recreational and educational facilities, that will provide residents and visitors with about 550 acres of open space.

The plan's success depends on active private sector involvement in the public realm. The Hudson River Park Conservancy (HRPC), a state agency created specifically to oversee the revitalization of the waterfront, intends to generate money from select commercial ventures within the Hudson River Park and use that revenue to help fund park

Beck's Studio

DEVELOPMENT TEAM

Developer

Chelsea Piers LP
New York, New York

Architect

James G. Rogers III
Butler Rogers Baskett Architects PC
New York, New York

General Contractor

AJ Contracting Company, Inc.
New York, New York

Mechanical/Electrical Engineers

Cosentini Associates
New York, New York

Structural Engineers

Thornton-Tomasetti
New York, New York

Project Manager

Cushman & Wakefield, Inc.
New York, New York

construction, maintenance, operations, and programs. The Chelsea Piers Sports and Entertainment Complex's 1.7 million square feet is the first large-scale commercial venture to be completed under HRPC's purview and is a happy marriage of convenience that satisfies a recreational need for Manhattanites and provides revenue to HRPC.

BACKGROUND

Entrepreneur and investor Roland Betts's young daughter was a champion figure skater, and the only place she could skate in Manhattan was at Sky Rink, at the time the city's only year-round indoor ice rink. Located on the rooftop of a building on West 33rd Street, the rink was substandard yet in great demand. Eventually, Betts was asked to serve on the board of Sky Rink. He thought that a new home for the facility, large enough to hold two rinks, was the only solution to the overcrowding and declining conditions. In searching for a new location, he discovered Chelsea Piers, where the huge spaces (120 feet wide, 840 feet long, with no columns) were ideal for the purpose.

In early 1992, Betts pulled in David Tewksbury (a former development professional for Cushman & Wakefield), and they submitted a development proposal to the New York state department of transportation (DOT), which owns the site. The plans called for just one pier—Pier 61—to be converted into two skating rinks on the upper level, with parking on the lower level. Even though their contact at the DOT liked the plan, he could not offer them more than a 30-day lease, which was obviously unacceptable.

At about the same time, the state of New York decided to seek proposals for a development plan for three piers. Although it was more than Betts had bargained for, he brought along his business partner, Tom Bernstein, with whom he had been successful in the film financing business. Betts, Tewksbury, and Bernstein decided that it might be worthwhile to make a bid for all three piers. (The fourth pier, Pier 62, is being used temporarily by Chelsea Piers and will be part of the Waterside Park scheduled to be developed by the Hudson River Park Conservancy by 2003.)

The four piers were not blank slates when the developers began. They were connected by a five-block long headhouse; the two covered piers—Pier 60 and 61—held disintegrating two-story structures. Despite their dilapidated appearance, the structures retained impressive original steel trusswork that could not be recreated today. The developers realized that they could work with the existing structures and retain one of the existing uses

—the soundstage used by the television series *Law and Order.* (*Spin City* has since been brought to Chelsea Piers as well.) By retaining and expanding on that use, they could add a different sort of entertainment activity to the planned ice skating rink. After a little market research, they concluded that there was enough demand for sports other than ice skating to justify turning the rest of the project into multipurpose recreational facilities with amenities such as restaurants and sports equipment stores.

According to Bernstein, "We found out that New York City was starved for competitive sport space. Before we started the project we met with the eminent developer Jim Rouse, who told us that we would be overwhelmed by the response because we were programming into a vacuum. But we did pick the sports carefully. For example, there are no tennis courts at Chelsea Piers because Manhattan already has enough."

The proposal submitted by Betts, Tewksbury, and Bernstein offered the state of New York lower monthly rents than it would have received under some of the other ten proposals ($157,000, adjusted annually for inflation), but seemed to the state to present a more viable long-term use. The state signed a 20-year lease (later extended to 49 years) with the partnership, and thus began the Chelsea Piers Sports and Entertainment Complex.

PLANNING AND FINANCING

A remarkable aspect of the Chelsea Piers complex is that the developers were able to complete the project, from bidding to opening, in four years—an unusual feat in New York City. Betts first looked at the piers in November 1991, the building permit was issued in May 1994, construction began June 1, 1994, and the facility opened in phases beginning in fall 1995. Tewksbury attributes the speed of completion to "timing and luck and relative inexperience. We had no track record and no

Before the renovation, Chelsea Piers was a waterfront eyesore. Rollup cargo doors have been replaced by giant picture windows that provide spectacular views.

bad stuff. And no buildings were actually constructed."

The last point is the critical one. Although the developers had to get an extraordinary number of approvals and zoning changes (the chairman of the board of standards and appeals was quoted as saying that the proposal involved the most comprehensive series of zoning changes in the history of the city), the absence of new construction greatly reduced the price of the project as well as the number of community groups that had to be involved in the process. The developers took care to involve Community Board 4 in discussions, planning, and review, but the board had almost no formal role. As expected, there were some objections from the private sector, but for the most part, the public sector embraced the plan from the start. Both of the covered piers are on the state and national registers of historic places, and both groups ultimately approved of the productive use of the aging buildings, rather than leaving them to continue to disintegrate. Preservation groups also approved of the plan to leave the original steel trusswork intact and exposed in the renovation.

With high-tech programming, golfers never need to bend down or touch a golf ball. Each of the 52 heated and weather-protected driving stalls has a computerized program that raises the ball from ground level according to how the golfer has programmed the tee height.

Fred George

A full environmental impact assessment was conducted and showed almost no problems, except for a minor amount of asbestos. One of the biggest concerns was traffic, but it was already heavy because of the highway—and in the end, the concern was not strong enough to stop the project.

In order to finance the project, the partners and investors put up $17 million, and Morgan Stanley issued $45 million in mortgage bonds. But because the concept was relatively untried, money was hard to get, and the loan ended up being expensive. According to Betts, "Financing was a harrowing experience." Once the project was finished, Chelsea Piers Management, Inc., wanted to refinance $55 million of short-term, high-interest debt, basically junk bonds. The first step was to seek an extension of the 20-year lease, which, after a year-long campaign, was extended by the state to 49 years. In January 1997, Chelsea Piers Management began meeting with bankers, who were still wary of the project and its long-term viability. While the development was doing moderately well since it opened, the management group's

operating history—or lack thereof—and the average attendance were not impressive enough to convince a bank to take the risk. However, in 1997 attendance began to rise, with increases at virtually every venue. After a solid five-month increase, more banks became interested in the project and Chelsea Piers was refinanced by Starwood on much more favorable terms.

The final cost of the project was $90 million, with $25 million in improvements made by subtenants. (It originally had been budgeted at $25 million in 1992 and at $60 million in 1994). Revenues come from a variety of sources—memberships, user fees, rental fees, percentages from restaurants. Sponsorships also are an important source. The field house, for example, is plastered with banners from sponsors such as Reebok, ConEd, Pepsi, and IKON. Employees wear sponsors' clothing; logos decorate collateral materials.

The center is run as 14 separate businesses, each expected to be financially successful. For most of the time since Chelsea Piers opened, each has been in the black.

THE FACILITIES

Chelsea Piers provides an array of activities for adults and children—ice skating, roller skating, gymnastics, workout facilities, and golfing. The piers originally were designed for live loads of 600 pounds per square foot, but the condition of the piles lessened that somewhat; however, the live load capacity of 520 pounds per square foot still made it possible to construct swimming pools and other indoor sports facilities without compromising their size and usability.

One of the most unusual parts of the complex is the golf club at Pier 59, where a little bit of suburbia can be found in the middle of one of the most urban settings in the United States. A newly constructed, shingled clubhouse on the riverfront is home to a pro shop, locker rooms, meeting rooms, a bag storage area, and the Chelsea Brewing Company, a 300-seat waterfront microbrewery and restaurant.

But in addition to the country-club atmosphere, thrust into the river, is one of the most technologically advanced driving ranges and teaching centers in the world. A four-tiered structure provides 52 heated driving stalls that can be used year-round except in very high winds. Surrounding the fairways and the tiered structure is a 155-foot-high net, supported by 12 steel towers positioned on top of steel piles, some of which extend almost 300 feet into bedrock. "The piers are capable of accommodating substantial vertical loads but are incapable of sustaining any bending or twisting," said James G. Rogers III, of Butler Rogers Baskett, project architects. "With a net 150 feet in the air, you create a sail, and the pier has effectively no capacity to resist that bending movement. The result is that the towers that support the net are not supported by the piers or pier structure. Rather they are supported by individual 280-foot steel piles. We sawed holes in the pier deck and drove hollow-ended steel piles until we hit bedrock. Each cluster of piles (six at each tower) has built on top of it a concrete pile cap, and the base of each tower is bolted on top of that."

But even that structure can resist bending motions and lateral forces only to a point, so the nets, controlled by a sophisticated computer system, lower automatically when winds reach 50 miles per hour. If the nets were to ice over, they essentially would become solid, which in high winds would be dangerous.

Innovative technology allows duffers to practice their driving without ever touching a golf ball. A $15 debit card permits users to program their practice stall; 100 balls automatically tee-up one by one, and the golfer never has to bend down. Golf balls that have been hit onto the fairway are picked up by a small cart that deposits them into a network of chutes and pipes.

On the next pier, Pier 60, the existing two-story structure was transformed into a spectacular 150,000-square-foot sports center

The sports center— the length of three football fields— houses one of the longest indoor tracks in the world (one-quarter mile) as well as a banked, 200-meter competition track. In addition, the sports center houses 15,000 square feet of locker rooms fully equipped with saunas, steam rooms, and other amenities.

Fred George

on the second floor, with parking on the first. The sports center alone could be the centerpiece of the project, as it features premier equipment; a banked, six-lane, 200-meter competition indoor running track; a 4,600-square-foot rock-climbing wall, the largest in the Northeast; and a 10-by-60-foot bouldering wall. This 880-foot-long and 120-foot-wide center is the length of three football fields. The workout area itself encompasses 20,000 square feet. In addition, the center offers 4,000 square feet of studio space; a six-lane, 25-yard swimming pool; a whirlpool; a boxing ring; and an 18,000-square-foot flexible infield that accommodates track and field events as well as volleyball, indoor sand volleyball, and other special events. Unlike most workout facilities, this one has floor-to-ceiling windows throughout with dramatic views of the Hudson.

The new twin-rink facility on Pier 61, which is available to skaters of all ages and ability, operates 24 hours a day, seven days a week, year-round. With party rooms that overlook the Hudson River, Sky Rink is a popular spot for birthday celebrations and other gatherings.

The sports center also houses a sports medicine and performance center operated by a New York hospital and an Origins Feel-Good Spa (an Estée Lauder company). The spa provides an array of services, from massage to acupressure facials to treatment for jet lag.

In fall 1998, the last available space will be built out. The 40,000-square-foot Pier 60 event center will offer 20,000 square feet of ballroom space (up to four separate ballrooms) with 7,000 square feet of deck space. These ballrooms, which will be available for weddings, bar mitzvahs, corporate events, and so forth, will be completely surrounded by glass and water.

All this is housed in Pier 60, one of two buildings standing when Chelsea Piers Management, Inc., began development. To add visual appeal to the interiors of the nondescript structures, the developers and architect punched out the roll-up doors and replaced them with floor-to-ceiling windows that offer dramatic views of the Hudson, bringing the outdoors inside and making the sports center feels almost like a vacation resort.

The same could be said of Sky Rink at Pier 61. Floor-to-ceiling windows in the two ice rinks offer spectacular views of the Hudson. "I've played hockey all over the country," said Betts, "but until Chelsea Piers was finished, I'd never played with a window at all. You can't believe what a different feeling it is."

In addition, the new facility provides locker rooms; a pro shop; skate rentals; food service; meeting rooms; and seating for 1,600, including two skyboxes. An array of adult and junior programs is offered, from hockey to figure skating.

Roller skaters also have a spot at the plaza entrance to Chelsea Piers. The roller rinks, located on Pier 62, feature two outdoor, regulation-sized, professionally surfaced, in-line and roller skating rinks for general skating, hockey, and lessons. The roller rinks offer many programs for adults and youths, including roller hockey classes and leagues and in-line instructional and fitness classes. In 1997, a skate park and a skateboard curve were added between the two roller rinks. At the water end of Pier 62 is a public park paid for and maintained by Chelsea Piers Management, Inc. Pier 62 will become a public pier when the Hudson River Park is constructed.

A bus stop and taxi stand are at the plaza entrance, which has a small parking lot where cab drivers can park 20 minutes for free, use public rest rooms, and have a soda or make a phone call—a real luxury in Manhattan.

The headhouse stretches from 22nd Street to 18th Street and accommodates the management offices, offices for Silver Screen Studios (where two television series are produced by DreamWorks, whose New York office also is located at Chelsea Piers), a pro shop, a skate rental facility, a logo-wear shop, a café, Pier 59 studios, the Surfside 3 Marina, and a yacht dealership.

Also in the headhouse is a 90,000-square-foot field house. Located between Piers 61 and 62, the field house contains an array of athletic facilities: a 23,000-square-foot gymnastics training center, a rock-climbing wall especially designed for children and adult beginners, two basketball courts, two artificial-turf playing fields, and four batting cages.

The gymnastics facilities are the only ones in New York City sanctioned for competition by USA Gymnastics. The facility features at least two sets of equipment for each of the men's and women's Olympic events, as well as sunken trampolines and tumble tracks. A mezzanine overlooks the facilities to allow parents to watch their children.

The newest addition to the complex is a 40-lane, state-of-the-art AMF bowling facility with food service, a bar, and party rooms. Nightime "extreme bowling" is one of the most popular events at the facility. From Thursday to Sunday, lines form to bowl in a darkened facility to pulsating disco music on lanes bordered by red blinking lights. On weekend nights at midnight, 200 people may be dancing. This AMF bowling facility is the highest grossing anywhere.

The 23,000-square-foot gymnastics center features column-free competition spring floors, deep foam training pits, tumble tracks, and in-ground trampolines, as well as multiple sets of bars, beams, rings, horses, and vaults.

In total, 550 parking spaces are available on the first levels of Piers 59, 60, and 61. A 600-seat, $7.5 million seafood restaurant, the Crab House, has opened below Sky Rink. The Chelsea Brewing Company, a restaurant/microbrewery in Pier 59, seats 300. Additional food service is offered in Sky Rink and in the sport center.

Each of the five major sports facilities has a very different feel. The basic structures are fairly simple buildings, distinguished only by enormous steel trusses: the steel girders that support the second floor are five feet deep and reach 60 feet to either side. Architect Jim Rogers retained the original steel trusswork throughout. Instead of fighting the existing architecture, he simply designed each facility to look different from the others. The various facilities are connected by virtue of being located in one enormous structure on the waterfront, but according to Rogers, "This is not architecture for the architectural purist. It has to do with being appropriate to the

The waterfront site presented interesting construction and design challenges. For example, project architects had to deal with condensation control on the steel structure of the rinks and gymnastic training pits cut into the pier deck actually sit in water at high tide. In addition, construction had to take place without interfering with ongoing production in various soundstages.

energy and sense of action that is so much a part of the facilities. While all are part of the same entity, they're very different and for very different markets. The gymnastics facility is used mostly by kids and is painted in primary colors. The ice skating rink is all about moving fast and reacting quickly to things, and it has bright colors and a blue-and-white-diagonal checkerboard pattern, what I'll call high-energy coloration. The health club is more sophisticated, not directed toward children but toward adults who are prepared to spend a substantial amount of money and time working on themselves."

Pedestrians can walk through the entire project along Sunset Strip, a walkway that runs parallel to the river. From there they can enter any of the commercial spaces—the stores, the café, the seafood restaurant, or the microbrewery. They can watch outdoor sports, including roller skating and golf; they can sit in the park at the end of Pier 62; or they can sit on any of the benches that dot the esplanade. Chelsea Piers brings in about 8,000 to 10,000 visitors daily; a total of 3.1 million visitors came through in 1997. As of late 1997, the sports center had some 5,100 members.

The complex is kept immaculately clean, one of several management ideas that the developers freely admit that they took from the Disney Company. Badges for all 800 employees bear only a first name, and that goes for owners and managers as well as the 150 part-time employees. And while Chelsea Piers has its own security force, the limited entrances provide natural checkpoints. Bernstein says, "We tell our employees, 'You're all part of the security force.' Guest services and security go hand in hand. So in a sense we have an 800-person security force. However, security hasn't been a real problem. Since all venues have a water view, people don't feel like they're in New York, so they don't act like it either."

The owners are convinced that programming is the key to their success. In addition to regular programs at the field house, several free events are organized annually, such as an ice show, Holiday on the Hudson; a Halloween carnival with a costume contest; a flower show; art shows; an antique automobile show; a kids' performing arts day. These events attract people to Chelsea Piers and make them want to come back, and they enhance the project's reputation within the community. In 1997, a well-known New York fashion show, "7th on Sixth," was held at the piers for the first time.

The owners and staff work hard at making Chelsea Piers a place where people go not for just 50 minutes to work out but for two, three, or four hours to enjoy whatever is going on. Betts said, "We're tapping into the lifestyle thing. Good healthy sports. Most other entertainment complexes are sedentary—restaurants, retail, gimmicky things. We have almost no retail at Chelsea Piers. When we first started this, we were barraged by virtual-reality people. But it didn't interest us. We think competition fits the New York lifestyle." Bernstein added, "We believe this gives us staying power and that we'll stand the test of time where others might not."

The rock-climbing wall is an especially popular attraction for enthusiasts. Designed in Paris, the fiberglass-and-pulverized granite wall is 46 feet high and 100 feet long and features an overhang that extends out some 25 feet, so climbers are actually parallel to the ground.

The Jacuzzi and the waterside sun deck in the sports center have unparalleled views of the Hudson River, giving them a resort-like feel.

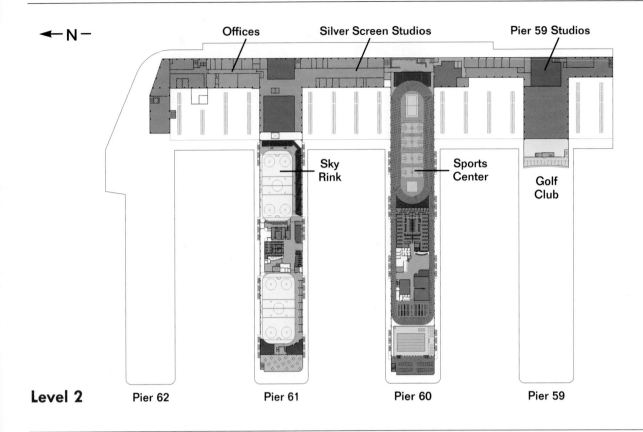

Level 2

N

Offices   Silver Screen Studios   Pier 59 Studios

Sky Rink

Sports Center

Golf Club

Pier 62   Pier 61   Pier 60   Pier 59

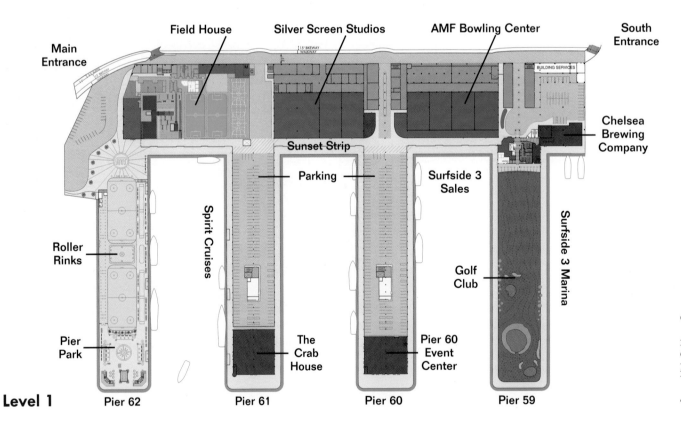

Level 1

Main Entrance   Field House   Silver Screen Studios   AMF Bowling Center   South Entrance

BUILDING SERVICES

Chelsea Brewing Company

Sunset Strip

Roller Rinks

Spirit Cruises

Parking

Surfside 3 Sales

Golf Club

Surfside 3 Marina

Pier Park

The Crab House

Pier 60 Event Center

Pier 62   Pier 61   Pier 60   Pier 59

Sonnenblick-Goldman Company

Piers 60 and 61, the enclosed piers, house primarily the sports center and the Sky Rink. The open piers, 59 and 62, are the sites of the golf club and the roller rinks. At the western end of Pier 62, Pier Park, which is open to the public, provides benches, picnic tables, and a wooden shade structure for visitors to take advantage of the spectacular river views.

134

Operating Information

Source of Revenues	Percent of Revenues
Golf	14.23
Sport center	17.07
Sky Rink	19.55
Roller rinks	3.49
Fieldhouse	9.96
Studios	8.65
Marina	2.87
Parking	4.16
Restaurants	3.66
Sponsorships	5.79
Special events	2.67
Office leasing	3.83
Company store	1.18
Other revenue	2.90
Location shoots	0.00
Total revenues	100.00

Source of Expenses	Percent of Expenses
Golf	5.14
Sport center	15.02
Sky Rink	9.16
Roller rinks	2.29
Fieldhouse	7.50
Studios	0.34
Marina	0.20
Parking	1.99
Restaurants	0.00
Sponsorship	0.40
Special events	0.66
Office leasing	0.00
Company store	0.52
Location shoots	0.04
Total expenses	43.26

Overhead expenses: 36.65%
Net income: 20.09%

Construction Costs[1]

Source	Percent of Costs
Sports center	24.39
Golf	16.37
Sky Rink	15.33
Studios	11.07
Service areas	10.86
Fieldhouse	4.87
Roller rinks	2.36
Marina	2.16
Other hard costs	2.12
Total hard costs	89.52
Total soft costs	10.48
Total construction costs	100.00

Note

1. Figures are based on total construction costs of approximately $80 million.

CocoWalk
Coconut Grove, Florida

Located in the heart of Miami's Coconut Grove commercial district, CocoWalk represents a specialized entertainment-oriented retail center that not only captures the spirit of its setting but also gives it new life. CocoWalk's 3.3-acre site is well situated at the approximate center of the trendy restaurant, shopping, and nightlife district. Yet for years the site was underused as a retail building and surface parking lot. In 1986, a French bank, Banque Worms, acquired the site and began to study potential market niches and redevelopment options. To assist, Banque Worms brought in another French company, Constructa U.S., a full-service real estate company with more than 25 years of experience in France and the United States. Working with the Baltimore-based architectural firm Development Design Group, Inc., Constructa came up with a winning concept that focuses on entertainment and leisure-time pursuits and a design that blends with the village-like scale and massing of Coconut Grove.

CocoWalk contains 162,532 square feet of leasable space in a four-story, U-shaped building. About 66 percent of the total floor area is leased to entertainment-related uses such as restaurants, nightclubs, and a 16-screen movie theater, most of which are located on the two upper floors. The center relates strongly to the outdoors, with a plaza on the ground floor, open-air sidewalks on the upper floors, and several terraces for outdoor dining or sitting. Although the tenant mix has continued to evolve, the center has remained virtually fully leased since opening in November 1990. With nearly 6 million visitors in 1996 and operating hours that span 19 hours per day, CocoWalk achieved average sales in 1996 of almost $450 per square foot, including the movie theater. Sales excluding the movie theater were close to $600 per square foot.

Development of CocoWalk was financed with a conventional construction loan from Banque Worms. Ownership of the property is held by Grand Oak Limited Partnership, which includes Banque Worms, Franko Florida Corporation (Kuwaiti French Bank), Al Khalife Al Sabah, and Virginia Management Corporation. The lenders' willingness to consider percentage rent as a significant source of income was important to obtaining financing.

DEVELOPMENT TEAM

Developer

Constructa U.S.
Coconut Grove, Florida

Architect

Development Design Group, Inc.
Baltimore, Maryland

When CocoWalk opened in 1990, the gross leasable area (GLA) was 138,441 square feet. After the addition of eight screens to the movie theater during Phase II (completed in September 1994), GLA of the center increased by 17.4 percent to 162,532 square feet. The addition of a five-level garage during Phase II increased the number of parking spaces from 522 to 865 to accommodate the increased number of theatergoers expected. Constructa expects to build another 18,000 to 20,000 square feet plus parking for 68 vehicles by 2001.

THE SITE

Coconut Grove, located about six miles south of downtown Miami, has long had a reputation for its bohemian lifestyle. Like New York's Greenwich Village, "the Grove" has attracted artisans and writers, as well as a host of activities such as the Coconut Grove Playhouse, restaurants, and music clubs. These small businesses line many of the streets that radiate from the project site. Although a diverse mix of architectural styles characterizes the neighborhood, most buildings tend to be simple, low-rise structures with a strong orientation to the street.

A notable exception to the relaxed, street-oriented nature of Coconut Grove is the Mayfair Hotel and shopping center located across Virginia Street from CocoWalk. Built in the early 1980s, the indoor, multilevel shopping center targeted exclusive, high-end retailers and an international clientele. That market failed to materialize, and the center was largely unoccupied from the mid-1980s to the early 1990s. Given that amount of adjacent retail space on the market, Constructa's

Street-level outdoor spaces open up to the neighborhood and blend with the village-like atmosphere of Coconut Grove. (Preceding page: The center relates strongly to the outdoors, with a wraparound plaza on the ground floor and open-air sidewalks on the upper floors.)

John J. Gillan

138

In addition to the elevators and escalators found in a typical shopping center, a grand Italianate staircase at the rear of the plaza provides access to the center's upper floors and creates a sense of drama.

challenge was to find a different niche in which to compete; the solution was to build on Coconut Grove's reputation as a social and entertainment hub by creating a place that would attract Miami's young and affluent as well as tourists. It can be argued that it was the success of CocoWalk that attracted the millions of dollars invested in the repositioning and renovation of the shopping center into the Streets of Mayfair, which now has tenants like Planet Hollywood, Regal Theatre, Borders Books/Music/Cafe, Ralph Lauren, Structure, the Limited, the Improv, and Virtua Cafe.

PLANNING AND DESIGN

In the design for CocoWalk, Constructa sought to reflect both the casual charm and low-rise scale of Coconut Grove. Although the site was zoned for up to 250,000 square feet of commercial use, Phase I originally contained only 138,441 square feet of gross leasable area, which was determined to be an acceptable critical mass for establishing

the project as a retail destination. It also allowed for creation of street-level outdoor spaces that would open up to the neighborhood and enable the project to exceed the 42,000-square-foot zoning requirement for open space. Phase II added another 23,091 square feet of gross leasable area, consisting solely of the expansion of the theater from eight to 16 screens. An additional 1.1 acres was acquired to accommodate the theater and the additional 343 parking spaces required.

At the core of the project is a large plaza that serves as CocoWalk's primary open space. To invite pedestrians into the center, brick pavers on the Grand Avenue sidewalk were extended to the full depth of the plaza. The plaza is surrounded primarily by fashion retailers but features also a restaurant and coffee bar with casual outdoor dining areas. The area is landscaped with large date palms and pots of flowering plants. Both escalators and elevators, as well as a grand Italianate staircase located at the rear of the plaza, provide access to the upper floors of the center.

John J. Gillan

CocoWalk's eateries feature numerous outdoor decks that are very popular because of Miami's typically warm climate. The decks not only generate a sense of excitement at the center but also create more dining space.

To have four floors and maintain compliance with the 50-foot zoning height limit, the building uses a post-tension structural system to achieve 12-foot floor-to-floor spacing, compared with the standard 16-foot spacing. The reduced spacing is compatible with older buildings surrounding the project and helped CocoWalk achieve the small building scale and massing desired. The scale of the structure is further reduced by stepbacks of the facade along Grand Avenue that also provide space for outdoor dining terraces.

A four-level garage accessed from Virginia Street provides parking for 522 cars. Another parking garage, which is accessed from Grand Avenue and provides parking for 343 cars, was added during the Phase II expansion (1993/1994). Due to the presence of ground-

water at 18 feet below grade, the entire complex was designed to "float" on a two-foot-thick concrete mat. Stormwater, most of which was required to be retained on site, is channeled through 150-foot-deep wells that pierce the water table and injected into the aquifer.

Prompted by the early success of Coco-Walk, in 1992 the owners acquired an adjacent 1.1-acre parcel located to the west. Initially used as a surface parking lot and containing two retail/restaurant buildings, the site was redeveloped for 343 parking spaces in a five-level garage (two below grade, one at grade, and two above grade), and the movie theater was expanded from eight to 16 screens.

MARKETING AND MANAGEMENT

Leasing, marketing, and management of CocoWalk are handled by Constructa; property, marketing, and security managers are located in an on-site office. Constructa also maintains its U.S. business office in Coconut Grove; it oversees CocoWalk and all properties and projects in North and South America.

The marketing/merchandising strategy is based on the placement of certain types of tenants at each level of the center. The street level includes national apparel retailers such as the Gap, Victoria's Secret, and Banana Republic. The second level is reserved primarily for gifts and accessories, although restaurants with outdoor decks are set at each end of the building facing Grand Avenue. The third and fourth levels provide space for entertainment uses, including a 16-screen AMC movie theater, a dance club, a nightclub, and a sports bar and grill. To promote both the business and the larger retail center, Dan Marino, a local celebrity, broadcasts a weekly television show during the football season from a glass-enclosed soundstage within the bar.

Marketing promotions include print and radio advertisements as well as special events held throughout the year. In its ads, Coco-Walk tags itself the "Heart and Beat of the Grove." Based on the premise that anyone visiting the neighborhood is likely to spend time at CocoWalk, the campaign strives to promote not only the project but also the entire Coconut Grove district. Constructa works closely with the local chamber of commerce in its promotional efforts, and center staff serve on the chamber's board of directors. Constructa also has become a strong supporter of the Greater Miami Convention and Visitors Bureau as well as many civic and philanthropic organizations, using its entertainment/retail facility to present additional special events that coincide with major South Florida events: the Orange Bowl, the Banyan Arts Festival, A Taste of the Grove, the Marlboro Grand Prix of Miami, the Super Bowl, the Coconut Grove Arts Festival, Make-A-Wish Foundation's fundraiser, the Doral-Ryder Open, the Royal Caribbean Golf Classic, the Lipton Tennis Tournament, and the March of Dimes Walk-A-Thon, to name but a few. CocoWalk engages educational activities also by hosting various events for the children at Coconut Grove Elementary School, such as "commissioning" the children to paint a barrier erected during construction of the new parking garage.

The management philosophy is to create and maintain a team spirit among tenants and property management staff. Because the center operates daily from 8:00 a.m. to 3:00 a.m., management functions such as cleaning and security must occur virtually around the clock. CocoWalk has a contract security staff, whose 24-hour services are augmented by off-duty Miami police officers Thursday through Sunday nights.

EXPERIENCE GAINED

▼ Entertainment-oriented projects such as CocoWalk experience far greater intensity of use than traditional retail centers and thus must withstand significantly greater wear and tear. Durable materials should be selected and greater allowances established for repair and maintenance.

▼ Developers of unanchored specialty centers need to understand the merchant's side of the business and be prepared to work closely with tenants in creating merchandising and marketing programs. The management team should visit tenants regularly and maintain a cooperative relationship.

▼ CocoWalk demonstrates that national chains can succeed in small specialty centers even when store sizes are smaller than in more traditional suburban centers.

▼ Although some existing businesses in Coconut Grove at first were concerned about the increased competition from CocoWalk, there has been no indication of negative effects. Instead, the project may have given tourists and residents more reason to visit the neighborhood. The advertising campaign run by CocoWalk has been effective in promoting Coconut Grove as an entertainment destination and has fostered goodwill in the community.

John J. Gillan

CocoWalk's low-rise configuration blends with the scale of the surrounding neighborhood. The bulk of the structure is reduced by facade stepbacks along Grand Avenue that also provide space for outdoor dining terraces and views of surrounding activity.

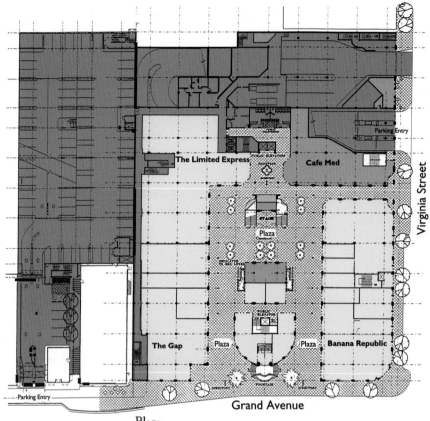

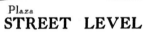

The Limited Express   Cafe Med

Parking Entry

Virginia Street

STAGE

Plaza

The Gap   Plaza   Plaza   Banana Republic

Parking Entry

Grand Avenue

Plaza

STREET LEVEL

CoCoWalk

0   16   32   48

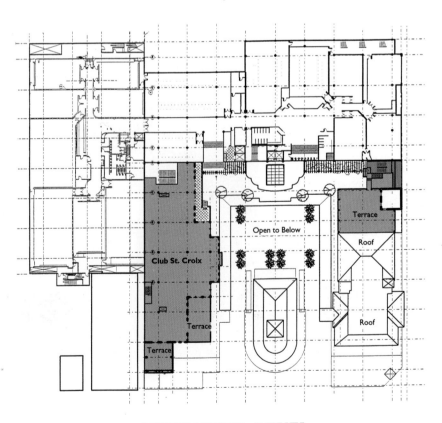

Terrace

Roof

Open to Below

Club St. Croix

Roof

Terrace

Terrace

Key:

Retail

Restaurants/
lounges/
nightclubs

Theater

Parking/service/
storage

MEZZANINE LEVEL

CoCoWalk

0   16   32   48

142

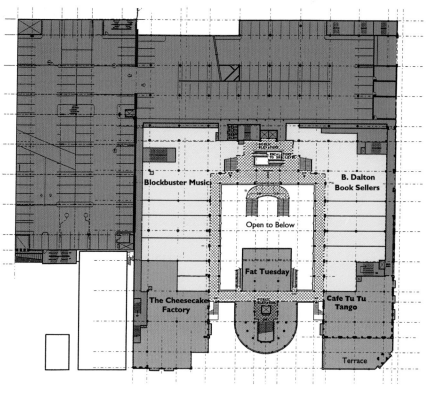

Blockbuster Music

B. Dalton
Book Sellers

Open to Below

Fat Tuesday

The Cheesecake
Factory

Cafe Tu Tu
Tango

Terrace

CoCoWalk

Veranda
SECOND LEVEL

0 16 32 48

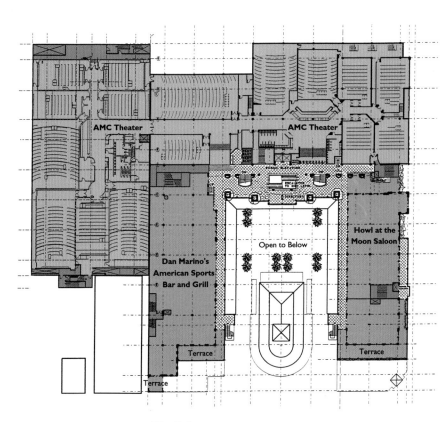

AMC Theater

AMC Theater

Open to Below

Howl at the
Moon Saloon

Dan Marino's
American Sports
Bar and Grill

Terrace

Terrace

Terrace

CoCoWalk

The Balcony
THIRD LEVEL

0 16 32 48

Land Use Information

Site area: 143,748 square feet
Gross building area (GBA): 184,458 square feet[1]
Gross leasable area (GLA): 162,532 square feet
Floor/area ratio (FAR): 1.28
Total parking spaces: 865

Development Cost Information

Phase I

Site Acquisition Cost: $8,800,000
Site Improvement Cost: $1,900,000[2]

Construction Costs	
Retail	$12,250,000
Parking	4,250,000
Tenant improvements	8,100,000
Total	$24,600,000

Soft Costs	
Architecture/engineering	$ 1,500,000
Project management	2,400,000
Marketing	1,500,000
Legal/accounting	300,000
Taxes/insurance	250,000
Construction interest/fees	5,100,000
Total	$11,050,000
Total (Phase I)	$46,350,000

Phase II

Land Cost	$3,347,681
Construction Costs (hard and soft)	8,105,474
Total (Phase II)	$11,453,155
Total Project Cost	$57,803,155

Development Schedule

Site purchased: February 1986
Planning started: June 1988
Construction started: March 1989
Leasing started: January 1990
Phase I opened: November 1990
Construction on Phase II started: November 1992
Phase II opened: September 1994

Notes
1. Exclusive of parking garage.
2. Estimated; includes on- and off-site improvements.

Retail Information

Classification	Number of Tenants	Percentage of Total	Total GLA (square Feet)	Percentage of GLA
Food/food service	6	16.7	35,174	21.6
Clothing and accessories	12	33.3	30,507	18.8
Home appliances/music	2	5.6	7,430	4.6
Hobby/special interest	5	13.9	10,723	6.6
Gifts/specialty	3	8.3	3,290	2.0
Jewelry	2	5.6	1,003	0.6
Lounges/nightclubs	3	8.3	22,845	14.1
Personal services	1	2.8	1,082	0.7
Shoes	1	2.8	1,055	0.6
Cinema	1	2.8	49,423	30.4
Total	36	100.0	162,532	100.0

Rental Data (1996)

Annual rents: Approximately $32.85 per square foot (net), including percentage rents.

Average base rent: $27.78 per square foot GLA

Average length of lease: Five to ten years

Typical terms of lease: Base rent plus percentage rent (above natural break point) plus extra charges (common area maintenance fee, promotion, real estate taxes, rent tax, and insurance)

Sales Data (1996)

Total center: $447.66 per square foot

Total center (without 16-screen cinema): $597.18 per square foot

First level only: $862.43 per square foot

Second level only: $625.48 per square foot

Third level only: $167.01 per square foot

ENTERTAINMENT CENTER AT IRVINE SPECTRUM
Irvine, California

The Entertainment Center at Irvine Spectrum (Phase I) is a $25 million, 260,000-square-foot (GLA), freestanding destination entertainment center located in Irvine, California, approximately 40 miles south of Los Angeles. The project is one of the first freestanding, entertainment-only centers in the nation. Instead of emphasizing shopping, the center responds to increasing consumer demand for exciting experiences and features signature restaurants (where high energy, good service, menu, and atmosphere are all of equal importance) and a variety of high-tech entertainment tenants. It is designed to offer consumers a complete, synergistic experience involving entertainment, food, people-watching, and shopping.

The Entertainment Center is anchored by the world's largest theater complex, the 158,000-square-foot, 6,400-seat Edwards Theater (known as The Big One), which features 21 state-of-the art motion picture screens, including the West Coast's first IMAX 3-D theater. The festive outdoor center also features a variety of entertainment-oriented tenants, including four world-class restaurants, a food court, a virtual reality center, book and music shops, a coffee shop, and colorful carts and kiosks; 4,100 surface parking spaces; and valet parking. Blending a Moroccan design theme with futuristic innovations such as computer-generated laser lighting, the center provides a memorable experience.

The project, which is nearly 100 percent leased, is averaging sales of $425 per square foot, excluding the theater. In addition, restaurants are averaging gross revenues 30 percent higher than their own projections, and 10,000 cars a day visit the center. The Entertainment Center's combination of location, demographics, tenant mix, and architectural theme has resulted in a project that is exceeding revenue projections dramatically.

Phase II, which broke ground in July 1997 and is expected to open in July 1998, will double the size of the existing center and greatly expand the entertainment and retail offerings. Dave & Buster's (a thirty-something–oriented place for dining, billiards, and a variety of games) will anchor Phase II, along with restaurants that are more affordable than those in Phase I. Additional parking already has been added in preparing for Phase II. Altogether, there will be 3,350 spaces on site and another 2,500 spaces in commercial areas next to the center; shuttles and expanded valet service also will be available for customers' convenience.

DEVELOPMENT TEAM

Developer

The Irvine Company
Newport Beach, California

Architect

RTKL Associates
Los Angeles, California

Landscape Architect

Burton Associates
San Diego, California

General Contractor

Snyder Langston
Irvine, California

THE SITE AND TRADE AREA

The project serves as an urban center for Orange County, California, and for Irvine Spectrum, a 3,600-acre master-planned business community developed by the Irvine Company. Irvine Spectrum currently has more than 100 industrial and commercial buildings totaling 7 million square feet and is home to more than 2,200 firms and 36,000 employees. The Entertainment Center site was zoned for a regional mall, with all entitlements in place.

The flat, 56-acre site is ideally located at the convergence of Orange County's two busiest freeways (I-5, the Santa Ana Freeway, and I-405, the San Diego Freeway). Known as the El Toro Y, it is the world's largest interchange, with 26 lanes across at its widest point. An estimated 500,000 vehicles drive by the center each day. Four exit ramps and 30 lanes of arterial roads feed directly into Irvine Spectrum.

In addition to outstanding visibility and accessibility, the Entertainment Center enjoys excellent demographics. Ninety percent of Orange County households (2.4 million people) are located within a 20-minute drive of the center. Residents of the center's trade area are affluent and well-educated. The average household income in the primary trade area is $86,000, and 30 percent of the households have an income of more than $100,000. Furthermore, 70 percent of all Orange County households with an income of more than $100,000 and 85 percent of households with incomes of more than $150,000 reside in the primary trade area. The center draws not only from Orange County (with its population of more than 2.8 million) but also from as far north as Los Angeles County and as far south as San Diego County.

PROJECT HISTORY

The project originated in response to the need for retail facilities (particularly places for people to meet and eat) to serve the 36,000 employees at Irvine Spectrum. The original plan was to locate several restaurants on the site. However, it was recognized that while the restaurants would have a built-in lunchtime business, it would be difficult to attract business in the evening and, therefore, to attract signature restaurants. An anchor tenant was needed to draw people to the area after business hours and on weekends.

The Irvine Company decided to pursue a multiscreen cinema as the anchor tenant and approached Edwards Theaters to discuss the concept of developing a ten-screen cinema adjacent to the proposed restaurants. Edwards Theaters had a record of great success in Southern California (currently operating 470 screens at 86 locations) as well as a strong working relationship with the Irvine Company. After reviewing the project's demographics, Edwards decided that it wanted to do more than a ten-screen theater and the original concept gradually evolved into a 21-screen complex with an IMAX 3-D theater. The cinema site was ground-leased to Edwards, and the project concept was expanded to include an entertainment center requiring about 30 acres to provide for the buildings, public space, and parking. RTKL Associates was hired to master plan the site and to implement the design theme set by Irvine's chairman Donald Bren. Bren envisioned the center as an escape, "a destination resort for those in search of a smile—a place that demands that you leave your cares in the parking lot." Burton Associates of San Diego was retained as landscape architect for the project.

Phase I, which started out to meet the lunchtime needs of the rapidly growing number of employees in Irvine Spectrum, evolved into a successful entertainment destination for a much wider audience. The more than five million visitors per year both from surrounding counties and from around the world, coupled with their eagerness to spend, resulted in sales per square foot of GLA of $425 in the first year of operation. In response to the unmitigated success of Phase I, the Irvine

RTKL Associates

Company broke ground for Phase II less than two years after the opening of Phase I.

PLANNING AND DESIGN

The primary planning and design objective for Phase I was to create an entertainment/retail destination with a distinct sense of place and a variety of vibrant, exciting spaces. It was achieved by using a Moroccan village theme featuring a unique blend of indoor and outdoor spaces and the bold forms and

A Moroccan village theme helps the center to achieve a distinct and vibrant sense of place.

rich colors of Moroccan and other North African cities. The Moroccan design was selected for its compatibility with Southern California's predominantly Spanish Mediterranean architecture as well as its ability to balance the more intimate, human-scale environment of the Entertainment Center's retail buildings with the massive cinema complex. The five one-story restaurant/retail buildings (containing 100,000 square feet) were designed to be one-and-a-half stories in height to provide the proper balance. All of the buildings in the center are outlined by

The center is anchored by the 158,000-square-foot, 21-screen Edwards Cinemas and 3-D IMAX theater. Grand public spaces near the cinema serve as a place for people to gather and orient themselves upon arrival.

RTKL Associates

five miles of neon lighting, enhancing the project's visibility and visual excitement after dark.

The heart of the project is the central plaza—a major public space in front of the cinema complex for people to gather and orient themselves upon arrival. The plaza is paved with splashes of color—copper, turquoise, and purple—and links the Edwards cinema building with the restaurant buildings, the tented food court, and the entertainment-oriented stores. The plaza also features the center's open bazaar, an area of carts and 15 kiosks. Near the cinema, the public spaces are wide and open, but the circulation network gently transitions into a series of more intimate paseos. Subdued patterns and clustered elements are used to outline gathering areas and to draw people into the heart of the project. The center was planned to be a series of spaces framed by buildings and landscape, and as much attention was given to designing spaces in which people can interact as to designing the buildings.

The layering of Moroccan-inspired elements enhances the sense of adventure for customers as they stroll through the center. Recurring domes in reds, greens, and golds; neon lighting around the buildings; intricately patterned paving; landscaping; fountains; bright graphics (including 150 banners in a variety of shapes and colors); a variety of portable kiosks and carts; narrow canvas-shaded passageways; 150 palm and 100 olive trees; and a tented food court provide visual excitement and a fantasyland escape for visitors. Working closely with the city of Irvine, which has strict sign controls, the architects created an 80-foot-high Plexiglass pyramid to serve as the center's landmark. A computerized lighting system changes the colors of the pyramid by day and night. The pyramid is the only one of its type in the United States and provides a dynamic landmark for the center.

Overlooking the central plaza, the $27 million Edwards Theater building was envisioned as a Moroccan palace. Grand stairs connect the building to the central plaza and

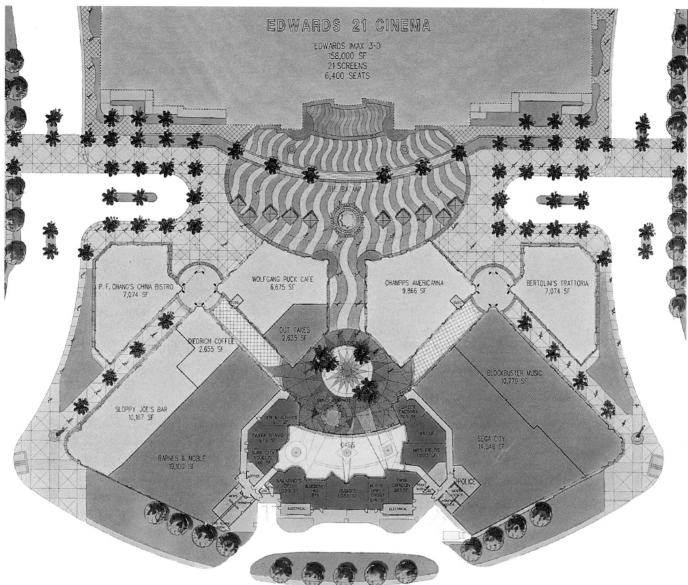

EDWARDS 21 CINEMA

EDWARDS IMAX 3-D
158,000 SF
21 SCREENS
6,400 SEATS

P.F. CHANG'S CHINA BISTRO
7,074 SF

WOLFGANG PUCK CAFE
6,675 SF

CHAMPPS AMERICANNA
9,866 SF

BERTOLINI'S TRATTORIA
7,074 SF

DIEDRICH COFFEE
2,655 SF

OUT TAKES
2,635 SF

OASIS

BLOCKBUSTER MUSIC
10,779 SF

SLOPPY JOE'S BAR
10,167 SF

BEN & JERRY'S

PASTA BRAVO

SURF CITY SQUEEZE

OFFICE

SABATINO'S DELI

BLUEBERRY HILL

RUBIO'S

N.Y.'S UPPER CRUST

TWIN DRAGON

SWEET FACTORY

MRS. FIELDS

SEGA CITY
14,548 SF

BARNES & NOBLE
19,100 SF

OASIS

POLICE

ELECTRICAL

ELECTRICAL

Phase I leasing plan.

the rest of the center. The building's facade features twin 80-foot towers with vertical, cantilevered blade signs. A cornice frieze with decorative 3-D patterns wraps around the entire building. Inside, the 42-foot-tall, 15,000-square-foot lobby evokes images of the grand movie palaces of the 1920s and 1930s, with 40-foot-tall mosaics and murals, bright neon piping, seven concession stands, and brass and marble finishes. Each of the four giant-screen (40-by-80-foot) theaters in the complex features a design theme (Hollywood, ancient Egypt, imperial China, and a 1920s movie palace). The theater complex also houses the Edwards IMAX 3-D theater (with

a 90-foot-tall screen) and two large theaters with tiered stadium seating.

The design of Phase II was inspired by the Alhambra, a 13th-century castle in Granada, Spain, that features an exotic blend of classic architecture with the colorful overlay of Moorish detailing. The buildings of the Alhambra are connected by magnificent courtyards, including the Court of Lions and the Court of the Myrtles. Similar courtyards will become a main feature of the new center.

The Entertainment Center's Court of Dorado will include a shadow-lit bell tower, the highest point of the center. The Court of Lions will feature a fountain inspired by the lion fountain at the Alhambra, along with colored arcades and giant palms. In the Court of the Myrtles, architectural elements will include a reflecting pool with arching jets of water, arcades, and seating areas shaded by palms.

The "souks"—or shopping streets between the courts—will feature special overhead trellises and hanging awnings that will cast shadow patterns on the decorative pathways both day and night. The souks will connect the three courts.

Tenant Mix

In selecting tenants, three general categories were pursued: high-tech, interactive multimedia tenants; trend-setting eateries; and specialty retail stores focused on entertainment and recreation. One of the key objectives was to locate viable, high-quality merchants with extensive experience and the demonstrated ability to innovate and adapt to changing consumer preferences. Also sought were unique tenants that would do whatever they do in an entertaining way and offer a participatory experience to consumers of all ages. To minimize financial risk, 33 restaurants and stores were leased before construction started on Phase I. Five of the tenants have established their first California operations in the center. Phase II also was significantly preleased prior to ground breaking.

Major tenants in Phase I include four signature restaurants, each with a different theme, which were selected both for their presentation and for the quality of their food. Bertolini's Authentic Trattoria, Champp's Americana, P.F. Chang's China Bistro, and the Wolfgang Puck Cafe all provide a one-of-a-kind dining experience. The eleven tenants in the upscale Oasis food court offer a variety of gourmet items. The center has 50,000 square feet of restaurant space with 1,700 seats, including outdoor seating for 400. Entertainment retail tenants include a 20,000-square-foot, two-story Barnes & Noble Superstore. Barnes & Noble is connected to Diedrich's, an upscale coffee shop, and features cozy couch settings and book and poetry readings. A Blockbuster Music store includes a state-of-the art CD listening bar. Other key tenants include Sega City (a 15,000-square-foot virtual reality center) and California's first Sloppy Joe's Bar, a dance bar modeled on the bar frequented by Ernest Hemingway in Key West, Florida. The center also features 1,600 square feet of specialty retail space in carts, kiosks, and wall shops.

Similar tenants were sought for Phase II. Dave & Buster's, a 55,000-square-foot complex, will anchor Phase II. The Dallas-based entertainment restaurant chain markets itself as the ultimate place for "big kids" to play, combining upscale quality dining with classic and state-of-the-art amusements. Dave & Buster's includes two full-service bars, world-class pocket billiards, "Play-for-Fun Blackjack," full-swing golf simulators, table shuffleboard, and a "Million Dollar Midway" with more than 200 interactive amusements, including virtual reality games, classic carnival games, and simulator rides.

Restaurants that are more affordable than those in Phase I in were pursued to round out the dining opportunities. Among the full-service restaurants are the Cheesecake Factory, Hansen's Juice Creations (juice and sandwiches), and Johnny Rockets (hamburgers). Rounding out the retailers will be Coffee Bean & Tea Leaf, Wetzel's Pretzels, Skechers (family shoe store), Dapy (gift shop), and Glow (gift shop).

Experience Gained

▼ It was important to stay focused on an entertainment theme in creating the tenant mix. The customer is not confused about the center's purpose; it is clearly a place to dine and enjoy movies and other attractions. Opportunities to buy are all entertainment related.

The design for Phase II was inspired by the Alhambra, a 13th-century castle in Granada, Spain, that features an exotic blend of classic architecture with a colorful overlay of Moorish detailing.

Souks—the shopping streets between the courts—will feature special overhead trellises and hanging awnings.

▼ An entertainment center requires a trade area with a population that has the disposable income to spend on entertainment and that is large enough to supply good repeat business. A key factor in the success of the project was the critical mass of jobs and affluent households in Irvine Spectrum and Orange County.

▼ The center must feature only viable merchants with high-quality operations, preferably with national stature and experience at keeping up to date and staying ahead of trends.

▼ Safety and security (and the perception of safety) are important considerations in an entertainment center. Including a police substation within the center and working with the local police department to provide uniformed officers at appropriate times ensures that customers feel comfortable returning to the center on a regular basis.

▼ A strong anchor with the ability to draw from a large trade area was essential to the center's success. The Edwards Theater complex, the largest movie theater in the world and the most advanced IMAX 3-D theater in the country, fulfills this role.

▼ Conventional shopping center parking ratios are not adequate for an entertainment center that includes a mega-theater. Counting the center's original 1,350 surface on-site parking spaces and the 2,000 spaces in adjacent shared lots, the center had more than three times the code-required parking (5 spaces per 1,000 square feet). However, to meet demand, 1,000 new spaces were added on site three months after the opening of the center. The project now has a parking ratio of 17 spaces per 1,000 square feet.

▼ An entertainment center draws people who want to be entertained, not conventional shoppers. Originally, some of the carts and kiosks in the plaza were stocked with too many conventional clothing items and accessories instead of merchandise that appeals to the customer's sense of fun and to the impulse to buy.

▼ Larger service areas and a larger on-site management office should have been provided. The higher-than-anticipated customer traffic has placed increased demands on center operations, specialty retail (carts and kiosks) maintenance, and security. Allowing additional space for service areas would have allowed all deliveries and service to be confined to designated service areas.

▼ More and larger trash compactors should have been provided. High-volume stores

As people wend their way through the center, the circulation network changes into a series of more intimate paseos.

RTKL Associates

154

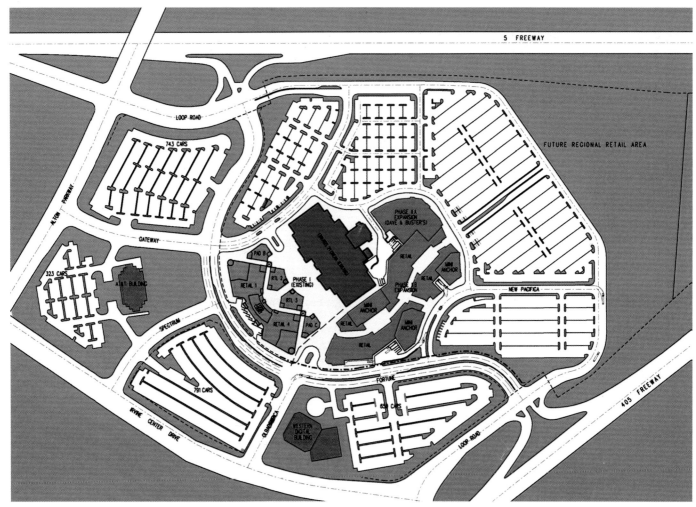

Site plan.

and restaurants generate a lot of trash, leading to higher operating costs due to more frequent trash service.

▼ In planning the center, the frequent use of valet parking was not anticipated. Many customers (more than 13,000 cars per month) are taking advantage of the convenience of valet parking, even in a center where surface parking is available within a reasonable walking distance.

▼ If the physical layout of the site and the surrounding road system permit, main vehicular entrances should be kept away from pedestrian areas. This is particularly true in a project such as the Entertainment Center, where the vehicular traffic volume is very high.

▼ Entertainment options must be well rounded. The center needed to offer enjoyment to consumers of all ages—from the business person looking for relaxation on a lunch break, to the thirty-something professional stopping by after work, to the family on weekends, to the Southern California tourist.

PROJECT DATA

Land Use Information

	Phase I	Phase II	Total
Site area (acres)	29	27	56
Gross building area (square feet)	277,050	228,500	505,550
Gross leasable area (square feet)	258,728	221,600	400,328
Floor/area ratio (FAR)	0.205	0.205	0.205
Number of levels	1 (with some mezzanine space)	1 level	1 (with some mezzanine space)
Parking			
On-site surface spaces	2,247	1,108	3,355
Off-site shared spaces	1,857	650	2,507
Total	4,104	1,758	5,862

Land Use Plan (Phases I and II)

	Acres	Percent of Site
Buildings	11.39	20.5
Service and amenity areas (plazas, paseos)	8.59	15.5
Paved areas (surface parking/roads)	29.40	53.0
Landscaped areas	6.11	11.0
Total	55.54	100

Retail Tenant Information

Classification	Phase I Total GLA (square feet)	Phase II Total GLA (square feet)	Phases I & II Total GLA (square feet)
Cineplex	158,000	55,000	213,000
Entertainment/retail	48,228	129,100	177,328
Restaurants	40,900	35,000	75,900
Food court	10,000	0	10,000
Specialty retail (carts, kiosks, wall shops)	1,600	2,500	4,100
Total	258,728	221,600	480,328

Lease Information

Average length of lease: Five to ten years

Typical lease provisions: Minimum rent plus percentage of sales, common area expenses, real estate taxes, and promotional fund

Annual rents: $28 to $60 per square foot

Average annual sales: $425 per square foot (excluding theater)

Development Cost Information

	Phase I	Phase II
Site Acquisition Cost	–	–
Site Improvement Costs	$6,132,000	$10,648,000
Construction Costs		
Building costs	$8,681,000	$18,936,000
Graphics/specialties	$890,000	$710,000
Tenant improvements	$3,487,000	$9,018,000
Total	$13,058,000	$28,664,000
Soft Costs		
Architecture/engineering	$2,042,000	$3,806,000
Project management	$667,000	$301,000
Marketing	$150,000	$400,000
Legal/accounting	$75,000	$160,000
Taxes/insurance	$100,000	$342,000
Fees/permits	$709,000	$1,675,000
Construction interest and fees	$1,045,000	$1,828,000
Leasing	$954,000	$1,714,000
Total	$5,742,000	$10,226,000
Total Development Cost	$24,932,000[1]	$49,538,000

Annual Operating Expense (Phases I)

Taxes	$884,000
Insurance	82,000
Services	720,000
Maintenance	488,000
Janitorial	619,000
Utilities	159,000
Legal	50,000
Management	1,036,000
Miscellaneous	117,000
Total	$4,155,000

Development Schedule

	Phase I	Phase II
Site purchased	–	–
Planning started	December 1993	April 1996
Leasing started	February 1994	September 1996
Approvals obtained	July 1994	February 1997
Construction started	January 1995	July 1997
Project opened	November 1995	July 1998 (scheduled)

Note

1. Excludes theater development costs of approximately $25 million. Theater transaction is a ground lease; all theater development costs were paid by the lessee.

THE FORUM SHOPS
AT CAESARS PALACE
Las Vegas, Nevada

The "Shopping Wonder of the World," reads the Forum Shops' advertising copy, and with sales exceeding $1,200 per square foot, the words are no idle boast. Lured by its Ancient Rome–themed "streets," its vaulted cloud-painted ceilings lit to reflect the changing colors of the sky, and its animatronic sculptures that simulate human movement, some 50,000 visitors flow through the center each day—almost 20 million visitors a year.

And when not looking at the "sky," listening to Bacchus, or watching the sinking of Atlantis, a good number of the 20 million shop. For the well-heeled and the lucky roulette players, there are shops offering fashions by Gucci, Bernini, and Louis Vuitton. For the rest, the Forum Shops includes less patrician retailers, such as Guess, Brookstone, and Victoria's Secret, and, in a bow to the emerging family atmosphere in Las Vegas, a Warner Bros. Store and a Disney Store.

Phase II has a similar tenant mix, with strong name-brand retailers such as Abercrombie & Fitch, DKNY, Hugo Boss, Diesel, Lacoste, Nike-Town, Polo/Ralph Lauren, Virgin Megastore, and Bernini Collections. Completing the mix are high-profile restaurants such as Spago, Planet Hollywood, and the Stage Deli. The center is anchored by Caesars Palace Hotel and Casino.

The Site

The Forum Shops is situated on a 12-acre site just north of Caesars Palace on land that formerly was used for employee parking and as a Grand Prix racetrack. Phase I of the center is L-shaped, with the long leg facing Las Vegas Boulevard and the short leg abutting and tied into the Olympic Casino of Caesars Palace. Phase II extends the long leg of the center westward from the Fountain of the Gods. The center's shops are primarily on one level, raised above the lower-level vehicle circulation area, which leads to the valet parking entrance as well as a self-parking area in the rear. A Cyberstation (games arcade) and Cinema Ride (a motion simulator 3-D ride) also are located on the lower level.

From the street outside, one approaches the Forum Shops on a one-way moving walkway that passes through a series of five triumphal

arches. Inside, the visitor proceeds along the Roman "street" as it bends and turns, passing through a series of gathering points—piazzas—and eventually exiting directly into the casino. Going the other way, hotel and casino patrons pass through a monumental portal into the Forum Shops. As a result of a grade change as well as the one-way moving walkway at the end of the "street," a journey through the Forum Shops that starts at the casino also ends back at the casino.

DEVELOPMENT PROCESS

Back in the late 1980s, as lavish new hotels were booming all around Caesars, it became clear that employee parking was not the highest and best use for eight acres facing Las Vegas Boulevard. The "Street of Dreams," as the Forum Shops was initially conceived, represented to Caesars the opportunity to reestablish its preeminent place in the pantheon of hotel-casinos by offering the most unusual, most upscale shopping environment in Las Vegas. Not incidentally, the plan also was intended to drive more people through the casino. Simon DeBartolo Group and

DEVELOPMENT TEAM

Developer

Simon DeBartolo Group, Inc.
Indianapolis, Indiana

Gordon Group Holdings, Ltd.
Las Vegas, Nevada

Architect

Marnell/Corrao Associates
Las Vegas, Nevada

Interior Designer

Dougall Design Associates, Inc.
Pasadena, California

Gordon Group Holdings, Ltd., developers of premier shopping centers across the country, were brought in to realize the vision.

The Forum Shops was constructed on land leased to the project by Caesars World. Construction for Phase I was financed by Yasuda Trust and Banking Co., Ltd., along with equity contributions from Simon DeBartolo Group. In 1996 the United Bank of Switzerland (UBS) provided permanent financing for the project.

Development of the specialized architectural and entertainment elements of the Forum Shops involved the efforts of a wide range of designers, artists, and artisans working under the direction of Dougall Design Associates and Marnell/Corrao, the center's design/build architect and contractor. To achieve the complex special effects and authentic-looking faux finishes envisioned for the project, the design and construction process required an extended series of models, mock-ups, and material samples.

Because of the project's complexity, Simon DeBartolo Group retained Marnell/Corrao under a design/build arrangement. As executive architect, Marnell/Corrao developed the construction documents from Dougall Design Associates' models; thereafter, as contractor, Marnell/Corrao was responsible for building the project for a guaranteed maximum price. As a further control, Simon DeBartolo Group placed two of its in-house construction personnel on site for the duration of construction.

The primary difficulty encountered in the otherwise smooth construction process involved unanticipated delays in the completion of storefronts because of the extensive number of castings and faux finishes required and the limited number of firms retained to do this specialized work.

DESIGN AND ARCHITECTURE

Both in materials and layout the Forum Shops is intended to evoke the feel of a Roman city.

The fantasy design of the Forum Shops reflects a classic Roman theme with columns, pilasters, balconies, and statuary. Storefronts are two stories tall, with display windows below and Roman streetfront facades above. The vaulted ceiling is painted to look like a cloud-filled sky.

Just north of Caesars Palace and fronting on the Strip, the Forum Shops is situated on land that formerly was used for employee parking and as a Grand Prix racetrack.

The Fountain of the Gods piazza contains the Temple of Neptune. Roman statuary crowns the store and café facades along the piazza.

FAO Schwarz is but one of many strong brand-name retailers—such as Abercrombie and Fitch, DKNY, Hugo Boss, Diesel, Lacoste, NikeTown, Polo/ Ralph Lauren, Virgin Megastore, and Bernini—to take space in Phase II.

The common-area floors, for example, are of stamped concrete, patterned to look like the rough stone of a Roman street. The storefronts are two stories high, with display windows below and Roman streetfront facades above, replete with shuttered windows, balconies, lanterns, and tile roofs.

Arching over the "street" is a vaulted ceiling painted to look like a cloud-filled sky. Computer-controlled devices light up the "sky," changing its appearance from that of an orangy dawn to a clear blue midday to a purple dusk, all in a one-hour rotation. The layout of the Forum Shops also contributes to its varying ambience. The narrow street scene alternates with wider piazzas, and the "street" itself bends, producing a series of vistas as one proceeds along the route.

The first highlight of the procession— judging by the crowds—is the Festival Fountain, a large rotunda and fountain with figures of Bacchus, Apollo, Venus, and Pluto, who come to life once an hour through the magic of audio animatronics. For seven minutes, the characters are heard chatting, moving their lips and other parts of their bodies in sync.

Offering more sedate charms is the larger Fountain of the Gods piazza. In addition to some of the upscale shops, the Fountain of the Gods offers an "outdoor" café (Bertolinis) at which customers can sip coffee and watch the passing parade. Roman statuary crowns the facades along the piazza.

Phase II is a seamless integration of more entertainment and shopping options into the existing fabric. The centerpiece of the new addition, which extends westward from the Fountain of the Gods, is the Roman Great Hall; of heroic proportions, it measures 160 feet in diameter and 85 feet high. Located within the great hall is a spectacular new Atlantis attraction featuring both humans and talking statues in a mind-boggling display that combines cutting-edge technologies in projection, animation, and hydraulics. It has been designed to draw crowds into the new shopping area with regularly scheduled performances of the sinking of Atlantis, Las Vegas style. The expansion also includes a 50,000-gallon marine aquarium designed to represent the legendary sunken city of Atlantis. Overseen by three staff biologists, the aquarium contains a wide variety of fish from a geographic range of 10 to 15 degrees north latitude, just above the equator in the Caribbean. Many new statutes made of fiberglass and weighing between 1,500 and 2,000 pounds each adorn Phase II's Piazza IV, including four large horses, a winged siren, two warriors, and a lion.

Marketing and Management

Marketing the Forum Shops to financiers as well as potential tenants before development was not the easy sell that in retrospect it might seem. In their favor, the developers had a strong location, a strong concept, and quotable sales figures from retailers in Las Vegas. On the other hand, at that time Las Vegas was known to most retailers as a casino market, not as a shopping market or family market. By opening day for Phase I, however, the center was 90 percent leased. Phase II, which opened four years later, also was nearly leased at opening.

Construction activities were the source of much of the initial publicity for the center, and hard-hat tours were organized for the news media to cover events such as the painting of the sky ceiling. In addition, the development team marketed the center through airport displays, billboards, in-flight magazines, tourist publications, and, to a lesser

Many famous retailers line the narrow street bustling with activity between Piazza IV and the Roman Great Hall.

extent, radio and television. The team also staged a series of preopening events, including separate hosted evenings for the local chamber of commerce, taxi and limousine drivers, and Caesars Palace employees.

More than 15 million people visited the center in its first year—50 percent more than initially projected. Almost all of the center's tenants have exceeded projected sales, and several are the leading sales locations in their chains. Only one tenant (a restaurant) has failed, and two have been bought out and replaced with new tenants.

The shops typically are open from 10:00 a.m. to 11:00 p.m. and until midnight on weekends. The common areas remain open 24 hours a day, 365 days a year. Because of the extended hours and the large crowds, maintenance and security are critical, and management and security personnel are on duty around the clock. Nearly 50 employees

are on staff, including management office personnel, security officers, building engineers, and housekeeping staff. To support these operations, common-area maintenance (CAM) charges are high, but, as a percentage of sales volume they are not unlike those in more typical centers, according to Deborah Simon of Simon DeBartolo Group.

Due to Phase I's record sales and numbers of visitors, Phase II broke ground just four years after the opening of Phase I. The 276,000-square-foot expansion, which opened in August 1997, effectively doubles the size of the center. The entertainment and shopping experience has been enhanced by the recreation of the sinking of Atlantis as well as by the addition of 35 strong name-brand tenants. Unlike for Phase I, little marketing was required for Phase II. The unmitigated success of Phase I and the promise that Phase II would offer even more shopping

The Festival Fountain, a large rotunda and fountain with figures of Apollo, Bacchus, Venus, and Pluto, delights shoppers as the statues come to life once an hour through the magic of audio animatronics.

THE FORUM SHOPS AT CAESARS

and entertainment options were the keys to marketing Phase II. Ninety percent of the new retail space was preleased, and it is now completely leased. Referring to the record sales at the Forum Shops, David Salz, CEO of Alfred Dunhill USA, an upscale men's wear store, said, "I would have to be catatonic not to do business in this center" (*Daily News Record*, September 5, 1997).

EXPERIENCE GAINED

▼ Both entertainment and environment attract visitors to the Forum Shops. The center's architectural theme and its sup-

porting amenities, including the animatronic displays, combine to create a "must see" attraction in Las Vegas.

▼ Design and development required extensive production of custom finishes and complex installation procedures, increasing both hard and soft costs and prolonging construction. These finishes, however, significantly contribute to the innovative design theme that has played an invaluable role in the Forum Shops' success.

▼ Through creative design and tenanting, the integration of retail and entertainment can serve as a valuable complement to a casino and hotel complex, creating a strong identity in a crowded market.

PROJECT DATA

Land Use Information

	Phase I	Phase II
Site area (acres)	8.4	3.6
Gross leasable area		
(GLA; square feet)	250,000	276,000

Number of levels: One retail level with valet parking entrance and video arcade on a sublevel. Several tenant spaces include mezzanine levels.

Total parking spaces: 2,100

Retail Tenant Information

Tenant Classification	Number of Retailers (Phase I)	Number of Retailers (Phase II)
Food	3	0
Food service	6	3
Clothing and accessories	24	13
Shoes	6	2
Hobby/special interest	3	0
Gifts/specialty	8	2
Jewelry	5	3
Other retail	13	9
Personal services	2	1
Recreation/community	2	1
Total	72	34

Tenant Classification	Phase I GLA (square feet)	Phase II GLA (square feet)
Food	2,967	0
Food service	52,062	29,729
Clothing and accessories	81,606	77,428
Shoes	21,739	3,261
Hobby/special interest	0	10,515
Gifts/specialty	22,014	1,707
Jewelry	3,766	3,146
Other retail	31,058	109,354
Personal services	851	100
Recreation/community	13,436	23,200
Total	240,014	247,925

Average length of lease: Ten to 12 years
Annual rents: $70 to $200 per square foot
Average annual sales: $1,200 per square foot

Annual Operating Expense for 1995 (Pre-Phase II)

Taxes	$471,996
Insurance	218,000
Services	65,100
Maintenance	1,074,000
Janitorial	496,900
Utilities	301,000
Management	225,352
Miscellaneous	2,694,419
Total	$5,545,767

Development Cost Information (Phase I)

Site Acquisition Cost	$5,000,000[1]

Site Improvement Costs (on- and off-site)

Excavation/grading	$500,000
Sewer/water/drainage	250,000
Paving/curbs/sidewalks	200,000
Landscaping/irrigation	100,000
Fees/general conditions	200,000
Other	750,000
Total	$2,000,000

Construction Costs

Superstructure	$11,000,000
HVAC	3,000,000
Electrical	4,000,000
Plumbing/sprinklers	2,000,000
Elevators	200,000
Fees/general conditions	6,200,000
Finishes	15,800,000
Graphics/specialties	500,000
Parking structure	5,000,000
Tenant improvements	17,000,000
Total	$64,700,000

Soft Costs

Architecture/engineering	$2,500,000
Project management	100,000
Marketing	1,500,000
Legal/accounting	1,000,000
Taxes/insurance	500,000
Construction interest and fees	7,600,000
Other	600,000
Total	$13,800,000

Leasing and Development Fees	$4,500,000
Total Development Cost	$90,000,000

Development Schedule

	Phase I	Phase II
Site purchased	Ground lease	Ground lease
Planning started	1988	1992
Sales/leasing started	1988	1992
Construction started	February 1990	May 1995
Project completed	May 1992	August 1997

Note

1. Reimbursement to Caesars Palace for existing site improvements.

MALL OF AMERICA
Bloomington, Minnesota

Mall of America in Bloomington, Minnesota, is the largest enclosed entertainment/retail complex in the United States. Opened in August 1992, the center totals 4.2 million square feet—the equivalent of 78 football fields—of which 2.8 million square feet is devoted to retail tenants. The mall's 2.9 miles of corridors form a three-level rectangular ring around the development's marquee element, the seven-acre Knott's Camp Snoopy theme park, with additional entertainment and dining on a partial fourth level.

Mall of America is a synthesis of two development types: the shopping mall and the theme park. Although these components remain physically and operationally segregated, they are intended to work synergistically to maximize total visitation and length of stay at the complex. This is achieved by extending the market area from which the development draws visitors and by offering alternative experiences that appeal to various members of a visiting group. The retail elements, for example, have high appeal with adults and the theme park has high appeal with children. The combined effect is that Mall of America is a family-oriented leisure destination. Although Mall of America is built on a grand scale that is not likely to be widely replicated, melding entertainment and retail—at every scale—is a prevailing trend.

Common UEC entertainment components include cinema complexes, arenas, and family entertainment or high-tech game centers with interactive "software"-based attractions. These venues serve the visitation requirements of UECs as they draw repeat visitors regularly. In contrast, theme parks with fixed rides such as roller coasters and log flumes like those found at Knott's Camp Snoopy do not usually inspire frequent repeat visitation. Normally, participating residents will visit an area theme park perhaps once or twice a year, which is an inadequate rate for a super regional shopping center, especially one with 2.8 million square feet of retail space and a resident market of only 2.7 million persons. Thus, like the Forum Shops at Caesars Palace in Las Vegas, Mall of America is an example of a UEC complex that depends on tourists.

THE MARKET

Mall of America was built on the 78-acre site of the former Metropolitan Stadium, which was home to the Twins baseball team and Vikings football team until they moved to a replacement stadium in downtown Minneapolis in 1982. The site is only minutes from the Minneapolis/St. Paul International Airport. The 13-county metropolitan area surrounding the development is home to 2.7 million people. Moreover, the mall draws from—and fuels—Minnesota's visitor base of more than 15 million annually. Between residents and visitors, Mall of America has become the Midwest's leading tourist destination. With nearly 40 million visitors per year, it is visited more than Walt Disney World, the Grand Canyon, and Graceland combined.

A recent study found that about half of the mall's visitors were residents of the metro area; 10 to 15 percent came from within 150 miles, excluding the metro area; and the balance came from farther than 150 miles. The same study found that about half of all mall customers visited the mall at least once a month, while about a third were first-time visitors. Surprisingly, for a development with high tourist appeal, 20 percent of mall visitors came once a week or more. Other findings were that metro area visitors spent an average of just over $60 and two hours per visit, while nonresidents spent an average of about $140 and 3.5 hours.

DEVELOPMENT TEAM

Developer

Simon DeBartolo Group, Inc.
Indianapolis, Indiana

Owners

Simon DeBartolo Group, Inc.
Indianapolis, Indiana

Triple Five Corporation
Edmonton, Alberta, Canada

Teachers Insurance and Annuity Association
New York, New York

Architect

The Jerde Partnership
Venice, California

Korsunsky Krank Erickson Architects, Inc.
Minneapolis, Minnesota

Hammel Green Abrahamson, Inc.
Minneapolis, Minnesota

Construction Manager

PCL Enterprises, Inc.
Denver, Colorado

ENTERTAINMENT ATTRACTIONS

Entertainment attractions at the mall include the Knott's Camp Snoopy theme park, which targets families with children and is busiest during the day, and the Upper East Side, an adult-oriented nexus of nightclubs, eateries, and a 14-screen General Cinema on a partial fourth level that is most active at night. This area originally included a cluster of nightclubs operated by America Live! that were later joined by other amenities, including a Planet Hollywood. Other mall attractions include Golf Mountain, a two-level, 18-hole miniature golf course; the LEGO Imagination Center, a 6,500-square-foot hands-on exploratory play area; Starbase Omega, a futuristic laser tag facility; and UnderWater World, a journey through a 400-foot acrylic tunnel within a 1.2 million gallon aquarium.

Knott's Camp Snoopy is a $70 million indoor theme park that melds rustic North Woods architecture and landscaping with characters from Charles Schulz's Peanuts comic strip, including Snoopy, Charlie Brown,

and Woodstock. The seven-acre pay-as-you-go park was designed and has been operated by Knott's Berry Farm of Buena Park, California. To provide protection from the elements, the park features a ceiling of glass skylights 100 feet overhead, while massive columns, trusses, and ducts are painted a pale blue-gray, allowing them to disappear against the abundant daylight. Its beautiful natural landscaping—which includes nearly 400 trees, some up to 35-feet tall; 30,000 blooming plants; streams; and fountains—distinguishes Knott's Camp Snoopy from other indoor parks and gives it the prestige of being the largest indoor planting in the world.

At nighttime, old-fashioned street lamps and lanterns illuminate the twisting trail-like paths while hundreds of thousands of sparkling lights create an enchanted atmosphere.

Although there are a variety of noises and sensory effects associated with the rides and games in the park, the park still serves as a relaxing, natural escape from the relatively geometric and discordant retail spaces.

Admission to each attraction is on a point-pass basis. The passes are coded with a predetermined number of points in a variety of increments. For instance: Woodstock Pass, five points; Charlie Brown Pass, 10 points; Snoopy Special Value Pass, 35 points; and Peanuts Special Value Pass, 45 points. Each point-pass is worth 50 cents, and admission varies from two to five points per attraction. Attractions include 16 major rides, among them a 60-foot-high, 2,600-foot-long roller coaster and a log flume with a 40-foot drop. In addition, there are seven other attractions, including a shooting gallery and panning for

The largest shopping center in America has four shopping corridors that form a square with Bloomingdale's, Macy's, Nordstrom, and Sears at the corners.

Knott's Camp Snoopy, a specialized indoor amusement park, occupies much of the center of the mall.

gold, and three theaters featuring musicians and costumed-character stage shows. A total of 14 food locations and seven shops selling logo and character-based souvenirs round out the park's offerings.

Paying participants in the park number about two million annually, with a greater number strolling through, enjoying the landscaping and themed ambience without spending any money. A survey of Knott's Camp Snoopy visitors found that the average length of stay in the park was about an hour and the average amount spent by visitors was between $20 and $25, with little variation between residents and nonresidents. The study also found that more than half of park visitors made the decision to visit the park during their visit to the mall. This indicates the important role of impulse-entertainment sales at entertainment retail centers. These sales rely on dynamic on-site marketing and exposure. For instance, Knott's Camp Snoopy

can be accessed from nine separate entrances throughout the mall, meaning visitors are continually exposed to the park as they navigate the corridors laden with retail shops.

FOOD AND BEVERAGE SERVICES

Food and beverage services are ample in both supply and diversity at Mall of America. The mall features 30 full-service restaurants, including the original Rainforest Cafe, a Hooters, and a Planet Hollywood, along with many lower-profile brand-name eateries. The mall also features 30 fast-food outlets, a majority of which can be found within two food courts on opposite sides of the mall. The role of food and beverage at Mall of America is key, as is typical with entertainment retail developments due to the extended length of visits associated with them. The time spent at the mall is almost certain to include at least one mealtime. Furthermore, the tempting impulse foods that are available, like frozen yogurt, cinnamon rolls, and pretzels, are difficult to resist and are in keeping with visitor's leisure orientation.

RETAIL TENANTS

Retail tenants include anchor department stores such as Bloomingdales, Macy's, Nordstrom, and Sears, which are located at the four corners of the mall's four major multistory corridors, or "avenues." Along these avenues, which feature distinctive design treatments and are designated "North Garden," "East Broadway," "South Avenue," and "West Market," are nearly 400 additional stores and dozens of carts. Among these are a large number of entertainment-oriented retailers, from Disney and Warner Bros. Studio Stores to FAO Schwartz and Scientific Revolution. These stores sell interesting novelty and collectible merchandise within dynamic theme environments, adding to the overall entertainment appeal of the center.

The mall reportedly has pursued several alternative strategies for using vacant space, including establishing its Entrepreneurial Partnership Program. That initiative has assisted at least 22 enterprising proprietors in opening their own in-line boutiques by providing education and training as well as store design and merchandising assistance.

OTHER AMENITIES

Other mall amenities include eight guest service centers offering such items as baby strollers, wheelchairs, and rental cellular phones. There also is a tram service on the third level. These features aim to make the mammoth-sized development accessible by guests with varying mobility constraints. There are two seven-level parking decks and four surface lots, for a total of 12,750 spaces; because of Minnesota's harsh winter weather, no parking space is more than 300 feet from a mall entrance. In addition, a transit station designed for the mall in conjunction with the Regional Transit Board and Metropolitan Transit Commission receives more than 6,000 motor-

Because of Minnesota's harsh winters, no parking space is more than 300 feet from the mall's entrance.

Lego Imagination World, a Danish entertainment attraction for young children, is based on a popular line of toys.

coaches and tour buses annually. Often, passengers on prearranged tours are greeted with a Mall of America shopping bag, directory, special guest sticker, and a book of values from participating tenants.

DEVELOPMENT AND MANAGEMENT

Mall of America originally was conceived by Triple Five Corporation of Edmonton, Alberta, Canada, the developers of the similar West

Edmonton Mall. At 5.2 million square feet, the West Edmonton Mall remains the world's largest enclosed entertainment/retail development. In 1985, the city of Bloomington accepted a proposal by Triple Five to develop a super mall on the former site of Metropolitan Stadium near Minneapolis and St. Paul, Minnesota, the "twin cities." In 1987, Melvin Simon & Associates of Indianapolis joined the project. Ground breaking occurred in June 1989, and construction continued on a fast track until August 1992, when opening ceremonies were held.

Of the development's $680 million total investment, $650 million came from Teachers Insurance and Annuity Association, based in New York, while the balance came from the other two parties. In order to obtain tax advantages, Mall of America ownership was apportioned to two entities, Mall of America Company and Minntertainment, which are mirror-image partnerships comprising Teachers Insurance and Annuity Association, Melvin Simon & Associates, and Triple Five. Basically, Minntertainment represents ownership of nontenant Mall of America attractions such as Knott's Camp Snoopy and Golf Mountain, while Mall of America Company represents ownership of the traditional "mall" assets.

Mall of America is operated by Melvin Simon & Associates, a privately held real estate development and management corporation founded in 1960. Along with Mall of America, the company has an interest in more than 200 shopping center developments in 33 states, including the Forum Shops at Caesars Palace in Las Vegas. The Knott's Camp Snoopy theme park has been operated under contract by Knott's Berry Farm of Buena Park, California, where the company's signature theme park is located. In October 1997, Knott's Berry Farm announced that it was being acquired by Cedar Fair of Sandusky, Ohio, owners and operators of such parks as Cedar Point in Sandusky, Ohio; Dorney Park & Wildwater Kingdom, Allentown, Pennsylvania; Worlds of Fun and Oceans of Fun,

Kansas City, Missouri; and Valleyfair! in Shakopee, Minnesota.

Most recent average annualized sales per square foot for the retail portion of Mall of America was about $375. Retailers less than 14,000 square feet in size averaged $455 and those greater than 14,000 square feet averaged $241. Department stores at the mall averaged $249 per square foot.

EXPERIENCE GAINED

▼ The combination of entertainment and retail is undeniably a successful and synergistic formula. However, the exact contribution of entertainment to overall retail success cannot be precisely measured.

▼ The benefit of combining entertainment and retail is due in part to their counter-cyclical performance patterns. The theme park is popular during the day, while the nightclubs and cinema attract business in the evening. Over the course of the year, the retail portion tends to boom during the winter holiday buying season, while the theme park booms during the summer vacation season.

▼ Developments of the magnitude of Mall of America are more likely to depend on a broader spectrum of markets than typical retail developments in order to achieve the necessary visitation levels. These may include both residents and tourists, who have widely varying demands. Thus, orchestrating appropriate, interdependent, and complementary amenities can be challenging.

▼ The complexity of these developments necessitates active, specialized management. In addition to issues associated with retail mall tenants, issues more typically associated with theme parks must be addressed, including long-range planning, reinvestment, and rejuvenation through new attractions; marketing to tourists and the travel industry; corporate sponsorship; and the provision of visitor amenities like on-site hotels and transit terminals.

▼ While the climate of some areas may make large indoor developments like Mall of America appealing, they are not necessarily appropriate for all locales. In the United States, few projects of this type are likely to be developed, especially given their extraordinarily high capital requirement. However, this development type may make particular sense in other areas of the world. For instance, in Asia, there may be high potential for all-day shopping and entertainment in climate-controlled environments.

▼ One of the most publicized operational issues at Mall of America has been teen misconduct. The combination of entertainment and retail makes these developments exceedingly attractive as a teen "hang-out." From the mall's opening, proactive measures were taken to address this issue, including stationing a Quick Response Team on-site to deal with problems when they erupted and creating community liaisons to speak to kids about proper behavior at the mall. Unfortunately, the teen problem continued as the number of teen visitors climbed over the years, climaxing with a series of major incidents. In 1996 the mall instituted a somewhat controversial policy banning teenagers under 16 years of age from the mall on Fridays and Saturdays after 6:00 p.m. unless they are accompanied by an adult over the age of 21. A program that employs "Mighty Moms" to defuse potential problems also was initiated when it was found that some teens interacted better with "moms" than with uniformed guards.

NAVY PIER
Chicago, Illinois

Stretching 3,000 feet into Lake Michigan, the 50-acre Navy Pier represents the rebirth of a Chicago landmark. The project includes the painstaking restoration of historic structures combined with new construction, all designed to preserve skyline and lakefront views. The project offers a mix of commercial and public uses, providing residents and tourists with year-round entertainment, recreation, and meeting facilities. Major attractions on the pier include an IMAX theater, a children's museum, year-round and seasonal retailers, an indoor botanical garden, two outdoor parks, a 1,500-seat outdoor theater, a 150-foot-tall Ferris wheel, a musical carousel, a 170,000-square-foot exposition hall, and a beautifully restored grand ballroom.

One of the principal objectives of the $200 million renovation was to ensure the pier's continued use as a public promenade. Earlier redevelopment plans failed in part because they either focused too greatly on private commercial development of the pier, abandoning its historically public nature (and thus failing to gain political or popular support); or they focused too heavily on public use of the pier, ignoring the fiscal realities of modern cities and the need for revenue generation. The redevelopment of Navy Pier exhibits a balance between commercial and public uses in much the same fashion as when it first opened more than 80 years ago.

SITE HISTORY

Municipal Pier, as it was then called, opened to the public in 1916, realizing in part architect Daniel Burnham's master plan for Chicago, which envisioned as many as five public pier facilities. A monumental brick headhouse served as the pier's formal entrance, while upper and lower sheds serving both passenger and freight lines extended along both sides. Unique in its time, the pier also included a recreational section featuring the Terminal Building, with a cafeteria and concessions, and the Shelter Building, with a pavilion, rooftop garden, and grand ballroom with observation towers. The pier was then the largest construction project of its type in the world, and it was the only to combine commercial and recreational uses.

Following service as a barracks and Red Cross station during World War I, the pier became home to its own streetcar line, a theater,

(Preceding page:
Aerial view of
Navy Pier with the
Chicago skyline as
a backdrop.)

DEVELOPMENT TEAM

Developer

Metropolitan Pier and Exposition Authority
Chicago, Illinois

Architect

VOA Associates, Inc.
Chicago, Illinois

restaurants, and an emergency hospital, while continuing to serve both freight and passenger traffic. In 1926, annual attendance at the pier peaked at 3.2 million visitors. The following year the pier was officially renamed Navy Pier as a tribute to navy personnel who served during World War I.

Cultural and recreational use of Navy Pier continued with the onset of the Great Depression, even while freight and passenger service declined. In 1941, the pier again was put into military service when the city of Chicago leased it to the U.S. Navy for use as a training center. More than 60,000 recruits from six countries were trained at the pier during World War II.

Following the navy's departure after the war, Navy Pier became home to the University of Illinois, which transformed the facility into a two-year undergraduate branch campus with 52 classrooms, 21 labs, and four large lecture halls. The navy's main mess hall was converted to a library billed as the largest reading room in Illinois. The university remained at the pier until 1965.

Through the 1950s and 1960s, Navy Pier served as a location for major trade shows and exhibitions, but in 1960 it was supplanted by McCormick Place as Chicago's major exhibition hall. It continued, however, to handle smaller shows. In 1959 the pier was widened by 100 feet and, with the opening of the St. Lawrence Seaway, became the focal point of the Chicago World Port. In 1964 Navy Pier was billed as the greatest inland port in the world, handling as many as 250 oversized vessels annually.

In the 1970s the pier entered a period of general decline and disuse. City officials briefly turned their attention toward the pier as the historic East End Ballroom underwent a painstaking renovation as part of the country's bicentennial celebration. Successive city administrations attempted various redevelopment plans for the pier, none of which came to fruition. Even during its commercial decline, however, Navy Pier continued to function as a public gathering place, drawing hundreds of thousands of visitors to ChicagoFest celebrations with music, food, and entertainment. These celebrations highlighted both the affection that Chicagoans had for the pier and the need for its redevelopment.

It was not until 1989, following the recommendations of an Urban Land Institute advisory services panel, that concrete measures for Navy Pier's redevelopment began to take shape. Acting on one of the panel's most important suggestions, the state legislature established the Metropolitan Pier and Exposition Authority (MPEA), composed of city and state appointees, to manage and operate both Navy Pier and McCormick Place, the country's largest convention facility.

PLANNING

Plans to redevelop Navy Pier began in earnest in 1979, when Jane Byrne was mayor. Recognizing the appeal of Navy Pier as a recreation and entertainment destination during ChicagoFest celebrations, Byrne entered into discussions with officials from the Rouse Company, which had successfully redeveloped Fanueil Hall in Boston and Harborplace in Baltimore into waterfront entertainment and retail projects.

In 1982, the city council gave preliminary approval to Rouse for a $277 million redevelopment plan for the pier. The plan included retail uses, a hotel, an art center, a 400-slip marina, a maritime museum, and a 2,500-car parking garage.

The Rouse plan suffered a setback, however, when Byrne failed to win reelection, losing in 1983 to Harold Washington. While Washington wanted the pier to be redeveloped, he was more interested in linking any development efforts to Chicago's neighborhoods. He also was a political reformer, which put him at odds with the city council. In 1984 the city council voted to end lease negotiations with Rouse. Mayor Washington then appointed his own task force to consider new redevelopment options for Navy Pier.

The task force recommended redevelopment of Navy Pier into an urban park featuring cultural, educational, and community activities, along with limited retailing. Reflecting Washington's emphasis on neighborhoods, the plan focused on the community-wide appeal of the pier and its potential to reflect Chicago's diversity. The sudden death of Harold Washington in 1987, however, once again put redevelopment plans for Navy Pier in limbo.

In 1988, Mayor Eugene Sawyer created the Navy Pier Redevelopment Authority, which requested the Urban Land Institute to send an advisory services panel to Chicago to generate plans for the pier's future redevelopment. The establishment of the authority and the introduction of an advisory services panel were the first steps toward depoliticizing the redevelopment process. The panel was asked to consider the highest and best use of the pier for the city as whole, not simply for private interests. The panel presented its findings in May 1989.

The panel proposed a balance of public/private and commercial/noncommercial uses. The most important recommendation was for the formation of a city/state master development authority that would work both to depoliticize the project and to tap the state's funding capacity. Heeding the panel's advice, later in 1989 the city and state established the Metropolitan Pier and Exposition Authority as an independent municipal corporation. The MPEA board would be composed of an equal number of state and city appointees

Gateway Park, at the entrance to Navy Pier, features a computerized, black granite fountain that sends jets of water in random designs into the air. Funded by the National Park Service, the park serves as a buffer between pedestrians and vehicular traffic.

and would manage both the pier and McCormick Place.

Plans for the redevelopment of Navy Pier were aided by allies in political office at the city and state level. In 1989 Richard M. Daley was elected mayor of Chicago. In addition to having memories of visiting the pier as a boy, Daley believed in the ability of large-scale projects to promote economic growth. And at the state level, the governor's mansion now was occupied by Chicagoan James R. Thompson, who happened to be an alumnus of the University of Illinois' Navy Pier campus. The city of Chicago agreed to sell Navy Pier to the MPEA for $10. The state, for its part, provided a $150 million "Build Illinois" grant for the redevelopment effort.

PREDEVELOPMENT

Throughout the planning and development process, MPEA approached the project in much the same fashion as a private developer. However, the authority began by working with a pro-bono team of well-known Chicago-based architects; Trkla, Pettigrew, Allen & Payne, Inc. (TPAP, a local planning consultant); Jerome Butler (former commissioner of public works); and others for more than a year to develop a concept for redevelopment of the pier. Meetings were held with the city planning department and park district staff, the Army Corps of Engineers, the state of Illinois, and other consultants to solicit their participation in the planning process. Numerous community meetings also were held to respond to questions and concerns of nearby residents. (Navy Pier is located adjacent to one of the highest-income neighborhoods in Chicago.)

Based on the input of all those involved in the process, TPAP and Butler produced design guidelines to direct Navy Pier's ultimate development. The team then produced alternative conceptual designs and models based upon the design guidelines and their own creativity and expertise. A local planned unit development (PUD) ordinance was passed, defining general development para-

The south dock of the pier, Dock Street, serves as the pedestrian entrance and features seasonal merchants, free street entertainment, and access to recreational water vessels. Vehicular traffic is routed to the pier's north dock.

Several excursion vessels offer dining and entertainment opportunities for visitors. Options range from large, high-speed power boats to elegant dinner cruise boats to graceful sailing ships.

meters. In 1991, MPEA approved a conceptual plan for the pier as a mixed-use public activity center.

MPEA then issued a request for qualifications (RFQ) from architectural firms. Twelve of 28 architectural firms responding to the RFQ were invited to submit proposals. The MPEA selected the team of VOA Associates, Inc., and Benjamin Thompson and Associates, Inc., a firm that had extensive experience in commercial waterfront development. The design team worked closely with local civic and planning organizations in developing the new pier design. The team also visited other successful waterfront entertainment projects throughout the country.

DESIGN

In 1991, work began to upgrade the structure of the pier. A new, modern utility core was added, including storm and sanitary sewers, electrical and water lines, and telecommunications. About half of the $150 million grant was spent on infrastructure upgrades and stabilizing the pier. As it was, the soil beneath the pier would not have supported new construction. A new precast concrete platform supported by concrete caissons drilled into load-bearing clay material to a depth of about 70 feet was built on top of the existing platform.

It was decided to demolish the steel sheds that had for so long extended the length of the pier, serving passengers and trade shows. Although there were calls to renovate the sheds as historic structures, the degree of deterioration made the cost prohibitive. More important, the many columns and trusses present throughout the two-level structure would not allow the long clear spans and high ceilings expected by contemporary trade show exhibitors.

One of the most contentious redevelopment issues was traffic and parking. In order to provide separate vehicular access as well as accommodate the pier's new buildings, the north dock was widened by 50 feet for the entire length of the pier. Two bus and automobile turnarounds were constructed at grade level at the north dock. An early idea to construct a parking garage at the pier's headlands was quickly "nixed" by citizen groups unwilling to allow development on Chicago's historically open lakefront. Instead, an enclosed, 1,040-space parking garage that stretches two-thirds of the length of the pier is concealed beneath its buildings. An additional 700-space structure now is being constructed on top of a portion of the pier; its height will not exceed the height of existing buildings.

The overriding principle behind the redesign of Navy Pier was to maintain it as a public facility, open to all socioeconomic groups and offering public amenities as envisioned in Daniel Burnham's master plan for Chicago. It was determined early on that there would be no admission fee. In that spirit, the pier was redeveloped as a Chicago neighborhood. Brick towers incorporated into the buildings break the pier into blocks and streets.

Nineteen-acre Gateway Park buffers the pier entrance on the west from nearby residential and commercial development and separates pedestrian from vehicular traffic. Gateway Park is anchored by a computerized, state-of-the-art, black granite fountain that sends jets of water into the air in varying designs. Development of the park was funded with a $3.65 million grant from the National Park Service.

The completely restored brick headhouse is home to Navy Pier's administrative offices and security staff. It also serves as the formal entrance to the pier and as the main entrance to the newly constructed Family Pavilion. The pavilion features 40,000 square feet of restaurant space and unique, entertainment-oriented retailers as well as a five-story IMAX theater, the 50,000-square-foot Chicago Children's Museum, and a food court.

Adjacent to the pavilion are the 32,000-square-foot Crystal Gardens. The six-story glass structure houses botanical gardens with fountains, exotic flowering plants, palm trees, and other tropical foliage intended to establish the year-round nature of the development and to offer visitors a tropical retreat during Chicago's notoriously harsh winters.

Just east of the pavilion and gardens is Navy Pier Park, an outdoor landscaped area featuring more gardens and fountains, a reflecting pool that doubles as an ice skating rink in the winter, and the 1,500-seat Skyline Stage. The stage, visible for miles along the lakefront, boasts a dramatic vaulted roof, retractable side enclosures, and a landscaped outdoor patio. A radiant-heated floor extends the stage's concert season from early spring well into the fall.

Navy Pier Park also is home to the pier's most visible attraction, a 150-foot-high Ferris wheel modeled after the world's first Ferris wheel, which was built for the 1893 Columbian Exposition in Chicago. The wheel, which offers spectacular views of the lakefront skyline, can hold up to 240 passengers and is illuminated by thousands of lights. Also located in the park area is a musical carousel that recalls Navy Pier's golden age during the 1920s. The carousel has 36 hand-painted animals that represent the different styles used throughout the history of the carousel. The rounding boards of the carousel feature hand-painted scenes depicting the history of the pier.

A grand outdoor staircase leads from Navy Pier Park down to Dock Street, a pedestrian thoroughfare running the length of the pier's south dock. Free entertainment, such as jugglers, mimes, comedians, and musicians, is featured in four performance areas. Running along Dock Street beneath Navy Pier Park is an all-weather, glass-enclosed walkway packed with retail shops, food vendors, and crafts by local artisans. In season, the walkway is opened to become an extension of Dock Street. In winter, the glass doors are closed, creating an indoor market area.

Dock Street recalls the historically public nature of the pier. Decorative lampposts are a reminder of the pier's history, as are the several excursion ships docked alongside the pier—four dinner cruise ships, a sightseeing boat, a schooner, and two 150-seat speedboats. On less-crowded days, Dock Street is open to rollerbladers and bicyclists. Dock Street is a place to wander among other people, or perhaps fish, while enjoying a view of Chicago's downtown skyline.

Located just east of Navy Pier Park is Festival Hall, a 170,000-square-foot trade and exhibition center. The center is divisible into two separate areas, one of 56,700 square feet and the other of 113,400 square feet, and it offers ceiling heights of up to 60 feet; a minimum height of 30 feet is maintained throughout the structure. Distance between column spaces is 90 feet at the center and 60 feet on the sides. Festival Hall also includes 36 meeting rooms totaling 48,000 square feet, many of which are located on a mezzanine above the exhibition floor. Riva's, a destination, white-tablecloth restaurant, also is contained within the building. Another restaurant, the Dock Street Cafe, is located beneath the hall.

Exhibition Hall offers modern, well-equipped meeting and exhibition space, maintaining the pier's role as a trade and exhibition venue for medium-sized shows and meetings.

Adjoining Festival Hall, two historic structures, the 18,000-square-foot Shelter Building and the 12,000-square-foot Recreational Building, provide additional space for breakouts and receptions. The easternmost structure on Navy Pier is the magnificent 18,000-square-foot Grand Ballroom. Part of the original pier, the beautifully restored structure—which features an 80-foot domed ceiling, a five-foot elevated stage, and a 9,700-square-foot balcony —continues to serve as banquet and performance space.

Period light fixtures, numerous flags, picnic benches, and wide pedestrian promenades are the dominant features of the easternmost end of the pier. This far end of the pier was left free of development, enabling visitors to enjoy spectacular, unimpeded lakefront and skyline views as in the past.

TENANTS

Because of the emphasis placed on continued public use and enjoyment of the pier, the development team made a conscious effort to include in the plan elements that would appeal to a broad socioeconomic spectrum. While the ability to generate revenue was important, the fact that the development was beginning debt free (thanks to the state grant of $150 million) enabled the MPEA board to approach tenanting in a different light.

The board issued a request for proposals from retailers wishing to locate on the pier. The MPEA wanted family-oriented retailers that, rather than drawing people to the pier, would serve them once they were there. Still, the pier needed unique anchor tenants to attract visitors. One of the first anchor tenants to sign on was the Chicago Children's Museum, which represented an ideal tenant for the pier because it is family oriented and draws both local residents and tourists. Attracting more than 550,000 visitors annually, the museum features 13 age-appropriate exhibits, such as the Inventing Lab and the

InfoTech Arcade. The museum occupies a total of 55,000 square feet on three floors of the Family Pavilion; it also operates a store on the first level that offers books, music and art supplies, science toys, and videos. Since the museum relocated to the pier, its annual attendance has tripled.

The other large anchor for the project is the Navy Pier IMAX theater. The board had decided early in the process that it wanted the project to include a large-screen, 3-D theater, built and operated by MPEA if necessary. Members of the board felt strongly that this type of attraction was needed to establish the pier as an entertainment destination. The theater was constructed, and after much negotiation, Cineplex Odeon agreed to sign on as operator.

Located in the Family Pavilion near the entrance to the pier, the theater has Chicago's largest flat movie screen, 60 feet tall by 80 feet wide. Each of the theater's 395 seats is equipped with its own lightweight headset with liquid crystal lenses that create the three-dimensional effect, and each headset features its own digital sound system, which enhances the theater's system. Though primarily designed and programmed for 3-D entertainment, the theater recently began a series of late-night 2-D films.

In selecting the remainder of the pier's 14 permanent retail tenants, the board purposely avoided traditional retailers in favor of uncommon and specialty concepts, resulting in an eclectic group of stores unique not only in Chicago, but, in some cases, in the nation. Among the tenants is Magic Masters. The store, one of only four in the country, is fashioned after Harry Houdini's personal library and offers magic tricks, antique magic books, photographs of famous magicians, and other memorabilia. Other tenants include the Sports Store, offering sports apparel and souvenirs; Winston's Game Company, offering hundreds of games, card tricks, and puzzles; Alamo Flags, selling flags from nearly every state and country along with more than 10,000 flag-related items such as key rings, stickers, ties, watches, and jackets; and Animal Mania, specializing in stuffed animals and animal-related novelty gifts.

One of the most unusual stores on Navy Pier is the Illinois Market Place. The combination tourist center/retail store features Illinois-made merchandise, including museum pieces, jewelry, food, and other goods. It also features a large video wall, interactive kiosks, banners, and souvenir salvage items from the city of Chicago.

Navy Pier is served by a wide variety of restaurants to suit all palates and pocketbooks. The food court in the Family Pavilion is home to more than ten eateries offering American, Chinese, Greek, and Mexican fare as well as candy and baked goods. Nine other restaurants occupy sites along the Dock Street side of the pier, including a 7,500-square-foot McDonald's The Future, which features laser light shows, videos, and electronic gadgets to entertain visitors of all ages. The only restaurant of its kind in the

Chicago area, it also contains a retail store selling novelty items and clothing.

The Navy Pier Beer Garden, located near the east end of the pier, is open seven days a week from Memorial Day through Labor Day. Presented by Miller Lite, the Beer Garden offers a selection of beers, soft drinks, and

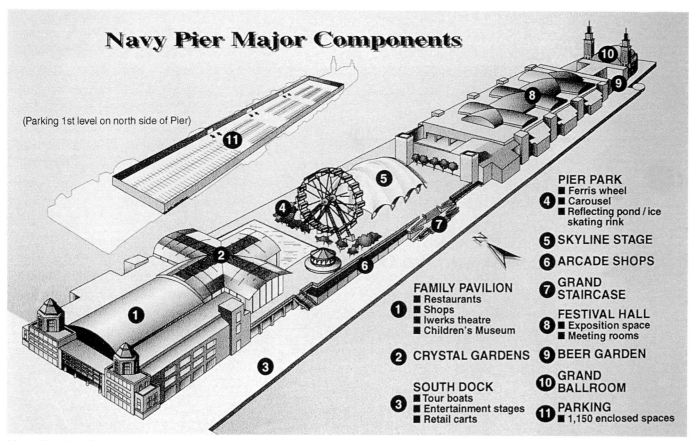

Navy Pier site plan.

concessions, along with live entertainment on weekends. Other restaurants on the pier offer various kinds of food and entertainment. Joe's Be-Bop Cafe & Jazz Emporium serves up barbecue along with Chicago-style jazz seven days a week. It also presents special children's concerts. The Wave Runner Bar & Grill offers year-round dining inside beautiful Crystal Gardens among Washingtonia palm trees. For more discriminating palates the pier offers Riva, a white-tablecloth restaurant that recreates the ambience of the Italian Riviera and specializes in fresh seafood, steaks, and pasta. Plates autographed by celebrity diners, including President and Mrs. Clinton, adorn the walls of the restaurant.

Management and Operations

The retail operations on the pier are managed in much the same fashion as those in a shopping center. The MPEA works with an outside leasing consultant to help manage the location of tenants and to negotiate lease terms. In most cases tenants typically pay a base rent plus a percentage of sales; rents currently range from a low of $20 per square foot to $80 per square foot. Annual sales

on the pier average an impressive $350 per square foot.

Providing trade show and exhibition space remains one of the primary functions of Navy Pier. MPEA was created with the intention of continuing the pier's traditional role of hosting small- and medium-sized trade shows that were too large for hotels but not big enough for huge McCormick Place, and it combined the management and operation of convention services at McCormick Place with those at Navy Pier.

In keeping with the pier's role as a public venue, the MPEA board schedules numerous public shows in Festival Hall throughout the year, including Chicago's famous annual flower show and international art show. Sensitive to nearby hoteliers' desire for trade shows and visitors, the pier's management endeavors to schedule public shows—which generally do not draw outside visitors—at times when the hotels tend to be full with other in-house events.

Two factors enable MPEA to keep the pier's focus on public use. The first is the state's initial financial commitment of the $150 million "Build Illinois" grant, which enabled the project to start debt free; as a result, the board was not forced to overemphasize commercial development. Feasibility studies concentrated only on the pier's ability to meet its own operating costs, rather than on debt retirement, which would have required much higher revenues.

The other factor is the board's decision to pursue corporate sponsorship of pier facilities and events. Revenues from these sponsorships go toward the pier's operating costs and help underwrite a variety of free attractions and entertainment. There currently are seven year-round corporate sponsors, including McDonald's, Pepsi, the *Chicago Sun-Times*, American Airlines, CitiBank, Miller Brewing Company, and WGN-TV. In exchange for their sponsorship, the companies' visibility on the pier is maintained through permanent signage, banners, and entertainment and hospitality opportunities. McDonald's for instance, is allowed to sport small golden arches on each of the Ferris Wheel gondolas. Other firms sponsor specific seasonal events throughout the year.

The board was careful to exercise restraint in the use of sponsorships in order to avoid excessive commercialization. Some sponsorships are traded for in-kind services that promote the pier rather than cash. McDonald's, for example, issues collectible cups. The pier realizes about $1.3 million per year in revenue, plus additional in-kind services, through corporate sponsorships.

Conclusion

The MPEA has successfully redeveloped Navy Pier into a major entertainment destination in Chicago while maintaining it as a public promenade. In fact, the south side of the pier remained open throughout redevelopment. Because MPEA was able to begin the project debt free, it could balance public and private uses and temper commercial offerings with public entertainment. That combination has made the pier a draw for city residents, suburbanites, and tourists, each of whom accounts for roughly one-third of visits.

Projected to cover its own operating expenses within five years of operation, the project currently is on track to reach that goal in four years. Attendance has grown steadily since the pier's opening—20 percent in 1997 alone. MPEA plans to add other revenue-generating facilities, possibly including a 250-boat marina and a year-round theater.

Retail tenants on the pier generally have been quite successful. Only two of 50 seasonal retailers have left the pier since its opening. Festival Hall also has achieved its goals, reaching 70 percent occupancy in its first year of operation. But the biggest draw remains the pier itself, as it has for the past 80 years, and the redevelopment guarantees that it will remain a favorite gathering place of Chicagoans for many years to come.

Experience Gained

▼ MPEA's commitment to maintaining Navy Pier as a public promenade must be carefully balanced against the need to meet its operating budget. In offering corporate sponsorships the board was careful not to try simply to raise the maximum amount of cash.

▼ In some cases it has made more sense for MPEA to have services on the pier privatized, as in the case of parking, because union contracts are very restrictive. Due to its technical nature, operation of the IMAX theater is privatized.

▼ Traffic has been, and will continue to be, a problem. Although at least six bus lines currently serve the pier, automobiles continue to be the transportation of choice for many visitors. While a garage currently under construction on the pier will alleviate some of the congestion, it is not a long-term solution. MPEA would eventually like to operate a remote shuttle bus from parking facilities at nearby McCormick Place.

▼ To maintain its vitality, an entertainment destination project should never be considered complete. MPEA continues to explore new ideas to make the pier a more interesting and exciting place to visit.

PROJECT DATA

Land Use Information

Site area: 50 acres

Gross Building Area (GBA)	Gross Square Feet	
	Existing	**Planned**
Retail, entertainment, restaurant, and office	345,000[1]	75,000
Exhibition	475,000	0
Public park[2]	920,000	0
Parking	630,000	0
Radio station	25,000	0
Total	2,395,000	75,000

Leasable Area	Square Feet	
	Existing	**Planned**
Office[3]	27,000	0
Retail	28,000	5,000
Entertainment[4]	110,000	70,000
Exhibition/meeting space	275,000	0
Radio station	25,000	0
Total	525,000	75,000

Land Use Plan

Use	Acres	Percent of Site
Buildings	18.9	38
Streets	4.9	10
Landscaping/open space	25.8	52
Total	49.6	100

Retail Information

Tenant Classification	Number of Stores	Total GLA (square feet)	Summer cart/arcade
General merchandise	0	0	46
Food service	20	61,000	12
Clothing and accessories	3	3,500	7
Gift/specialty	11	24,500	0
Jewelry	0	0	4
Cinema	1	16,000	0
Other entertainment	1	45,000	1
Total	36	150,000	70

Percent of GLA occupied: 100 percent.

Annual rents: Approximately $20 to $80 per square foot.

Average annual retail sales: Approximately $350 per square foot.

Average length of lease: Seven to ten years.

Typical lease provisions: Typical commercial lease terms, consistent with prevailing market trends.

Financing Information

100 percent publicly financed.

U.S. Department of Interior (park development)	$3.5 million
State of Illinois ("Build Illinois" program)	150.0 million
Metropolitan Pier and Exposition Authority	43.3 million

Development Cost Information (in $ millions)

Site Acquisition Cost — —

Construction Costs

Basic Project Cost

Demolition

Utilities

Pier stabilization

Pier widening

Buildings

Total $150

Skyline Stage 8.80

Dock Street enhancements 6.10

Ferris wheel 3.20

Carousel 0.40

Miscellaneous upgrades 0.90

Fountains, art, etc. 6.10

Restaurant improvements 5.80

IMAX theater 4.50

Food service equipment 1.50

Festival Hall upgrades 1.30

Spire restoration 1.30

Fiber-optic capability 1.10

Architect and engineering 2.30

Gateway Park development 3.50

Initial investment (1995) $196.8

Current work (parking addition) 20.0

Projected investment $216.8

Annual Operating Expenses
(for year ending June 30, 1997; in $ thousands)

Taxes	$0
Insurance	1,031
Maintenance	4,326
Janitorial	2,839
Utilities	2,385
Legal[5]	0
Management[6]	2,878
Miscellaneous[7]	20,694

Development Schedule

Site purchased: 1989

Planning started: 1990

Construction started: August 1992

Sales/leasing started: December 1992

Phase I completed: July 1995

Project completed: Enhancements continually in progress

Notes

1. Includes the following: Family Pavilion, South Arcade, Skyline Stage, and Riva Restaurant.

2. Includes the following: Gateway Park, Crystal Garden, and Navy Pier Park.

3. Includes the following: Navy Pier administrative offices.

4. Includes the following: Chicago Children's Museum, IMAX Theater, and Skyline Stage.

5. Legal costs absorbed by Metropolitan Pier and Exposition Authority.

6. Includes finance, general manager's office, materials management, and marketing.

7. Includes food and beverage, telecommunications, parking, transportation, entertainment, pier park attractions, convention services, Skyline Stage, space rental costs, safety and security, and other miscellaneous costs.

PARK MILLENNIUM AT LINCOLN SQUARE
New York, New York

Located in the Upper West Side of Manhattan and rising 47 stories (545 feet), the Park Millennium, which includes the Millennium Towers, is an 800,000-square-foot, mixed-use urban entertainment and residential center. The 400,000-square-foot, mixed-use base features a number of public amenities and entertainment options, including a 110,000-square-foot, 13-screen Sony theater that houses the first commercial 3-D IMAX theater in the United States. The base also features the Reebok Sports Club/NY, a 120,000-square-foot fitness center on six floors that contains state-of-the-art fitness equipment, a salon and spa, and a widely acclaimed restaurant. While memberships are available to the general public, residents of the Park Millennium and Millennium Towers (as well as residents of the other two buildings in the Lincoln Square complex, of which the Park Millennium is a part) are guaranteed memberships if they desire them, and the initiation fee often is waived. The Park Millennium has about 110,000 square feet of retail space; tenants include the Gap and Coconuts Music. A 35,000-square-foot space owned (but not yet used) by the United States Postal Service also is contained in the base of the building.

The residential component of the Park Millennium comprises a 38-floor residential tower containing 281 luxury condominiums and rental apartments. The upper 12 floors, known as the Millennium

The Park Millennium tower (brick building at center) spans a block between Broadway and Columbus Avenue near Lincoln Center on Manhattan's Upper West Side. (Preceding page: Second floor of the Sony theater.)

Towers, have their own lobby and elevator bank. They were sold as condominiums to a partnership that included Goldman Sachs, the Zeckendorf Company, and Sumitomo Realty. Another block of condominiums (six floors) was sold to J.P. Morgan for use by its senior executives and trainees. At $45 per square foot, rents in the Park Millennium are among the highest in the city. Nevertheless, the market can support them, and the building is fully occupied.

The relationship between the entertainment and residential components is interdependent and supportive. Residents create a built-in audience for the entertainment center. Indeed, many of residents' shopping and entertainment needs can be met without their ever having to go farther than their own building or one of the other buildings in the three-building Lincoln Square complex, and the income of the theater, health club, and stores is greatly enhanced by residents' patronage.

Lincoln Square Complex

The Park Millennium and Millennium Towers are part of a larger real estate project and revitalization success story known as the Lincoln Square complex because of its proximity to the Lincoln Center for the Performing Arts. The Park Millennium building is one block east and two blocks north of Lincoln Center, just a stone's throw away. The complex currently includes three high-rise structures, each containing both an entertainment/ retail and residential component. Altogether, these three buildings account for 1.6 million square feet of space.

Millennium Place, the second building in the project, is located just south of the Park Millennium, bounded by 66th Street to the south, 67th Street to the north, Broadway to the west, and Columbus Avenue to the east. (The Park Millennium is directly across 67th Street from Millennium Place and is bounded by 68th Street to the north.) The 30-story, 345,000-square-foot building has a total of 144 residential units. Some are rental units that are being converted to condominiums. Rents are more than $40 per square foot, close to those commanded at the Park Millennium. The building is 100 percent occupied. A 56,000-square-foot, four-story Barnes & Noble bookstore and café are located at the southwest corner of the building; Eddie Bauer has 13,000 square feet on the west side. On Columbus Avenue, stores include Speedo, Nine West, and Nick & Toni's.

The Grand Millennium, the last of the three buildings, opened in early 1997. The 31-story, 600,000-square-foot building is located directly across Broadway to the west of Millennium Place. The Grand Millennium houses a 56,000-square-foot Tower Records

Development Team

Developer/Manager

Millennium Partners
New York, New York

Owner of Commercial Component

Millennium Partners
New York, New York

Architect

Kohn Pedersen Fox Associates
New York, New York

Theater Interior Design Firm

Gensler and Associates
San Francisco, California

superstore as well as a new, 20,000-square-foot Pottery Barn. Also included is the Phillips Club, the prototype of a new breed of residential hotel to be leased and operated by Millennium Partners nationwide to accommodate visitors on extended stays. Phillips Club guests have immediate membership at the Reebok Sports Club/NY. In addition, they have access to a 24-hour business center and on-site boardroom and advanced telecommunications systems. In Phase II of the Grand Millennium, Millennium Partners will construct a building on the current site of the Chinese mission to the United Nations, which abuts Phase I on the west side of 66th Street. The purchase of the site from the government of the People's Republic of China—in exchange for Millennium Partners' construction of a new mission complex on First Avenue nearer the United Nations headquarters— represented an unusual transaction between a private American company and the Chinese government. Some possibilities for the building on the site include a post office on the ground floor and an extension of the Phillips Club above.

THE SITE

Located just north of the Lincoln Center for the Performing Arts on Manhattan's fashionable West Side, the site for the Park Millennium is bounded by 67th Street to the south, 68th Street to the north, Broadway to the west, and Columbus Avenue to the east. The site is located within walking distance of major cultural attractions, among them the Lincoln Center, which is home to the Metropolitan Opera Company, the New York City Opera, the New York Philharmonic, several ballet companies, and the Vivian Beaumont Theatre. Carnegie Hall is a ten-minute walk away, and the Broadway theater district is easily accessible. Also within walking distance to the east of the site is Central Park, an 840-acre tract of land that combines beautifully landscaped areas with a large variety of recreational options such as tennis courts, running paths, bicycle routes, an ice skating rink, theatrical performances, musical concerts, and a zoo. Times Square also is nearby. Many renowned institutions lie within close proximity to the site, including the Julliard School at the Lincoln Center, Columbia University, and Fordham University. Some of the best medical facilities in the New York area also are close by.

In addition, a variety of transportation alternatives connect the site to locations throughout Manhattan, New York City, the surrounding suburbs, and the world. Many subway stops are within walking distance, including the Lincoln Square stop at the intersection of Broadway and West 66th Street, and the West Side Highway is connected to Interstate 95 and the Henry Hudson Parkway, both of which are major regional arterials. New York City is served by three major airports, all of which are located within 15 miles of the Lincoln Square complex.

Despite its proximity to amenities, cultural activities, and transportation, until the early 1990s the history of the area just north of Lincoln Center and south of Broadway and 72nd Street was largely one of underdevelopment. Prior to that, Broadway between 67th and 68th Streets had held a small branch bank; the Cinema Studio 1 and 2; an old, low-rise office building with a rundown luncheonette on street level; a vacant former restaurant; a low-rise post office; and, around the corner on Columbus Avenue, a small ABC television studio that had been used to tape soap operas. Now, the three buildings of the Lincoln Square complex have utterly transformed the Lincoln Center neighborhood, turning it into one of the city's top shopping and residential areas.

PLANNING AND DESIGN

The overall planning objective was the revitalization of the area along Broadway between 66th and 72nd Streets. Until the early 1990s, this area was an oasis of underdevelopment nestled between two bustling areas to the north and south. Millennium's initial vision of the vehicle for revitalization—a mixed-use, urban entertainment and residential center—was supported by subsequent market analysis of the area's demographics and economics that revealed very high incomes but limited housing choices for high-income individuals wishing to live in Manhattan and few entertainment options for nearby residents or visitors to the Lincoln Center.

One advantage for urban entertainment centers is that downtowns typically have their own housing stock, which provides a built-in audience. It is easier to target an existing market, creating an entertainment center where people who already live nearby can spend their leisure time.

However, the Lincoln Square complex was surrounded largely by offices and mixed uses, not the built-in neighborhoods commonly found in downtown areas. Millennium had to create its own residences and neighborhood, which hardly seemed like much of a risk in a city with a well-documented housing shortage. However, most developers were reluctant to build residences, particularly high-priced ones, between 66th and 72nd Streets.

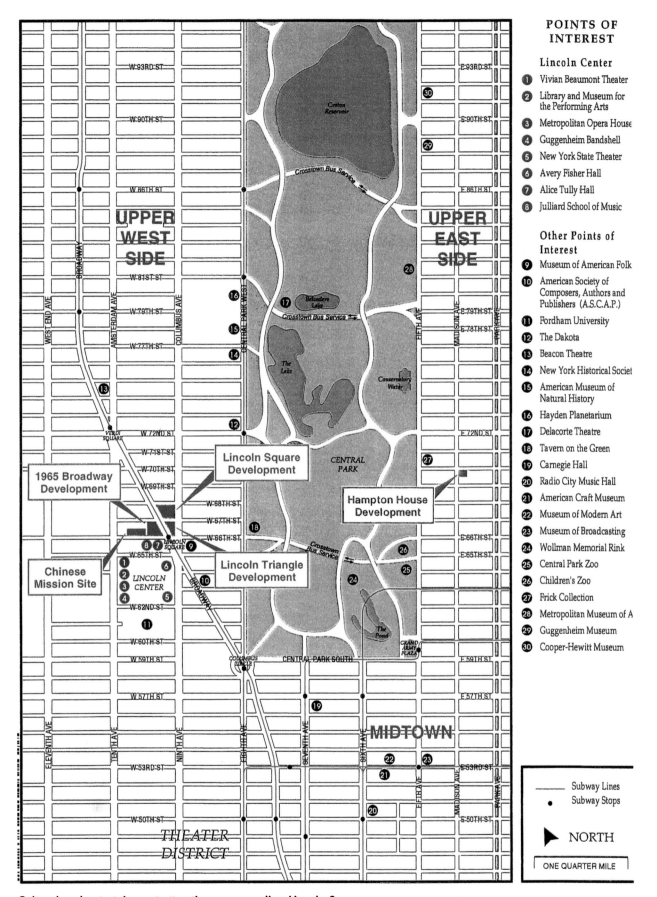

Lincoln Center

1. Vivian Beaumont Theater
2. Library and Museum for the Performing Arts
3. Metropolitan Opera House
4. Guggenheim Bandshell
5. New York State Theater
6. Avery Fisher Hall
7. Alice Tully Hall
8. Julliard School of Music

Other Points of Interest

9. Museum of American Folk
10. American Society of Composers, Authors and Publishers (A.S.C.A.P.)
11. Fordham University
12. The Dakota
13. Beacon Theatre
14. New York Historical Societ
15. American Museum of Natural History
16. Hayden Planetarium
17. Delacorte Theatre
18. Tavern on the Green
19. Carnegie Hall
20. Radio City Music Hall
21. American Craft Museum
22. Museum of Modern Art
23. Museum of Broadcasting
24. Wollman Memorial Rink
25. Central Park Zoo
26. Children's Zoo
27. Frick Collection
28. Metropolitan Museum of A
29. Guggenheim Museum
30. Cooper-Hewitt Museum

Subway Lines
Subway Stops

NORTH

ONE QUARTER MILE

Cultural and entertainment attractions surrounding Lincoln Square.

Exercise bikes
viewed from above
in the Reebok Sports
Club/NY.

Tom Reiss

Expensive housing heretofore had been concentrated on the East Side and Central Park West, where it was not unusual for condominiums to sell upward of $2 million. Nonetheless, market research by Millennium showed that this area was ready for residential development. Moreover, Millennium was able to convince investors, including J.P. Morgan, to purchase condominiums in the buildings before a public offering was made, thereby eliminating a great deal of risk.

The residential section of the building comprises 38 floors, beginning on floor 20. There are 282 residential units in all, including one unit for the resident manager. The residential floors are divided into three main sections—low-rise (floors 20–25), mid-rise (floors 26–43), and high-rise (floors 44–56). There are two entrances with lobbies and elevators on 67th Street—one for the low- and mid-rise sections and a separate one for the high-rise section.

Millennium Partners hired Kohn Pederson Fox as design architect for the building.

The exterior of the building integrates well with nearby residential areas including tree-lined 67th Street and with retail store-fronts along Columbus Avenue. The contribution of the building to the entertainment and retail district is reflected in the facade facing Broadway and Columbus Avenue, with its storefront retail and Sony Theaters. The upper floors are clad in a composition of brick, metal, and glass.

RETAIL/ENTERTAINMENT ATTRACTIONS

The Park Millennium's retail and entertainment components were designed to meet the needs and desires of its residents as well as of the larger community. And the wide array of shopping and entertainment options make the Lincoln Square complex a destination rather than just a stop on the way to the Lincoln Center. The Gap and Coconuts Music, along with retail tenants in the other two buildings in Lincoln Square (Eddie Bauer, Barnes & Noble, Tower Records, Pottery Barn), provide shopping opportunities to residents and nonresidents alike. The Sony multiplex theater is designed to serve the entertainment needs of both Lincoln Square residents and theater-goers from around New York City. It is located on the northwest corner of the building; its entrance is on Broadway. The theaters occupies portions of the first floor, first mezzanine, second floor, second mezzanine, and third through eighth floors of the Park Millennium.

Simply touring the theater, which celebrates the star-studded history of filmmaking, is tantamount to visiting a museum. The design of the theater reflects that of the old Loews theaters, now owned by Sony. Architectural details replicate movie palaces of the 1920s and 1930s, and the main theater is patterned after a Loew's theater that itself was patterned after a Hindu temple. The ceiling is designed for optimum acoustics. In addition to 13 screens, the theater has two retail shops and four concession areas.

Located at the southeast corner of the building with an entrance on Columbus Avenue, the Reebok Sports Club/NY, a full-service health club, occupies portions of the third through the eighth floors. It was designed to meet the needs of residents of the Park Millennium and Millennium Towers as well as nonresident sports club members with state-of-the-art equipment; personal trainers; exercise classes; a junior Olympic swimming pool with underwater music for lap swimming; two regulation-size basketball and volleyball courts; a 45-foot rock-climbing wall; a running track around the perimeter; and a salon and spa. The child care center allows members to leave their children with child care professionals while they exercise. The sports club also provides two restaurants and a Reebok store (open to the public). A roof-top garden is part of the health club.

The spectacular Sony theater complex lobbies overlook Broadway and offer dramatic views to patrons riding the escalators.

Hedrich Blessing

197

Views from upper-floor residences are unobstructed since the Park Millennium is the tallest building in the neighborhood.

FINANCING

Millennium Partners took a calculated risk and in so doing revitalized the Lincoln Square area. The availability of two largely vacant contiguous blocks, an anomaly in many large urban areas, facilitated the decision. The blocks were owned by Capital Cities/ABC, whose offices were across the street. Property values had plummeted in the real estate recession of the late 1980s and early 1990s, and vacant properties were selling at drastically discounted prices.

While the credit crunch made financing new commercial development nearly impossible, particularly projects proposed for such high-risk areas, Millennium Partners was able to find a formula that worked. By creating numerous alliances, the group obtained financing with a conservative debt-to-equity ratio. "The key was having capital when no one else did," said Christopher Jeffries, principal and founder of Millennium Partners, in a December 2, 1996 *Barron's* article. "The key to getting that is twofold: First and foremost, have a great idea. The second concept is not being afraid to bring in tenants and partners to whom you can give up a significant ownership position so that they can participate in your success." Limited partnerships, in which Millennium Partners was the general partner, were formed with investors like J. P. Morgan and Peninsular & Oriental Steam Navigation Company of London, the parent of its contractor, Lehrer McGovern Bovis. Other major project participants included Fleet Bank and a consortium of German banks and insurance companies. Millennium Partners also brought in well-known retailers like the Gap, the Reebok Sports Club, and Sony Theaters as creditworthy long-term tenants. So compelling was Millennium Partners in convincing prospective tenants of the dearth of entertainment and residential options despite a growing demand for them that Sony and Reebok spent tens of millions of dollars on their prospective spaces in the Park Millennium.

A 20,000-square-foot Coconuts music store selling music, compact discs, and videos is located at the southwest corner of the site with entrances on both 67th Street and Broadway. The 50,000-square-foot Gap has an L-shaped configuration that wraps around Coconuts, and it has entrances on both 67th and Broadway as well. Each retailer has portions of the first floor for selling and merchandising and portions of the cellar and subcellar levels for inventory storage.

With creditworthy tenants and investors lined up, debt financing was not difficult to come by. Millennium obtained construction financing from Bayerische Hypotheken-und-Wechsel Bank of Munich and the Sudwestdeutsche Landesbank Girozentrale of Stuttgart. In return for a limited partnership, Millennium received a completion guarantee from the Peninsular & Oriental Steam Navigation Company.

OWNERSHIP AND MANAGEMENT

The developer retains ownership of the commercial parts of the building. The Gap, Coconuts, the Sony multiplex theater, and Reebok Sports Club/NY all lease their spaces from the developer. Commercial common area expenses, services, and so forth whose benefits accrue only to the commercial tenants are paid for on a pro-rata basis by the commercial tenants exclusively. The base of the building also contains about 40,000 square feet owned by the U.S. Postal Service. This space is currently vacant while the U.S. Postal Service evaluates the highest and best use for the site within guidelines prescribed by the developer.

Residential common area expenses, services, and so forth whose benefits accrue only to the residents are paid for on a pro-rata basis by the residents only. By the fall of 1996 (two years after completion), the developer had sold all 281 residential units in the condominium, except for a handful of units to which the developer through a limited partnership is retaining ownership.

EXPERIENCE GAINED

▼ The rewards for taking calculated risks in areas slightly off the beaten path can be great. Until Millennium Partners developed the Lincoln Square complex, the area between 66th and 72nd Streets and Broadway had been largely neglected by developers;

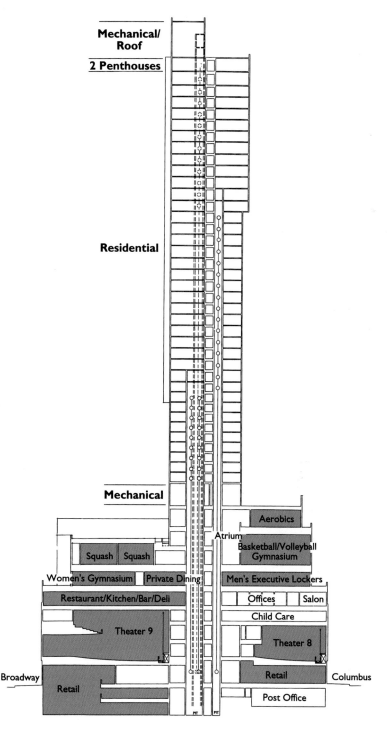

Cross-section of the Park Millennium tower showing residences above and retail/entertainment uses below.

however, the demographics and economics of the area indicated that it was ready for development. More than 2.5 million people patronized the Sony theater in 1996. This was good not only for Sony but for Millennium Partners as well, which receives per-

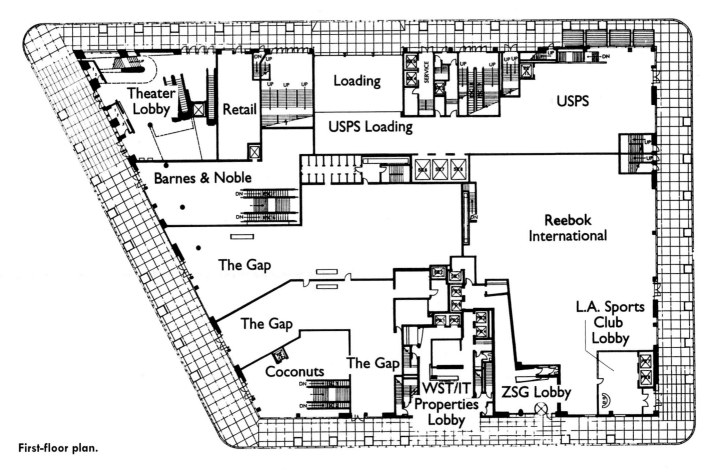

First-floor plan.

centage rents in addition to base rents from the theater in a highly unusual leasing arrangement. Nearly all residential units have been sold or rented for amounts previously seen only in the East Side and Central Park West.

▼ A developer with a great idea should galvanize investors at the beginning of the project and take a large equity stake in the project to show confidence in its potential success. Giving tenants and partners significant ownership interests can create a win-win situation for both outside investors and the developer. Investment partners share in the profits, while the developer obtains the initial financing required to get the project off the ground.

To this end, Millennium Partners formed several limited partnerships with notable investors such as J. P. Morgan and Peninsular & Oriental Steam Navigation Company of London to bring in capital and construction completion guarantees.

▼ Once the developer establishes a track record for success, it is much easier to enlist investors in similar projects around the country. Millennium Partners had little trouble finding investors willing to participate in other retail/entertainment projects it is developing around the country, including projects in San Francisco's Yerba Buena Gardens area and in an affluent Detroit suburb.

PROJECT DATA

Land Use Information

Gross Building Area (GBA)	Square Feet[1]
Retail	110,000
Residential	384,279
Sony Theater	130,812
Reebok Sports Club	133,820
Other (primarily U.S.P.S)	41,089
Total GBA	800,000

Retail and Entertainment Infromation

Tenant Classification	Number of Units	Total GLA (square feet)[1]
Clothing and accessories	1	50,140
Music/video	1	20,169
Cinema	1	130,812
Health club	1	133,820
U.S.P.S.	1	41,089
Total		376,030

Residential Unit Information

Unit Type	Number of Units
1 Bedroom	82
2 Bedroom	131
3 Bedroom	25
4+ Bedrooms	43
Total	281[2]

Notes

1. Figures are approximate.

2. Does not include one unit reserved for resident manager.

RESTON TOWN CENTER
Reston, Virginia

The importance of the entertainment component of Reston Town Center may at first be underestimated. Of the 2.1 million square feet of Phases I and II of the town center, less than one-fifth comprises retail, restaurants, and entertainment options. By contrast, nearly two-thirds is office space. Furthermore, Phase I and II constitute less than one-half of the designated 85-acre urban core and only 7 percent of the 460-acre Reston Town Center District. Looking at the relative size of the retail/entertainment component of the town center alone as a measure of its importance in the overall development would be misleading.

The importance of Reston Town Center, and in particular the entertainment and shopping components, lies in what it is designed to be and to do. Reston Town Center is designed to be the "downtown"—reminiscent of the Main Street of days gone by—of Reston, one of the premier neotraditional master-planned communities in the United States. Based on Robert E. Simon, Jr.'s vision of an alternative to conventional suburban development, Reston was begun in 1963 on 7,400 acres 18 miles southwest of Washington, D.C.; it now has nearly 100,000 residents and 3,500 businesses. The town center of such a community should be characterized by hustle and bustle. It should be where people come to shop, to eat, to see a movie, or simply to socialize and relax. In order to attract Reston residents and create that atmosphere, the town center offers a wide array of shopping experiences and other leisure activities.

Not only residents come to Reston Town Center to shop and enjoy themselves. Visitors living within a 60-mile radius and others from even farther away regularly come to explore the full range of the town center's offerings, which include nearly 45 stores, nine restaurants, an 11-screen multiplex cinema, a luxury 514-room Hyatt Hotel, and invigorating public spaces. The centerpiece is Fountain Square, an open-air civic plaza that contains a large fountain, outdoor seating, artwork, and in winter, an ice-skating rink. Plans are underway for a new parking structure with stores and possibly additional theaters at the bottom. Phase II's nearly 94,000 square feet of retail and Central Park, a park planned in the spirit of famous American town squares such as

In the wintertime, the ice skating rink in Fountain Square is Reston Town Center's central feature. (Preceding page: Market Street, the main commercial street in Reston Town Center, resembles a traditional downtown streetfront shopping district.)

Rittenhouse Square in Philadelphia and Union Square in San Francisco, will provide even more opportunities for residents and visitors alike to shop, socialize, and simply enjoy themselves. (Phase II will break ground in 1998.) Enticing after-hours entertainment and specially designed lighting make the town center vibrant and enjoyable at night. Although small in size, the retail/entertainment component of Reston Town Center is a significant presence in the community. And because it was designed from the start to be an inseparable part of Reston's downtown, not a stand-alone project like most other urban entertainment centers, it can be used as a model for other suburban communities to follow as they urbanize and mature.

DEVELOPMENT STRATEGY

In 1981, nearly 20 years after Reston was started, Reston Land Company (RLC), a subsidiary of Mobil Land Development, realized that the community could support its own downtown. RLC established an in-house task force to refine the concept for the Reston Town Center District and to consider development alternatives. The task force consid-

ered three options for developing the 85-acre urban core of the 460-acre district: development by the company, piecemeal land sales to other developers, or coventuring. After approving an initial plan for the district, Mobil agreed that RLC should seek a codeveloper to undertake the first phase. The task force recognized that while RLC was well qualified to ensure that the town center would respond to the demands of the community and the marketplace, it lacked the expertise necessary to develop a sophisticated mixed-use project.

After interviewing dozens of candidates, RLC chose Himmel/ MKDG in 1984 as codeveloper. The company's principals had experience creating such dynamic mixed-use projects as Copley Place in Boston and Water Tower Place in Chicago. Forming a general partnership known as Reston Town Center Associates (RTCA), Himmel and RLC joined staffs to execute the development. Mobil elected to purchase Himmel's interest in the partnership when the project was completed but retained Himmel as development and property manager.

Throughout the development process, RLC remained adamant about committing only to the first phase so that future phases could reflect evolutions in the marketplace. In 1996 and 1997, a change in ownership occurred that RLC could not have foreseen. By early 1997, portions of Phase I and II of the town center were sold to three separate owners. (The office and retail portions of Phase I were sold to Sam Zell's Chicago-based Equity Office Holdings, L.L.C. The hotel portion of Phase I was sold to New York–based Blackstone Real Estate Group. The undeveloped land on which Phase II will be built was sold to Westbrook Partners' Westerra Communities in a deal that included Mobil Land Development and RLC.) The development horizon for the urban core originally was about ten years.

PLANNING AND DESIGN

In February 1982, RTKL Associates, Inc., a national architectural firm that had provided planning assistance for Reston's neighborhoods and villages during the 1970s and early 1980s, devised a development concept and master plan for the Reston Town Center District.

The plan incorporated positive characteristics of both urban and suburban development—pedestrian-scaled streets, a variety of uses and services, open spaces, easy vehicular access, and ample parking. Before deciding on a traditional street grid, RTKL evaluated organizational schemes to make the core distinct from the rest of Reston. RTKL also looked at ways in which other communities created public spaces and integrated automobile use.

The plan was presented to a panel of ULI members in 1983. The panel challenged RLC to decide whether the project should be urban or suburban and then to stretch its limits. To create an urban center, the panel recommended higher densities and the inclusion of a hotel and a cultural and civic component along with the already planned retail and entertainment components. During 1984 and 1985, working with the new RTCA part-

nership, RTKL refined the core-area plan, responding to the panel's recommendations.

In 1986, in national invitational competition, RTKL produced the winning design for the first phase and became project architect. The firm designed Phase I's five structures simultaneously, establishing a visual and stylistic vocabulary that provided a strong identity for the new town center.

Sasaki Associates, the landscape architect, designed a streetscape plan that recalls Euro-

DEVELOPMENT TEAM

PHASE I

Codevelopers/Managers

Reston Town Center Associates (formerly Reston
    Land Corporation)
Reston, Virginia

Himmel & Co.
Boston, Massachusetts

Master Planner and Architect

RTKL Associates, Inc.
Baltimore, Maryland

Landscape Architect and Urban Designer

Sasaki Associates, Inc.
Watertown, Massachusetts

PHASE II

Developer

Westerra
Reston, Virginia 20190-5604

Design Architect

Keys Condon and Florance Architects (formerly
    Florance Eichbaum King Architects)
Washington, D.C.

pean shopping streets and public squares as well as American prototypes such as Country Club Plaza in Kansas City. Custom-designed paving and benches complement the architecture, providing for accessibility and comfort, and large trees and seasonal plantings give the streets and plazas a lively, mature look. The streets and sidewalks are proportioned to allow for spaciousness and ease of movement on an intimate, human scale. The sidewalks are wider on the sunny side of the street, and the cartway is narrow, encouraging pedestrians to cross from one side of the street to the other.

The developers realized that a variety of storefronts would help create a vibrant pedestrian experience. They engaged Philip George, a New York–based retail designer, to plan the layout of food, entertainment, and specialty retail establishments and to identify the visual characteristics critical to their success. The buildings then were designed to accommodate a continuum of storefronts at the ground level of every building with variations in setbacks, entrances, awnings, bay windows, and signage to create the impression that the town has evolved over time.

Reston Town Center's retail is located primarily along Market Street, the urban core's pedestrian spine, which extends east/west through Fountain Square. It is a private street and usually is open to one lane of traffic in each direction but can be closed for community events and concerts.

The hotel also was intended to contribute to the street-level vitality of the town center. RTKL and the developer edged the hotel's streetfronts with restaurants and shops and provided numerous entrances, making the hotel's public areas as much a natural gathering place as those in an elegant downtown hotel. The developers wanted the hotel's interiors to convey a residential intimacy; they achieved that effect through the use of richly textured fabrics and rugs, carefully placed antiques, and accent lighting.

The developers also recognized that cities that grow and prosper over time achieve a richness of detail rarely found in new projects. RTKL therefore was charged both with designing the directional and informational signage and with developing ornamentation to add visual texture to the town center. At the entrance to Market Street from Reston

Dining alfresco is a popular leisure activity at Reston Town Center.

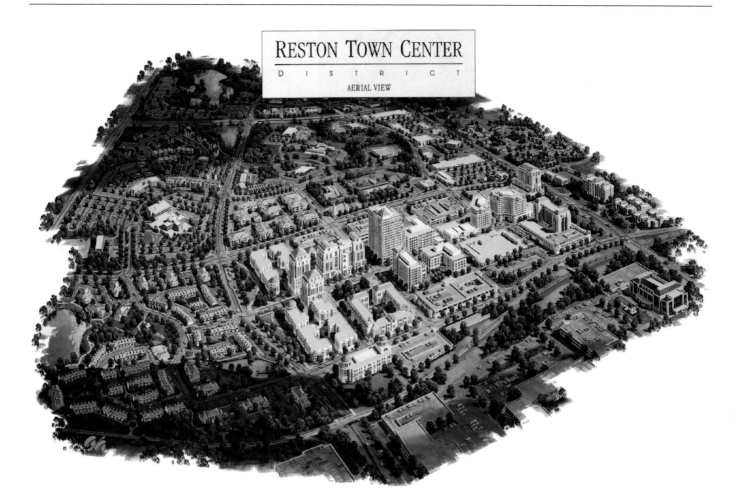

RESTON TOWN CENTER

DISTRICT

AERIAL VIEW

Parkway, for example, RTKL placed a row of eye-catching wind sculptures that evoke traditional weather vanes. For each side of the entrance, RTKL designed gold-colored orbs, each more than seven feet in diameter, reminiscent of medieval astrolabes.

To respond to the cultural needs of the community, the developers integrated museum-quality art into the project. For example, the sculpture of Mercury that graces the central fountain was commissioned from artist Saint Clair Cemin following an invitational competition, and the hotel's public spaces are filled with contemporary art from around the country.

Phase II builds on the best qualities of Phase I and addresses some new issues that affect how contemporary downtowns function and how individuals pattern their lives. An example of the new level of importance accorded automobiles without compromising the pedestrian-friendly nature of Reston Town

Center is that motor lobbies will form head-houses for garages, which will front onto motorcourts. These paved and well-landscaped plazas will lend the town center a sense of urbanity.

Phase II is designed to blend in with Phase I while establishing its own identity. The exterior materials used in the four structures in Phase II will be the same as those used in Phase I—brick, precast concrete, glass, and metal. New colors, however, will be subtly introduced. The tradition of offices with ground-level retail and entertainment will be continued in Phase II.

GOVERNMENT APPROVALS

The project required rezoning from Fairfax County. The process, which began in 1984, took approximately three years and involved several revised submissions. RLC's initial re-

Retail/entertainment tenants occupy the streetfront spaces in the Town Center District. This aerial view shows the district at completion.

The Hyatt Regency Hotel overlooks the skating rink and outdoor activities area in the town center.

zoning request for the 460-acre town center district was for permission to develop 8.4 million square feet of commercial space and between 1,400 and 2,000 residential units.

The predominant issue was traffic. Negotiations led to rezoning for a minimum of 6.8 million square feet of commercial space (including 1.3 million square feet of retail/entertainment space and 5.5 million square feet of office space) and 1,400 residential units. Up to 1.6 million square feet of additional office space will be permitted if RLC's traffic forecasts prove to be accurate and if the project meets RLC's trip-generation objectives. Transportation "proffers" (developer-funded and -implemented improvements), including pavement and right-of-way, are valued at approximately $30 million for the minimum program and $40 million for the maximum program.

As part of the approval, a shared-parking agreement was negotiated to recognize the efficiencies of the mixed-use project, thereby reducing the parking requirement for Phase I from 4,100 to 3,100 spaces. RLC also agreed to establish a transportation management association to educate the public on transportation alternatives, refine regional transit routing to the development, and advocate various

demand-reduction strategies. In addition, RLC proffered the provision of a cultural center within the project. This element will bring a civic, noncommercial dimension to the downtown.

The county was concerned that the retail and residential components were too small and that the residential component was not sufficiently integrated with the commercial development. RLC committed to expanding the retail component (thereby reducing office and/or hotel components) if demand proved sufficient. RLC also argued that since Reston already had a strong and diverse residential base, it was not necessary for the town center to be self-sufficient; the parties also agreed to defer residential building in the urban core until after the amenities necessary to support an urban lifestyle were in place. The maximum floor/area ratio for the urban core is 0.94; there is no density limit on specific parcels within the urban core.

LEASING

Phase I of the town center came on the market at the onset of one of the region's most severe economic downturns. Nevertheless, retail and entertainment space was 85 percent leased at project opening and is now more than 92 percent leased. For the purpose of preparing a leasing plan, the project's retail was considered a separate component that would compete directly with shopping centers in the area. It was determined that a critical mass of at least 110,000 square feet of fashion and general goods stores would be required to draw consumers from the primary trade area, which extends five to ten miles in all directions. It also was determined that the project could initially support at least six restaurants, a multiscreen cinema, and retail services, including banks and an office supply store.

Once the best locations for each tenant category were identified, a two-tiered approach was employed to attract merchants. Three years before completion, national tenants were approached by the developer's leasing director and an exclusive agent. At first, national tenants needed to be convinced of the project's merits because it was classified as an anchorless mall; several leases with national tenants were signed with cotenancy clauses. Second, the leasing team targeted distinctive local and regional tenants that could add variety to the center. Average sales are around $315 per square foot.

Restaurants were somewhat easier to attract, and RTCA was able to be selective in bringing together a variety of themes, price points, and cuisines. Restaurants were expected to average sales of more than $600 per square foot in the first year. The cinema complex was designed to contemporary standards, with four theaters on the ground floor and seven above. National Amusements, Inc., operates and manages the complex under a lease with RTCA. Plans for another theater currently are underway.

Until 1996, the hotel was owned by RTCA, which had a management agreement with Hyatt Hotels for the hotel and two restaurants. RTCA received profits from hotel operations, minus Hyatt's management fee. The hotel achieved approximately 60 percent occupancy during its first year of operation due to the slow overall market. By 1996, occupancy had risen to 80 percent. In 1996, the hotel was sold to New York–based Blackstone Real Estate Group, which maintained the management agreement with Hyatt.

Office leasing was significantly below projections, with nearly half the total space vacant almost two years after the first office building was ready for occupancy. The project has been successful in attracting premier corporate tenants from outside the Washington region. In the early 1990s, despite premiums of $1 to $4 per square foot, gross effective rents averaged about $17, well below original pro formas. Office rents have rebounded and now, unlike during the early 1990s, few concessions are available. The increased office employment augurs well for Reston Town Center's entertainment component, as office employees generate much of its daytime business.

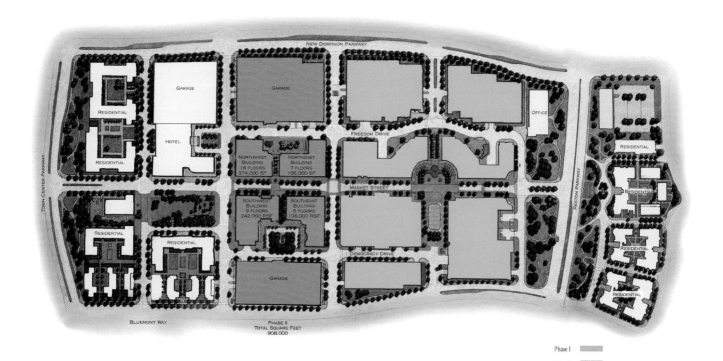

Reston Town Center urban core site plan.

Office leasing for Phase II has been underway for several years, well ahead of the expected ground breaking in 1998. Unlike the office market conditions that prevailed when Phase I opened, current office market conditions are ripe for the preleasing of Phase II, which is not expected to be ready for occupancy until 1999. Retail leasing for Phase II also is already underway.

MARKETING AND MANAGEMENT

Early marketing of Phase I focused on creating project awareness in users and brokers through media advertising, direct mail, and broker/community outreach programs. As the project approached completion, target audiences were blitzed with media advertising.

At project opening, marketing efforts shifted toward generating entertainment and retail consumer traffic by sponsoring high-profile events, beginning with a major holiday promotion that included an outdoor skating rink, extensive decorations, and six weeks of holiday entertainment including a Christmas parade and a 50-foot Christmas tree lighting on Thanksgiving. Continuing efforts focused on seasonal events (such as Easter egg contests, bike races, and a free summer concert series) have been made to generate retail traffic and sustain marketwide project awareness. Retailers are involved in event planning from the outset. Stores often sponsor individual events to attract customers (e.g., restaurant promotions),

The Big Apple Circus, which began in 1992, is an especially popular event that runs for two weeks in the fall. Looked forward to because of its reputation for inexpensive family entertainment, the circus donates all its proceeds to preserving and advancing the classical one-ring circus in America. During the summer, the Mobil Summer Concert Series presents a free concert every Saturday night.

Residents and visitors can obtain schedules for all events, movie show times, and hours of operation for retailers from the public relations packet available from RTCA and from brochures and flyers available from all town center merchants. They also can visit Reston Town Center's homepage on the World Wide Web at http://www.restontown-center.com. The homepage is updated daily and is linked to homepages for its merchants and the Hyatt hotel. Events are well attended because promotions are aimed at the entire region, which includes the secondary market of Montgomery County, Maryland, and Fairfax County, Virginia, and the tertiary market of Washington, D.C.

Community relations are maintained through extensive networks that include nonprofit community groups and arts organizations. For example, Reston Town Center hosts the Northern Virginia Fine Arts Festival, sponsored by the Greater Reston Arts Center. In 1996, the town center sponsored "Taste of the Town," an event in which town center restaurants and merchants offer delicious food and tempting sidewalk bargains. Proceeds were used to benefit the Fairfax chapter of the YMCA, which was planning to build a facility in the Reston area.

The entertainment needs of senior citizens are not overlooked either. On the fourth Wednesday of each month, the town center movie theater holds "Meet Me at the Movies," an event sponsored by Reston Association and Reston Town Center that draws about 300 senior citizens each month. They are transported free of charge by bus to and from the theater compliments of Multiplex Theaters Transportation Management Services, Inc. Caffe Northwest provides complimentary pastries, coffee, and orange juice.

The current owner considers the project a long-term investment and the culmination of the community's development. All aspects of asset management—building design, maintenance, equipment purchasing, tenant relations, and community outreach—are based on a commitment to create maximum long-term value.

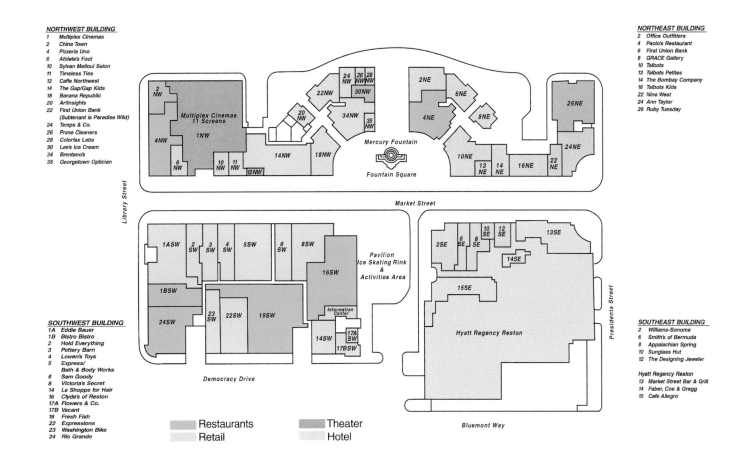

Restaurants
Retail
Theater
Hotel

Ground-level plan for Phase I of Reston Town Center.

EXPERIENCE GAINED

▼ Timing is critical to the success of the retail/entertainment component of a major mixed-use center. The density and mix of Phase I required the critical mass of population, employment, and income that Reston and the surrounding area had achieved by the late 1980s.

▼ It is important to define a project's market niche carefully and prepare the development plan accordingly. RLC knew that the town center would be neither a neighborhood shopping center nor a regional mall but was not sure what it should be.

▼ Development companies should recognize their limitations. RLC realized that it did not have the necessary background and conducted a nationwide search for a partner that understood mixed-use development with a retail/entertainment component.

▼ If a developer is confident in the overall market and the project's planning, it should not hesitate to be aggressive. The ULI panel advised RLC that the project was not dense enough to generate the level of pedestrian activity necessary to become a lively urban center with a successful retail/entertainment component. It was replanned, with positive consequences.

▼ RLC recommends securing entitlements as soon as the market and general plan can be quantified. Otherwise costs escalate, plans may be modified or downscaled, and opportunities may be lost.

Project Data[1]

Land Use Information

Site area: 20.6 acres[2]

Gross building area (GBA)	Square Feet
Retail	240,000[3]
Office	530,000
Hotel	430,000
Total	1,200,000

Gross leasable area (GLA)	Square Feet
Retail	240,000[3]
Office	530,000
Hotel	430,000

Floor/area ratio(FAR): 1.3
Maximum number of stories: 13
Total parking spaces: 4,000

Land Use Plan

	Acres	Percent
Buildings	5.7	27.8
Parking structures	2.5	12.2
Paved areas	6.5	31.4
Landscaped areas	5.9	28.6
Total	20.6	100.0

Development Cost Information
(in $ millions)

Land	$10

Construction Costs

One Fountain Square	$19
Two Fountain Square	21
Southwest building	10
Hotel[4]	41
Freedom Drive parking structure	7
Total	$98

Hotel Furniture, Fixtures, and Equipment Costs	$7

Soft Costs

Architecture/engineering	$11
Leasing	2
Marketing/promotion	7
Legal/finance/insurance/taxes	6
Management/fees	10
Construction interest	14
Other/startup	10
Total	$60

Total acquisition and development cost: $175 Million
Average development cost per square foot GBA: $145

Average construction cost per square foot GBA:
Office/retail: $60
Hotel: $85

Annual Operating Expense

Taxes	$1,440,770
Insurance	192,250
Maintenance	897,040
Janitorial	652,150
Utilities	879,400
Management/legal	527,470
Security	465,170
Landscaping	291,000
Miscellaneous	28,750
Total	5,374,000

Retail Tenant Information

Classification	Number of Tenants	Percent of Total	Total GLA (square feet)	Percent of GLA
Food/food service	12	27.3	54,186	29.4
Clothing and accessories	10	22.7	41,312	22.4
Shoes	1	2.3	1,359	0.7
Home appliances/music	5	11.4	13,642	7.4
Hobby/specialty interest	1	2.3	2,883	1.6
Gifts/specialty	6	13.6	9,690	5.3
Jewelry	1	2.3	1,140	0.6
Personal services	7	15.9	8,517	4.6
Cinema	1	2.2	51,511	28.0
Total	44	100.0	184,240	100.0

Average annual net rent: $25 per square foot

Average annual net rent (including percentage rent): $35

Average length of lease: Five years

Typical terms of lease: Base rent plus percent of gross sales

Average annual sales (1995): $314.51 per square foot

Ice Skating Rink Information

Size: 60 feet x 100 feet

Annual income: $287,000

Annual expenses: $213,000

Attendance (1995): 44,000

Office Tenant Information

Typical net rentable area per floor: 21,000 to 23,000 square feet

Average office tenant size (30 tenants): 9,397 square feet

Average annual rents: Approximately $23 to $27 per square foot

Average length of lease: Three to ten years

Development Schedule

Master planning started: February 1982

Design competition held: August 1986

Leasing started: January 1987

Application for rezoning and development approved: March 1987

Land purchased: April 1988

Phase I site preparation started: February 1988

Phase I office/retail construction started: June 1988

Hotel construction started: January 1989

First office building grand opening: September 1989

Phase I grand opening: October 1990

Phase II planning started: 1995

Phase II construction to begin: 1998

Notes

1. Project data are for Phase I only.

2. Does not include 15 acres used for 1,404 temporary surface parking spaces.

3. Includes entertainment and restaurant space.

4. Includes structured parking.

THIRD STREET PROMENADE
Santa Monica, California

Over a 35-year period, Santa Monica's Third Street area has gone from a failing downtown business district to a failing pedestrian mall to a spectacularly successful urban entertainment district. Running the gamut of post–World War II planning strategies, Third Street offers an interesting glimpse at the interaction between market economic forces and public planning, as well as at the limits and possibilities of public/ private partnerships.

The Third Street Promenade is a three-block-long pedestrian mall located three blocks from the ocean and the Santa Monica Pier in the heart of the central business district. The promenade is part of the nine-block Bayside District, which includes the three blocks of Second Street and Fourth Street flanking the promenade. A network of six public parking garages—one per block on either side of the promenade—and a system of passageways knits the district together into a cohesive whole.

Nearly 200 shops are located in the Bayside District, including 70 restaurants. In addition, four theaters with a total of 21 screens and approximately 5,000 seats are located there. Complementing the retail and entertainment uses are more than 900,000 square feet of office space and nearly 200 dwelling units. More than half of the 3.2 million square feet of space in the district (1.7 million square feet) has been constructed since the district's specific plan was completed in 1986.

Some of this development has occurred through renovation of the mostly two- and three-story existing buildings, many of which date to the early part of the century and are considered historic structures. Much of the development, however, has taken the form of new mixed-use, mid-rise structures, taking advantage of zoning incentives offered within the framework of the district's specific plan. Today, the promenade's problems are not so much how to attract development as how to manage success, how to maintain it over the long term, and how to extend it fully to the remainder of the Bayside District.

DEVELOPMENT

Like many small-city downtowns, Santa Monica's central business district found itself in steady decline by the 1960s. As elsewhere, traditional

Developer

City of Santa Monica
Santa Monica, California

Architect/Site Planner

Roma Design Group
San Francisco, California

Other Key Member

Bayside District Corporation
(formerly Third Street Development Corporation)
Santa Monica, California

New infill building housing the Disney Store, with dinosaur topiary sculpture in front. (Preceding page: Third Street Promenade, aerial view.)

urban retailers were losing ground to enclosed malls with acres of free parking. Santa Monica's first response, in 1965, was to create the Third Street Mall. The three blocks from Broadway to Wilshire Boulevard were closed off to automobiles, and new paving, benches, and lighting were installed, along with the six public parking garages. The 80- by 2,000-foot mall and related improvements were developed with the aid of municipal bond financing and eminent domain proceedings under the aegis of the local parking authority. The street was "prettier," in a sense, and more accessible, but focusing on physical planning only did little to alter its retail economy. The mall "didn't have the components to take people past the first or second visit," notes Jeff Mathieu, director of the city's resource management department.

In the 1970s, another approach was taken. In order to energize downtown and to bring people to the Third Street Mall, the city embarked on a redevelopment program to develop an *enclosed* downtown mall. After considerable debate and the usual turmoil associated with such projects, "Santa Monica Place" was built in the late 1970s by the Rouse Corporation at the foot of the Third Street Mall. The Rouse mall offered more than 100 shops, two department store anchors, and two multilevel parking garages.

Though successful in itself, Santa Monica Place did not contribute significantly to the prospects of the Third Street Mall or surrounding Bayside District retailers. Just the opposite, notes Mathieu: "The Rouse mall vacuumed up whatever retail activity was left. You could shoot a cannon off [down the Third Street Mall] and not hit anybody."

By the 1980s, something clearly needed to be done about Third Street, but the experience of the Santa Monica Place project had generated a fair amount of ill will toward government redevelopment planning. It was clear that the private sector would have to bear more of the burden and responsibility for improving Third Street and the surrounding area. While the city would commit re-

sources to support the district, this time the owners and merchants would have to be fully invested in the undertaking, both philosophically and financially.

With such a public/private partnership in mind, the city undertook a series of nearly 100 community meetings over 14 months to identify goals and objectives for the Bayside District and to develop a specific plan. The Third Street Development Corporation (TSDC) was founded, consisting of property owners, merchants, and others, and a consultant planner/designer, the Roma Group, was brought in to redesign the mall.

The Bayside District specific plan was completed in 1986, and in 1987 the city sold $13.2 million in assessment district bonds. Proceeds from the bonds funded reconstruction of the Third Street Mall—christened the Third Street Promenade—as well as improvements to Second and Fourth Streets and the addition of 275 parking spaces to one of the existing parking garages. Repayment of the bonds comes from assessments on property within the nine-block Bayside District. Three benefit zones and a hierarchy of assessment rates were established: the highest rates are in Zone 1, which consists of property fronting on the promenade; Zone 2 comprises property adjacent to Zone 1 (across the alley and fronting on Second and Fourth Streets); and Zone 3 consists of property on the far side of Second and Fourth Streets. In addition to proceeds from the assessments, the city pledged the six parking structures as collateral for the bonds.

PLANNING AND DESIGN

To the city planners in the 1980s, the flaws of the 1965 Third Street Mall were clear: physically, the nearly half-mile-long mall was just too large and undifferentiated in relation to the existing small-scale retail establishments available to populate it. And the elimination of the roadbed served only to make the mall more barren in the evening hours. There were no anchor tenants at the north end of the mall and little to induce patrons of Santa Monica Place to venture outside its doors.

To address these issues, the Promenade's designers reintroduced automobile lanes, to be open in the evening hours. To "put a street into a mall" was a somewhat ironic idea, notes Mathieu, after the 1960s efforts to ban

Third Street Promenade blends seamlessly into the surrounding downtown environment of Santa Monica, albeit with more graphics and street furniture.

the automobile. One lane in each direction was built, routed around market kiosks, fountains, and topiary sculptures. A variety of spaces was thus created. In some places, 30-foot-wide sidewalks big enough for outdoor dining were created; in others, islands were created, with benches and curbs available for sitting and people-watching. Though the traffic lanes helped to define these spaces, as the Promenade's popularity took off, the hours allotted for automobile use were scaled back and eventually eliminated altogether.

As the planners were evaluating alternative strategies for revitalizing the Third Street Mall, they noted a coincident upsurge in applications for permits to develop office buildings and movie theater multiplexes (a relatively new development type at the time) in scattered locations throughout the city.

As the idea of using theater multiplexes as anchor tenants for the Promenade began to take shape, the city placed a moratorium on new theaters outside the Bayside District until the specific plan could be finalized. Similarly, restrictions were placed on new office construction outside the district.

The specific plan that emerged in 1986 identified the desired characteristics of the Bayside District and provided a variety of zoning incentives and disincentives to achieve them. First, and perhaps foremost, the district was designated as the sole location in Santa Monica for new movie theaters. Complementing this focus, the plan enumerated other permitted uses for the district, primarily oriented toward retail and entertainment development. Service uses, such as banks, were excluded from the Promenade. To stimulate pedestrian interest, office tenants were banned from first-floor locations. Ground-floor uses were required to have substantial clear glass facades, and explicit rules were developed allowing for—and controlling—sidewalk dining.

To encourage mixed-use development, density bonuses in the form of increased floor/area ratios and height allowances were adopted. To encourage residential development, the specific plan allowed for residential square footage to be discounted by 50 percent in calculating maximum allowable floor area. Density bonuses also were enacted for the creation of mid-block passageways to link the Promenade with public parking garages. Food court uses were limited to passageways, and drive-through food service was banned altogether. In sum, the objectives for the Bayside District were to be achieved through zoning encouragements, rather than by direct municipal intervention, as had been done in the past.

MANAGEMENT, MARKETING, AND MAINTENANCE

With the specific plan in place and the bond issue improvements completed in 1989, the city had caught the crest of the 1980s development wave. The Third Street Promenade began attracting investment and visitors from the start. The first major project was the seven-story Janss Court, a mixed-use project that took advantage of the bonuses for movie theaters, mixed uses, residential units, and a mid-block passageway. (See ULI's *Project Reference File* case study of Janss Court, Volume 21, Number 3, January–March 1991.) By 1992, approximately $200 million of private capital had been invested in the district in addition to the initial $13 million bond offering.

In order to actively manage the district's burgeoning development, the Third Street Development Corporation was reconstituted as

the Bayside District Corporation (BDC). The nonprofit BDC has 11 members, appointed by the city council from the ranks of district stakeholders (property owners, merchants, residents, and others). The BDC, which has an annual operating budget of about $500,000, hires its own staff and retains a retail consultant in an advisory capacity.

The BDC functions in several official and quasi-official roles. The corporation reviews all issues affecting the district, including maintenance, operations, zoning and permit approvals. "The city encourages an advocacy role" for the BDC, notes Howard Robinson, economic development manager for the city, and encourages the BDC "to rattle our cage."

In addition to handling permit requests and other city actions, the BDC also takes a prospective view of matters. With the help of its retail consultant, the BDC works to identify specific kinds of development that complement the district's existing retail/entertainment mix and then identifies candidates for each use to be pursued. Instead of taking the more typical broker's role, the BDC's consultant works on a fee basis rather than on commission.

Another function of the BDC is to manage and monitor the Promenade's vending

Programmed street performances create a lively environment that draws people to the Promenade.

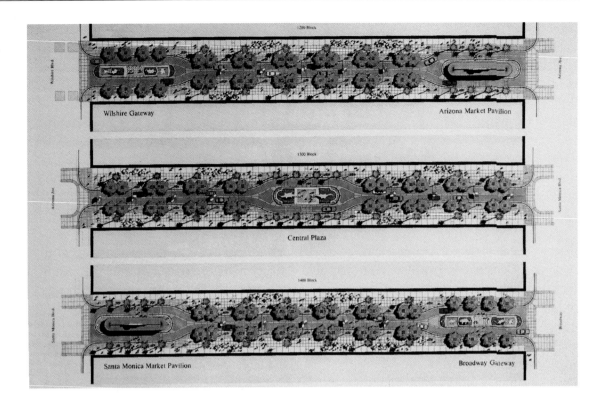

cart and street performer programs. The vending cart program includes 30 carts managed by a master operator under license with the city. Street performers are regulated behind the scenes. Specific performance zones are set aside on each block; the timing, maximum decibel level, and rotations are all set by regulation, and every performer has to have a city permit.

In addition to the entertainment/retail attractions, a farmers market is held on Wednesdays and Saturdays on Arizona Street, one of the district's three cross-streets. The market, which grosses approximately $80,000 per day, is one of the most successful of its type and greatly energizes the Promenade and adjacent streets. The BDC also organizes an annual slate of special events on the Promenade, including the Festa Italia, Book and Music Festival, and Seniors Day.

Maintenance work is done by regular city crews, supplemented by a special Bayside District crew. Routine maintenance includes daily power washing and mechanical scrubbing of the Promenade, landscape trimming, painting, minor maintenance, and repairs.

Similarly, security is provided through a combination of basic city police and fire services plus special services provided by additional personnel assigned to the district. Police patrol the district on foot and on bicycles, and a police kiosk is maintained on the Promenade. In addition, extra community service officers (CSOs) are provided in the district.

The BDC's operations, as well as maintenance and security, are funded in part by special assessments within the district. An operations and maintenance fee is charged annually to all district merchants. Initially, this fee was set at five times each merchant's business license fee, but eventually, in response to merchants' complaints, parking meters were installed in the district's municipal parking garages to defray the assessment. The assessment was reduced to three times the license fee and eventually to the amount of the license fee.

The city also charges property owners an "in-lieu parking fee" on all new construction in the district (including both wholly new buildings and additions to an existing building) for owners who do not provide on-site parking. This fee is set at one dollar per square foot per year.

The funds generated by these fees go to the city's general fund, not directly to the district. Rather, budgets for the BDC, for maintenance, and for security are set independently and administered by several city departments.

CONCLUSION

Activity on the Promenade has been so strong that the city council has had to act repeatedly to control its growth. In 1992, the city council revised the zoning code to limit the number of restaurants and establishments selling alcoholic beverages on a block-by-block basis. Most recently, in 1996 the specific plan was updated and amended to further control

growth on the Promenade, channeling it to the remainder of the district. Restaurants and liquor licenses are issued without limit off the Promenade, and additional floor/area bonuses are provided for residential uses.

The city also is grappling with a more philosophical sort of growth management issue. As national chains such as Pottery Barn, Barnes & Noble, and Borders move in at an increasing rate, leaving fewer and fewer independent retailers, the question that arises, as Howard Robinson notes, is "how can we keep the promenade from being like any other mall?" To date, the answer has not been to discourage the national chains. Instead, the city insists on "best of kind" retailers who will make substantial investments in the district and encourages flagship stores that are compatible with the district's architecture and that can strengthen its economic position.

Special lighting creates a romantic atmosphere for nighttime excursions for dinner, a movie, and browsing at the mix of entertainment-oriented shops.

Land Use Information (Bayside District)

Site area: 53.1 acres (including streets and alleys)

Gross Building Area (GBA/square feet)

Use	Existing	Planned
Office	944,222	40,000
Retail (including entertainment)	953,568	20,000
Residential	146,891	25,000
Hotel	75,267	–
Parking	900,000	–
Other (institutional)	173,462	–
Total GBA	3,196,410	85,000

Leasable Area (GLA/square feet)

Use	Existing	Planned
Office	944,222	40,000
Retail (including entertainment)	953,568	20,000
Residential	146,891	25,000
Hotel	75,267	–
Parking	900,000	–
Other (institutional)	173,462	–
Total GLA	3,196,410	85,000

Units	Existing	Planned
Residential	178	26
Hotel (rooms)	86	–

Floor/area ratio: 2.0 to 3.5
Number of levels: Three to six

Land Use Plan

Use	Acres	Percent of Site
Buildings	34.2	64.5
Streets/surface parking	15.6	29.3
Landscaping/open space (including Promenade)	3.3	6.2
Total	53.1	100.0

Retail Tenant Information

Tenant Classification	Number of Stores
General merchandise	3
Food service	70
Clothing and accessories	28
Shoes	7
Home furnishings	6
Home appliances/music	8
Hobby/special interest	1
Gifts/specialty	38
Jewelry	7
Personal services	19
Cinema	3
Health club	1
Other entertainment	2
Other retail	1
Total	194

Percent of GLA occupied: Ninety-five to 98 percent
Annual rents: $48 to $84 per square foot

Average annual retail sales: Approximately $400 per square foot

Range of retail sales: $300 to $1,200 per square foot

Average length of lease: Five to ten years

Typical lease provisions: Triple net. Landlord responsible for structural or seismic upgrading. No landlord credit for tenant improvements, but rent waived for 30 to 90 days of build-out period.

Office Information

Percent of NRA occupied: Ninety to 95 percent

Average tenant size: 1,000 square feet, with wide variations

Annual rents: $21 to $33 per square foot

Average length of lease: Five years

Typical terms of lease: full service, gross, or modified gross

Public Development Cost Information

Site Improvement Costs

Streetscape	$6,500,000

Construction Costs

Parking garage enlargement/street-level retail	5,500,000

Soft Costs

Bond issuance/miscellaneous	1,200,000
Total	$13,200,000

Financing Information

Financing Source

Assessment bond issue$13.2 million

While no financing was available from local agencies for individual owners/users, the city established an assessment district to fund streetscape and parking improvements. A business improvement district (BID) was set up to assist funding of maintenance, security, and promotional activities. City funds public nonprofit marketing and management organization.

Annual Operating Expenses

District operational responsibilities are not fully funded by BID. City provides all services but does not segregate costs for the district.

Development Schedule

Planning started: 1983

Construction started: 1988

Sales/leasing started: Ongoing

Phase I completed: 1989

Project completed: Ongoing. There is continuous capital investment by the city and private sector.

UNIVERSAL CITYWALK
Universal City, California

Universal CityWalk, in Universal City, California, is many things: part shopping center, part street, part entertainment destination, part tourist attraction. Perhaps because it is all of these, it has become—almost instantly—an immensely popular destination for visitors to Los Angeles and residents alike. Open since 1993, it is one of the area's biggest tourist attractions, as well as the place to go for a Saturday night date or a Sunday afternoon stroll with the kids.

The focus of CityWalk is entertainment, along a 1,500-foot-long street of architectural wonders. At one end is a cinematic thrill ride and an 18-screen theater complex, and at the other lies the Universal Studios Hollywood theme park. In between is a raucous collage of architectural forms and neon signs housing more than three-dozen specialty retail stores and restaurants as well as a neon art museum and the UCLA Extension Center. The purpose of CityWalk is to have fun, not to shop or dine. But with sales averaging more than $500 per square foot, there is no doubt that the fun translates into dollars.

One starts at Eastwalk, by the sand (which is real) beach of the Lighthouse Beach restaurant. Look up, and there is King Kong hanging off Sam Goody's, and beyond that, the Temple of Karnak Corinthian columns flanking the entrance to the music store's classical division. Go past the ships' masts of Gladstone's seafood restaurant and pass

Developer

Universal Studios
Universal City, California

Design Architect

The Jerde Partnership
Venice, California

Executive Architect

Daniel, Mann, Johnson, and Mendenhall
Los Angeles, California

Landscape Architect

Emmet L. Wemple & Associates
Pasadena, California

under a bridge (actually a second-story walkway) and you're in Center Court, a large, circular plaza topped by a giant, open-space frame structure. In the plaza is an interactive fountain, a mesmerizing, computer-driven water display that demands attention—or a walk-through—from young and old alike.

Finally, beyond the plaza, off at a tantalizing angle, is Westwalk. Greeting visitors from up above is Captain Coconuts, a giant wild-eyed bird, and the Hollywood Freezeway, with its upside-down car awning announcing "Ice cream this exit." Near the conclusion of this most unusual walk is a spaceship crashing into Things from Another World, a store for science fiction lovers, and the Current Wave, a clothing store with a surfboard for a roof and a wave machine moat at the door. Adding further pizzazz to the streetscape—if visitors have not had enough—are 21 vintage neon signs resurrected from a Los Angeles storage yard and a state-of-the-art, stadium-sized Astrovision™ video screen.

PLANNING AND DESIGN

Planning for CityWalk began soon after the adjacent Universal City Cinemas opened in 1987. With 18 screens, the movie theater complex was an instant success; two million patrons bought tickets in the first year.

With the success of the theater complex, Universal essentially had three anchors but no center. At one end of the 6.25-acre City-Walk site was the Universal Studios theme park, and at the other was the 6,200-seat Universal Amphitheatre and the 6,000-seat Universal City Cinemas. But each of these entertainment powerhouses was a stand-alone venture in a sea of parking. It became clear that the true potential of the site was in linking the existing venues to create a one-stop entertainment destination for adults and families where they could park in one place and spend the day or evening in an exciting and safe environment.

The Jerde Partnership, architects of innovative shopping centers around the country, was brought in by Universal to help articulate the vision. Working closely with Universal, the Jerde Partnership developed the City-Walk concept: the retail center as urban street, with all the architectural excitement and energy of a truly urban place.

The architects looked to real streets for design clues. The first and most striking element of the CityWalk concept is density. The street itself is relatively narrow, flanked by a towering jumble of building facades built at one-and-a-half-times normal scale to amplify the sense of urban density. The second element is the articulation of individual buildings. Avoiding the horizontal uniformity of the typical shopping center, CityWalk emphasizes individuality and verticality, encouraging each tenant to develop its own identity.

The third element is layering: the unfolding of vistas as one proceeds down the walk, passing under bridges and signs and through the central plaza. Also layered are building facade elements, from the facade given to each building by Jerde to the icons and neon signage added by each tenant. Inspired by the built-up energy of real city streets, the intent is purely to entertain.

TENANTING AND MARKETING

The concept of entertainment first was passed along to prospective tenants. Unlike at the typical shopping center, CityWalk's managers did not issue tenants a list of do's and dont's. Rather, prospective tenants were told to try what they always wanted but were never allowed to do.

Partly in response to desires expressed by Universal's Citizens Advisory Group, a loose collection of neighborhood residents, one of the first prospective tenants pursued by Universal was the University of California at Los Angeles (UCLA). The tie-in to a project like CityWalk is more likely than one might think. Adult education can be viewed as a form of entertainment since people take classes not only to advance their careers but to widen their horizons, meet people, or just have fun. The idea of a UCLA extension at CityWalk made perfect sense.

The UCLA extension center also has been active in the community by providing opportunities to underserved and often overlooked segments of the population. For example, a program called Entrepreneurial Business

A raucous and exhilarating collage of architectural forms and neon signs lines the street of specialty retail stores, restaurants, and entertaining features.

The Jerde Partnership

227

Odd-shaped creations and unique architectural and design features, many of which reflect in some way Los Angeles's heritage, mark the entrances to specialty restaurants and retailers.

Academy, sponsored by Universal CityWalk in partnership with the Los Angeles Unified School District (LAUSD), UCLA, and Communities in Schools—the nation's largest stay-in-school network—gives at-risk teenagers the opportunity to learn about business and marketing first hand. Under the program, 30 students from San Fernando High School and the Freemont Cluster in South Central Los Angeles are matched with restaurant and retail venues for a semester-long program of on-the-job training through paid internships in which the students work four days a week. One day a week the students take a business academy class at the UCLA extension center to supplement their on-the-job training. The students are not the only ones to benefit from the program. Universal CityWalk merchants get highly productive workers, and Universal CityWalk receives the positive publicity the program creates.

Universal also pursued highly regarded local restaurants like Malibu's Gladstone's For Fish and a Wolfgang Puck Pizza Cafe. They provide an architectural and gastronomic focus on the trademarks of the Southern California lifestyle. The merchants have benefited too; Gladstone's, for example, is among the top-grossing restaurants in the Los Angeles area. In 1997, the Hollywood Gaming Grill, a sports bar/cigar club/grill, opened, enhancing the restaurant and entertainment options available at CityWalk.

The more than 40 tenants brought together at CityWalk are a mix of popular or unusual local retailers and restaurants and upscale national chains. Retail shops include Out-takes, a video studio that, by the magic of computers, casts patrons in movies such as *Casablanca* and *The Wizard of Oz;* the Nature Company, with its own 40-foot-high rainforest; and the UCLA Spirit store, which sells Bruin-wear, university logo merchandise.

Restaurants include everything from B.B. King's Blues Club and Restaurant to Jodi Maroni's Sausage Kingdom. Entertainment offerings include Cinemania, a simulated ride by Showscan, Wizardz Magic Club and Dinner Theatre, and other restaurants combining dining and live performance. In the educational category are the UCLA Extension Center; Museum of Neon Art; Panasonic Pavilion; an interactive electronics display; and Scientific Revolution, a retail store selling educational gifts and toys. In charging ahead with its commitment to new technology and the environment, Universal CityWalk was the first entertainment complex in the United States to locate an inductive electric vehicle charging station on the premises. The station is the first of an expanded network of 90 charging stations to be located throughout Southern California, sponsored by General Motors, Edison EV, and the Los Angeles Department of Water and Power.

In addition, CityWalk regularly schedules street performers at assigned locations and provides a variety of planned events during the year—among them the International Street Performers Festival, the Los Angeles Parents/Kids Expo, Halloween trick-or-treating, and a Christmas season ice-skating rink.

MANAGEMENT AND OPERATIONS

Though CityWalk is like an urban street in character, it is mall-like in its management. Maintenance and security are serious business. The street is cleaned rigorously, and the management and security teams go to great lengths to keep CityWalk safe and orderly—no small task given the daytime crowds and nighttime concentrations of teenagers.

Much has been written about the safety factor at CityWalk. Admirers have pointed to the relatively crime-free environment—a street without the violence, panhandling, and homelessness of real city streets—as one of the attractions of CityWalk and a key factor in its success. Critics, on the other hand, have pointed to the sanitization of reality represented by CityWalk, for example, in its refusal to run certain controversial films.

From a retailing point of view, however, CityWalk has been an unequivocal success.

Phase I site plan.

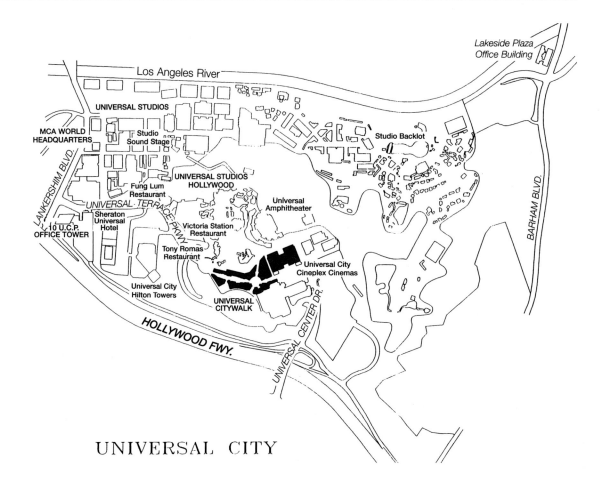

UNIVERSAL CITY

Phase I and future phases.

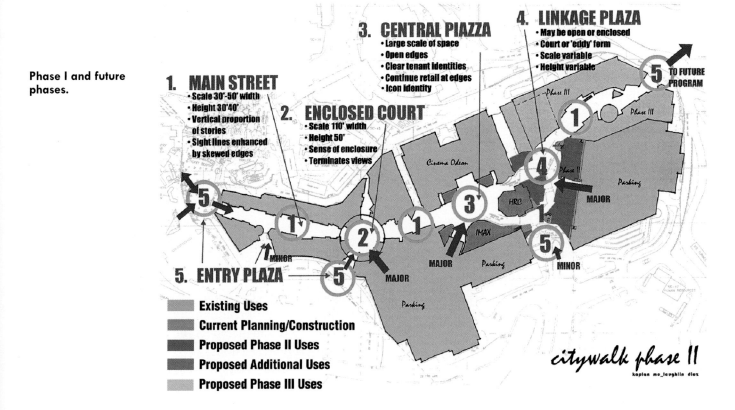

1. MAIN STREET
- Scale 30'-50' width
- Height 30'40'
- Vertical proportion of stories
- Sight lines enhanced by skewed edges

2. ENCLOSED COURT
- Scale 110' width
- Height 50'
- Sense of enclosure
- Terminates views

3. CENTRAL PIAZZA
- Large scale of space
- Open edges
- Clear tenant identities
- Continue retail at edges
- Icon identity

4. LINKAGE PLAZA
- May be open or enclosed
- Court or 'eddy' form
- Scale variable
- Height variable

5. ENTRY PLAZA

- Existing Uses
- Current Planning/Construction
- Proposed Phase II Uses
- Proposed Additional Uses
- Proposed Phase III Uses

citywalk phase II
kaplan mc_laughlin diaz

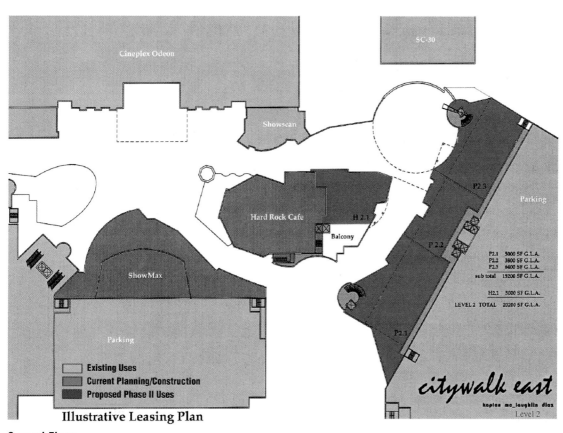

First Floor

Existing Uses
Current Planning/Construction
Proposed Phase II Uses

Cineplex Odeon

SC-30

Showscan

Hard Rock Cafe

ShowMax

Parking

Parking

citywalk phase II
kaplan mc_laughlin diaz
Option 1, Level 1

Existing Uses
Current Planning/Construction
Proposed Phase II Uses

Cineplex Odeon

SC-30

Showscan

Hard Rock Cafe

H 2.1

Balcony

ShowMax

Parking

P 2.3

P 2.2

P 2.1

Parking

P2.1   5000 SF G.L.A.
P2.2   3800 SF G.L.A.
P2.3   6400 SF G.L.A.
sub total   15200 SF G.L.A.

H2.1   5000 SF G.L.A.

LEVEL 2 TOTAL   20200 SF G.L.A.

citywalk east
kaplan mc_laughlin diaz
Level 2

Illustrative Leasing Plan

Second Floor

231

Though designed to be like an urban street, Universal CityWalk is managed like a mall. The management and security teams go to great lengths to keep the street clean, safe, and orderly.

The Jerde Partnership

According to Universal's surveys, more than 90 percent of the target market are aware of CityWalk, with relatively no advertising; more than 70 percent have visited CityWalk; and 80 percent of the latter group have visited more than once. Repeat visits by local residents average more than once a month.

The economic synergy of the project is evident in the statistics. Since CityWalk's opening, patronage at Universal City Cinemas is up 60 percent and the studio tour is up 15 percent. Similarly, when the amphitheater has a popular concert, CityWalk's restaurants are filled to capacity before, during, and after the concert. In general, retail sales levels at CityWalk have well exceeded both shopping center norms and Universal's original expectations.

EXPERIENCE GAINED

While success for CityWalk has resulted from creative design, programming, and management, it is clear that unlike many proposed urban entertainment centers, CityWalk started out with several advantages: it had three strong entertainment anchors already in place, with eight million annual visitors; Universal's name is widely known and is synonymous with entertainment; 10,000 people already were working on site and 3 million in the primary market area; and Universal had the management, marketing, and creative experience in house because of the company's other projects. In addition, funding for the development of CityWalk was provided internally by MCA, Inc., (now Universal Studios), the parent of the development company.

Nevertheless, the experience offers useful insights for future urban entertainment endeavors. Those contemplating new entertainment projects or trying to add entertainment to existing retail center should concentrate on the following four areas:

▼ Anchor Tenants: A good concept is not enough. Be careful not to confuse a good concept with an anchor! The test is simple: will the anchor bring customers back on a frequent and repeat basis and drive significant additional gross sales to other tenants?

▼ Uniqueness: CityWalk's success can be attributed in part to providing a different experience to the consumer, an escape from the sameness of shopping centers and multiplex movie theaters. Avoid the sameness that seems to be emerging with shopping centers and entertainment destinations seeking the same new chains. And work hard to stay unique, which is a temporary condition. What is today a unique retail or entertainment concept will likely become a national chain tomorrow.

▼ Technology: Technology is not entertainment. Virtual reality, ride simulators, high-definition TV, and CD-ROM all have exciting capabilities. But the technology must be managed in the context of the overall concept and target market.

▼ Entertainment: Keeping entertainment and restaurant concepts fresh is difficult but necessary. At the heart of a successful entertainment project there should be a reason to come back on a continuing basis. When targeting a local repeat customer rather than a tourist and especially when there is competition in the primary market area, do not assume a onetime capital cost with a long amortization period.

What lies ahead for Universal and City-Walk? A 100,000-square-foot expansion to the east of the 200,000 square-foot center has been approved, although a construction date has not been set. In addition, Universal is seeking approval for a $3 billion project that will more than double the developed land at Universal City and add a considerable portion to CityWalk in addition to the already

The Jerde Partnership

Center Court, a large circular plaza topped by a giant, open-space-frame structure, features a mesmerizing computer-driven water display.

approved second phase. True to its belief in working hard and investing the capital necessary to stay unique, Universal also is exploring other entertainment offerings, teaming with Marvel Entertainment Group Inc., and Planet Hollywood, Inc., to build the first Marvel Mania, a theme restaurant based on Marvel's comic book characters.

CHAPTER 6

FUTURE DIRECTIONS

The urban entertainment industry is evolving quickly as new projects, products, concepts, and plans are announced with breathtaking rapidity. It already is difficult enough to keep up with the entertainment development activity in cities around the world, and it may be almost impossible to predict accurately where the industry will head in the next few years. Unlike most Urban Land Institute books, which describe best land use and development practices based on a wealth of information, this one in some ways is ahead of its time in that there are few urban entertainment projects that have any track record at all.

Although a handful of successful urban entertainment projects are in place, no universally accepted models currently exist from which definitive development rules and practices can be drawn. As a result, some of what this book has to say is by necessity preliminary and in some cases based on emerging plans, concepts, and techniques for projects that have not yet opened. Thus, in many ways the entire book reflects anticipated future trends in the urban entertainment industry. It is a compilation of information, insights, and analysis from some of the industry's leading experts, a snapshot in time as the industry develops.

The following statements represent what the Urban Land Institute believes will be some of the most important trends over the next few years. Some already are apparent in major markets, and it is predicted that they will spread; others are more speculative, based on proposed activities and ideas that are bubbling just below the surface. Undoubtedly, in a few years new trends and ideas will appear as the industry matures. The industry's future is limited only by the imagination of its many talented creators.

Entertainment-enhanced retail development will be part of large-scale urban revitalization projects.

To date, urban entertainment projects have been developed in shopping centers; as adjuncts to casinos, sports facilities, and amusement parks; and as stand-alone developments. But in the future, entertain-

Entertainment-enhanced retail development will be part of large-scale urban revitalization projects such as CityPlace, which is being built by the Palladium Company in downtown West Palm Beach, Florida. (Preceding page: The planned Taichung entertainment center in Taichung, Taiwan.)

ment increasingly will be seen as a way to energize large-scale urban revitalization projects whose character is only partly oriented toward entertainment. These developments have the potential to create a new social and cultural center for urban communities that have lost theirs to blight and for suburban communities that never had one.

The forerunner of this trend is Reston Town Center, a new suburban downtown, which is primarily an office development but also includes a hotel, traditional retail stores, and an entertainment component. The success of this mix of uses in a neotraditional downtown setting has led to even more ambitious proposals to create large-scale, integrated downtown developments that include a major entertainment element.

Mission Bay is a planned, mixed-use project to be developed by Catellus in downtown San Francisco that will include 400,000 square feet of retail and entertainment uses plus residential development next to the new Pacific Bell Park, future home of the San Francisco Giants. Designed to be a component of a

much larger urban redevelopment area south of Market Street along the Embarcadero waterfront, the district will include 6,000 residential units; five million square feet of commercial development; a 500-room, first-class hotel; and an expansion campus for the medical and research facilities of the University of California, San Francisco.

CityPlace is a 600,000-square-foot town center retail and entertainment development planned for West Palm Beach, Florida, that will create a hub of cultural and social activity for the city. It is part of a much larger $375 million mixed-use development that includes residential, cultural, performance, hotel, office, and convention facilities. The developer, the Palladium Company, plans to roll out this concept in 11 additional communities by the year 2000.

These projects represent the cutting edge of a long-term trend that will recreate the essential elements of successful downtowns for the 21st century by incorporating entertainment-enhanced projects into the overall development program.

The public and private sectors will join forces to market collectively their urban entertainment attractions in urban districts.

Downtowns are favored locations for many urban entertainment developers and entertainment companies that want to showcase their attractions in locations with high visibility and access. But marketing downtowns is complex. Their image often needs polishing, and first their problems have to be overcome.

Cities increasingly will assume a direct role in creating the preconditions for marketing urban entertainment development. At the broadest level, more public/private partnerships will be set up as in Times Square in New York City and on Hollywood Boulevard in Los Angeles specifically to guide and facilitate the development of desired entertainment attractions in urban districts. Business improvement districts (BIDs) increasingly will be set up, as in the new downtown entertainment district of Washington, D.C., to improve the designated areas by providing heightened security and sanitation services, infrastructure improvements, direct marketing, and event coordination. And cultural districts increasingly will broaden their mandate to encourage entertainment attractions as well as the more usual museums and performing arts.

The entertainment providers will begin to team up to market jointly the districts in which their attractions are located rather than

SHANGHAI PLAZA

The Land of Oz meets H.G. Wells! Could this be representative of large-scale retail's new world order? The proposed Shanghai Plaza, in Shanghai, China, is an ambitious 8 million-square-foot megadevelopment that will offer an intricate combination of entertainment attractions as part of its mix of uses, from an underwater entrance world occupied by fish and submarines to markets in mythical settings and a courtyard of heavenly bodies and intergalactic delights.

Phase I, pictured below, is a 3 million-square-foot, six-level complex featuring retail stores, restaurants, virtual reality attractions, a water park, and high-tech entertainment components designed by RTKL. The theme of the project draws on the energy of natural and manufactured motion: waves, geysers, airplanes, rockets, and subway trains. State-of-the-art simulation systems will generate erupting volcanoes, crashing airplanes, and undulating rivers, bringing the project's various themed districts to life. The virtual traveler, designed as a merchandisable icon, will serve as the "tour guide" through these simulated worlds. The project has been designed to weave seamlessly into the urban fabric of Shanghai by a network of transportation systems running in and around the site.

Source: Daniel J. Brotman and Richard Yuan, RTKL.

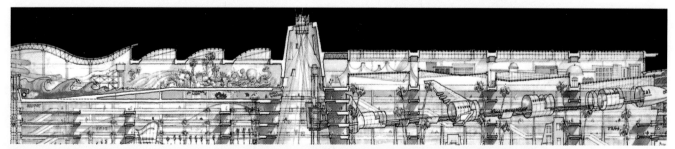

Shanghai Plaza, Phase I, a 3 million-square-foot, six-level retail and entertainment megadevelopment planned in Shanghai, China.

try to compete independently. For example, the Durst Organization, Forest City Ratner Companies, and Tishman Realty & Construction Company have agreed to jointly market Times Square as a single, enormous urban shopping and entertainment mall. This is expected to help all of them lease the remaining space in their retail entertainment projects under construction. One marketing technique that they will use with prospective tenants is a virtual reality CD-ROM walking tour of Times Square modestly entitled "Crossroads of the World."

Urban entertainment development will be linked to cultural, educational, and sports activities.

Cultural and educational institutions—from museums, performing arts venues, and universities to aquariums and zoos—and sports venues including stadiums and arenas are trying to adapt as they face strong competitive pressures from changes in societal and lifestyle trends and decreased public funding.

Entertainment offers an opportunity for these institutions to broaden their markets and compete more effectively for consumers' time and attention in a crowded marketplace. In turn, these institutions are beginning to provide entertainment development with a unique local character, cultural context, and educational aspect that is viewed by many experts as essential for long-term project success.

For example, science centers historically have been testing grounds for entertainment attractions. Virtual reality attractions, interactive entertainment technology, and large-format films are just some of the features that made the move from science centers to the world of mass entertainment. Today these centers are forgotten by many entertainment developers, and yet they offer great opportunities to create educational and cultural links.

Cultural facilities increasingly will be seen as anchors for downtown entertainment districts. This technique has been pioneered by several major cities, including the city of San Francisco at Yerba Buena, site of the new Museum of Contemporary Art, the Moscone Convention Center, and Sony's Metreon entertainment center. And in New York City, Times Square, site of the world's largest concentra-

Sports and entertainment will be linked at the planned L.A. Arena, future home of the NHL Kings and NBA Lakers in downtown Los Angeles.

NBBJ Architecture

238

tion of playhouses, also has several new urban entertainment centers along 42nd Street and numerous stand-alone entertainment attractions along Broadway. Smaller communities often have historic and cultural attractions in their downtowns that can be leveraged in the same way.

Entertainment/retail attractions also will be added to stadiums and arenas to create a more continuous customer draw for expensive downtown sites, to leverage the enormous crowds that are attracted to large-scale events, and to take advantage of these venues as anchors for entertainment/retail development.

In downtown Washington, D.C., entertainment is linked to sports and cultural attractions at the new MCI Center. Other sports and entertainment links are planned in San Francisco, northern New Jersey, Dallas, and Los Angeles, among other areas.

Universities often need gathering places that can provide essential retail and entertainment activities. Large lecture halls increasingly will be used for cinemas after classes are over for the day, as they are at the University of California, San Diego, and retail and entertainment uses will be collocated to take advantage of the captive student audience.

Entertainment will be added to all forms of shopping centers as they are repositioned to reflect 21st-century lifestyles.

In mid-1997 commercial real estate prices rose in almost all categories except that for shopping malls, and capitalization rates for malls are higher than they have been in almost ten years—11 percent or more for second-tier properties. Tenants and customers are difficult to find at many malls because of the overbuilding of retail space and the introduction of more competitive retail formats

like power centers, off-price megamalls, and outlet centers.

How can malls compete? Increasingly, their owners are adopting a lifestyle and entertainment orientation that makes the traditional shopping center more of a social gathering place that reflects the essence of its locale and caters to more than shopping needs. Early evidence suggests clearly that the environments that are being created bring more customers who stay longer, come more often, and spend more money—a retailing grand slam.

The introduction of entertainment can help revitalize many ailing malls as well as assist premium properties in maintaining their competitive positions. It is not a panacea, however, for malls that are poorly located, poorly merchandised, and too small to accommodate the needed changes.

At Circle Center, a new downtown mall in Indianapolis, Indiana, the Simon DeBartolo Group used entertainment—a cineplex, clubs, and restaurants—as one important element in creating a regional draw and has succeeded in bringing suburban customers downtown to shop and enjoy themselves. At Trizec-Hahn's Park Meadows Resort, a new mall in suburban Denver, the name reflects the broad appeal that shopping centers are striving for. It is designed to feel like a large Colorado ski lodge with wooden beams, fireplaces, and overstuffed sofas where people are encouraged to linger. At Tysons Corner Center in the northern Virginia suburbs of Washington, D.C., long one of the nation's premier suburban centers, an entire entertainment wing to be anchored by a megaplex and other specialized attractions is planned for construction in 1998. It will replace a 1970s era cineplex that is now woefully out of date.

James Martin Photo

Power centers and off-price megamalls also increasingly will include entertainment in their retail mix. The most extreme example to date is Ontario Mills in Ontario, California. Along with its massive collection of off-price and outlet stores are a megaplex, a Gameworks, a California Wilderness Experience, theme restaurants like Wolfgang Puck, and other specialized entertainment attractions. At Potomac Yards Center in Alexandria, Virginia, a new power center built where railroad yards existed a few years ago, a megaplex is planned to extend the center's hours and make it more of a community destination.

The bottom line is that as more entertainment features are added to shopping centers, the distinction between traditional malls and urban entertainment centers increasingly will blur until they include a seamless continuum of project types.

The variety of new location-based entertainment concepts and attractions will continue to expand dramatically in the next few years.

The number and variety of new entertainment concepts is truly astonishing. New ideas are being turned into prototypes and rolled out by large and small creative firms not only in New York and Hollywood but all over the world. In the future, the rise of home-based virtual reality equipment will force location-based operators to offer more highly themed and motion-based attractions. Bob Rogers, founder and chairman of BRC Imagination Art, predicts that these will be group oriented, allowing audience members to interact with each other, and that they will create a new kind of social experience. Film will become digital sometime in the next ten years, which means that operators will save money and scratchy film prints will be a thing of the past. In addition, new technologies and attractions will need to appeal to market segments that are currently overlooked and to the rapidly aging baby boomers.

But no matter how sophisticated the attractions and the technology become, the bottom line is still how entertaining the end product is and how often the "software" can be changed to keep people coming back.

Branding strategies will drive the development of urban entertainment destinations.

In the short time since urban entertainment centers were first introduced, branding has proven to be a powerful business generator. The major entertainment companies increasingly are using the power of their own brand images to deepen their penetration of the various entertainment market segments and create new markets altogether. Merchandise, interactive features, events, movies, music, television, publishing, and a range of location-based attractions from amusement parks to specialized, smaller-scale urban entertainment centers and stores are being strategically coordinated. Disney is leading the charge, and the other major entertainment companies are doing the same, to a greater or lesser extent. The nation's largest shopping center developer, the Simon DeBartolo Group, now is exploring how to market its brand. And cities with powerful images will exploit them to the fullest as they fight to rejuvenate their downtowns and historic districts. So far most of the action has centered around major locations like Times Square and the Las Vegas Strip, but many smaller communities soon will exploit their own identity on a smaller scale. Increasingly, the type and variety of features and attractions that define urban entertainment development will be determined by the branding strategies of the major anchors and the cities in which they locate.

The new-generation megaplex cinemas will render much of the nation's stock of movie screens obsolete and drive customers toward urban entertainment centers.

The new megaplex cinemas being developed by such giants as AMC, Sony/Loews, Cineplex Odeon, and Edwards will put intense pressure on the existing stock of movie screens that have been built over the last few decades. Hundreds of new megaplexes have been announced, and undoubtedly more are on the way; AMC Entertainment alone plans to build 60 megaplexes in the next year.

The new megaplexes offer from 24 to more than 30 large screens, state-of-the-art surround sound and projection systems, comfortable stadium-style seats, a great variety of food, dramatic lobbies, high levels of finish and detail, and strong architectural features like those found in the movie palaces of the 1930s. Because there are so many screens, movies start every few minutes, and the same movie is likely to be showing on several screens, thus obviating the need for customers to time their arrival or pick their movie in advance. They also create a strong sense of occasion that is enhanced by their prominent locations and the presence of other nearby attractions including theme restaurants and entertainment-oriented shops.

One of the newest developments is a screening room that is being incorporated into a planned cineplex at Country Club Plaza, in Kansas City, Missouri. This small, 30- to 40-seat cinema will have all the latest

The AMC Grand theater in Dallas, Texas, contains 24 screens and state-of-the-art cinema design.

Len Allington

Political and economic reforms in South American countries have paved the way for significant new development opportunities. Evidence of this fact is abundant in the entertainment industry, with many movie exhibitors zealously converging on South American countries to be part of urban entertainment complexes.

The excitement over South American entertainment development is spurred by the fact that most countries are underscreened and cinemas are the anchor attractions. Chile, for example, has only one screen per 150,000 people, compared with one screen per 9,000 in the United States. It is anticipated that within two to three years Chile and neighboring Argentina will be in the one per 30,000 range. Most of these new screens will be associated with cinemas in retail environments such as malls and power centers.

South American consumers are enthusiastically embracing new entertainment opportunities. Retail developments in Latin American urban areas are incorporating cinemas and other entertainment complexes into their projects at a rapid rate. The current development trend focuses on dense urban infill sites, rather than on the suburban sites preferred in the United States. Such infill sites are complex in nature, often comprising an assemblage of small adjacent sites and a mix of nonretail uses. The challenges posed by the locations are substantial. Harold Blank, managing

director of Hoyts Latin America, says, "With the hefty land costs and limited space availability, we are facing more vertical theaters" in entertainment complexes, which require auditoriums to be stacked one upon the other, as at the Patio Olmos mall in Cordoba, Argentina. The site resulted from the acquisition of two perpendicular ten-meter wide parcels. Three stories of theaters are arranged in a T-shaped plan, attached to the mall.

Another example is the San Agustín Cinema located in the center of Santiago, Chile's premier retail district. Ten screens had to be finessed into a small basement space filled with columns and shear walls supporting a 12-story tower and a 400-year-old church above. To better integrate the theater into the retail context, the design incorporated two entrances from a street-level plaza with the lobby of the subterranean cinema.

As in the United States, the most significant challenges in developing entertainment centers with multiplexes include parking, theater planning, and visibility. These issues are amplified in Latin America. Available parking is scarce in South American city centers, so while many projects are going up with stacked theaters, there also is a need to go down with stacked parking levels—at substantial cost.

Commenting on the differences in retail and cinema development between the United States and South America, Blank points out, "The dif-

ference is in the retail end of it. You don't see a lot of big anchor stores, just a lot of little shops." In the United States, cinemas often are considered an additional anchor, whereas in South America a cinema is usually the only anchor and is therefore a welcome addition to retail developments.

Going to the Movies

At present, going to the movies in South America is a much more formal event than in the United States. Movie going there is more accurately compared with an evening at the opera or ballet in America. This characteristic effects construction costs, because the South American public has higher expectations for materials and finishes in cinemas. For example, the Hoyts Cine 12 at Mercado de Abasto in Buenos Aires features high-tech stainless steel siding and a warm, wood-paneled interior, rather than the artificial stucco and drywall common to the U.S. market. As in the United States, going to the movies can generate an opportunity for synergy with dining out. At Showcenter in Buenos Aires, for example, the cinema shares an enclosed plaza with restaurants and other entertainment venues.

Codes and Regulatory Issues

In South America, zoning and building codes vary widely from country to country and often from city to city

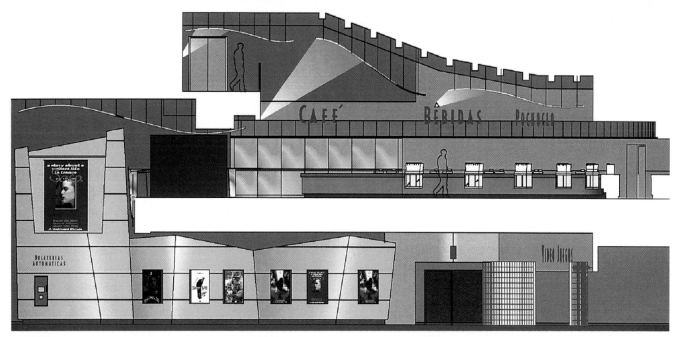

Mercado de Abasto, a Hoyts cinema-anchored UEC, is under construction in Buenos Aires, Argentina.

within a country. Many codes are quite old and written in a way that leaves them open to interpretation by local officials, requiring a great deal more negotiating with municipal authorities throughout the planning and design process. Accommodations for the disabled are only beginning to be addressed in many countries; however, it is generally accepted that accommodations are to be made.

Construction Issues

Building materials and methods vary widely from country to country. In Chile, for example, steel commonly is used for structural elements, while in Argentina poured-in-place con-

crete is the norm, even in high-rise construction. Labor rates in South America are lower than those in the United States, which substantially reduces the cost differential between expensive and inexpensive materials and systems. Masonry construction and plaster, for example, are typically used in lieu of studs and drywall.

Summary

In South America, as in the United States, placing cinema complexes within retail centers provides a wide range of experiences for the customer and creates an overall synergy that is financially beneficial for many retailers. Proper attention to detail and placement of the cinema will en-

sure creation of a successful entertainment complex that is seamlessly integrated with retail uses. The added variety makes a real difference in attracting the repeat local shopper and pays off in increased activity and sales.

Source: Robert S. Holt, AIA, and Dennis B. Carlberg, AIA, Arrowstreet Inc., Somerville, Massachusetts.

amenities, including stadium seating, and will show advance screenings of new movies to patrons who will pay a flat yearly fee rather than buy a ticket for each movie. The screening room will take reservations and have a separate entrance and valet parking.

Some experts have warned that the market for cinemas already is saturated and that there is no need for more. But this misses a critical point because, in many ways, the new megaplexes are a new form of entertainment, completely unlike most older cinemas, which offer functionally obsolete, small screens in isolated, leftover shopping center space or at stand-alone roadside locations. Many of these undoubtedly will close while others will begin to show specialty foreign and art films to survive the onslaught of the megaplex.

Stan Durwood, chairman of AMC Theaters, stated at ULI's annual meeting in New York City in November 1997 that up to 60 percent of the nation's 29,000-plus movie screens are functionally obsolete and at risk of being driven out of business by new-generation cinemas.

The proliferation of innovative theme restaurants now offers unprecedented choice, but will they all survive?

Theme restaurants are proliferating wildly throughout the urban entertainment indus-try. A trend that started in the 1970s with Hard Rock Cafe and later was reinforced by Planet Hollywood now encompasses at least 20 brand restaurant chains including such relative newcomers as BET Sound Stage, Race Rock, Cafe@Play, and Velocity Grill. Restaurant concepts are expanding to such an extent that they now can be grouped into broad categories, including Hollywood movies, sports, travel, television and radio, computers, music, adventure, and Americana. Within these categories are numerous restaurant concepts being rolled out as described in Chapter 2, and more are on the way.

Rochlis, DeMeyer and Rosen, a leading entertainment development firm in Los Angeles, reports that in 1997 there were about 150 new-generation theme restaurants in place around the United States, up from only 40 in 1992, and that the pace of construction is increasing. And this does not include the many one-of-a-kind restaurants with high concept design such as Cafe Casablanca in Joliet, Illinois, the Silver Diner in Fairfax, Virginia, and the Night Gallery in Greenwich Village, New York. Many of these restaurants are in stand-alone locations; others are located in urban entertainment centers. All of them require large, free-spending markets and high levels of repeat visitation.

Can the market support all of these concepts? It is too early to tell how many the market can support and which will have staying power, but some experts think that in markets such as New York City, Orlando, and Las Vegas saturation already may be near. Consumers inevitably will become more choosey as their dining options proliferate and the novelty begins to wear off. Jim Dunn, director of the New York Restaurant Group, said, "I think [the market] is already at the saturation point or close to it."[1] The restaurants that thrive will be those that offer environments that can be continuously freshened and that place a higher priority on the food they serve. In too many theme restaurants, food takes second place to the environment as a drawing card.

Another challenge will be to develop theme restaurant concepts that work where the demographics are less powerful than in major metropolitan markets and where the prices that people are willing to pay for dinner on a repeat basis make it difficult to create the type of elaborate environment that now is their main draw. Inevitably, new theme restaurants will emerge that will be structured to accommodate smaller market sizes. But in the meantime, many theme restaurant chains are accelerating their expansion into major overseas markets in order to sustain the growth demanded by their investors.

Live theater will be the next major new/old component of urban entertainment development.

For years pundits proclaimed that Broadway was dead or dying and that live theater did not suit modern audiences. It turns out they were wrong on both counts. Not only is live theater surging in New York City as Times Square is revitalized, but it also is on the verge of becoming a destination attraction in urban entertainment centers as well, although in different forms. In addition to Broadway, off-Broadway, and touring productions, there are family shows, theme park shows, casino shows, concert productions, and major events and pageants that entertainment centers can draw on.

Gaylord Entertainment opened Wildhorse Saloon in Nashville, Tennessee, in 1994. Seen regularly on the Nashville Network (TNN) and Country Music Television (CMT), this live performance/restaurant/retail venue has had enormous exposure through the media.

A revolution is reshaping the entertainment and leisure activities of American women. Women's roles in the family and the labor force and their attitudes, preferences, and level of education have changed to the point that the housewife of the 1950s is nowhere to be found in American culture today. These changes have profound implications for developers and builders in the United States. Nowhere are they more evident than in the leisure, entertainment, and specialty retail industries where the potential of the women's market is just beginning to be tapped.

The Women's Market

The women's market in the United States is characterized by its powerful and growing size, high education and income levels, and strong labor force participation rate. But women are pressed for time, have interests that are different from men's, respond differently to entertainment offerings, and increasingly are afraid to venture out alone at night.

▼ *Powerful demographics.* Working women represent a big, wealthy market that currently is underserved by the retail/entertainment industry. Women's earnings are no longer discretionary; they are essential to the household standard of living. In 1996, 51 percent of the U.S. population, or 135 million people, were women, and their incomes rose almost 50 percent between 1970 and 1995 in current dollars. Ninety-six million were working, and 4.4 million were earn-

ing more than $50,000 per year. The largest percentage of these high earners were women 35 to 54 years old, the peak wage-earning years. Working women with partners contribute at least half of household income 55 percent of the time, and in 18 percent of all households, employed women are the sole earners.

▼ *High education level.* Women in the United States are highly educated and their education level relates directly to their entertainment consumption: higher education levels correlate positively with movie going, patronage of the arts, and reading. The trend is only going to increase as incomes, education, and leisure time grow. In 1996, women accounted for the majority of bachelor's (56 percent) and master's degrees earned (51 percent). And the percentage of doctoral (39 percent) and professional degrees (41 percent) earned by women also continues to increase. As a result, future growth in the leisure and entertainment market has the potential to be strongly oriented toward women.

▼ *Strong labor force participation.* The number of women in the labor force has increased steadily in the past 30 years and will only continue to grow in the future. The biggest submarket of working women in the leisure and entertainment market is working mothers. By 1995, 59 percent of all women were in the labor force, and by 2005, the participation rate is expected to increase to 65 percent. By 1996, almost 8 mil-

lion women owned businesses, employing 18.5 million workers. Among women aged 25 to 49, at least 75 percent are in the labor force; however, the women most likely to be in the labor force are also most likely to be mothers. In 1994, of mothers with children aged six to 17, 78 percent worked either full- or part-time.

▼ *Time pressures.* Women are the primary purchasers of food, clothing, and household products in 85 percent of homes, and 73 percent of all mall shoppers are women, according to the Mass Retailers Association. It is no surprise that women feel pressed for time and stressed in their daily lives (88 percent according to a Louis Harris & Associates poll). Because of time pressures, women do not enjoy shopping as in the past; the percentage of shoppers who do so for enjoyment on the weekend declined to 32 percent in 1994. However, women tend to think of shopping in two ways: necessary shopping and fun/recreational shopping. The necessary shopping is drudgery, so women want fast service, quality products, and low prices. However, when shopping because they want to, women seek a fair price and a differentiated product at a more leisurely pace. This is when they may visit an urban entertainment center. Recreation and entertainment providers can capture their business by offering short-length-of-stay opportunities with lots of value or just by providing a fun experience that both mothers and children can enjoy together or at the same time.

▼ *Fear.* Fear is a way of life for many women. According to a University of Chicago survey, 60 percent of women are afraid to walk alone at night in an area near their home, while an American Research Group survey found that 60 percent of women also shop less at night because of fear. Entertainment venues must be sensitive to this concern and ensure a safe environment to attract the female customer at night.

▼ *Different preferences in leisure and sports.* Women's and men's favorite leisure activities are similar but not the same, according to the Louis Harris and Associates poll. Watching television ranks high for both, while golf and participating in team sports make it to the top five activities for men but do not appear on the top-ten lists for women. This may change, however, because women constitute the fastest-growing segment of new golfers and women are becoming big participants in team sports. For women, the top-five activities are walking, bicycling, aerobics, swimming, bowling, and calisthenics. Women exercise more than men. Think of the sales potential for retailers if sporting goods stores devoted more space to women's sporting goods, not just clothing!

▼ *Different responses to games.* According to numerous scientific studies, women's and men's brains tend to be different. Hard wiring makes sensitivity to color, light, and sound different in women and men,

The times....they are a changin'!

perhaps explaining why the noise of some old-fashioned game centers is offensive to many women and not to men. In addition, women tend to be better than men at rapidly identifying matching items; they have greater verbal fluency; and they outperform men in arithmetic calculation and in recalling landmarks from a route. Women also are faster at certain precision manual tasks. Men, on the other hand, perform better than women on spatial tasks. They have an advantage in tests that require

the subject to imagine rotating an object or manipulating it in some other way. They also outperform women in mathematical reasoning and in navigating their way through a route, and they also are more accurate in tests of target-directed motor skills, that is, in guiding or intercepting projectiles. The relevance of these differences for game designers is significant. No wonder men are the primary audience for the war-based projectile shooting games that are on the market!

(Continued)

Women's and Men's Ten Favorite Leisure Activities

Women's Favorite Activity	Percentage of Women	Men's Favorite Activity	Percentage of Men
Reading	39	TV watching	26
TV watching	24	Fishing	17
Spending time/playing with family and kids	14	Reading	16
Sewing/crocheting	13	Participating in team sports (i.e., basketball, baseball, etc.)	14
Gardening	11		
Walking	11	Golf	10
Going to movies	10	Spending time/playing with family and kids	10
Swimming	8	Gardening	8
Entertaining with friends	7	Hunting	8
Shopping	6	Entertaining with friends	7
		Going to movies	6

Source: Louis Harris & Associates, September 5, 1995.

New Entertainment Products and Ideas for Women

After weighing all the data on income, education, preferences, and family structure, a few entertainment and leisure companies are taking a chance on the growing women's market. They are putting dollars into research and development for sports, leisure, and entertainment products with women in mind.

Paul Allen established Purple Moon in 1995 to develop CD-ROM games for girls. After an effort that cost several million dollars and took a few years of targeted research, the company now is ready to roll out its first few CD-ROM games for girls. And lest one thinks girls do not like games, Fashion Designer Barbie, a CD-ROM game for girls under ten, sold more in its first month on the market than any other CD-ROM game in history. In Japan, one of the hottest new location-based attractions with girls is Print Club, a Sega arcade machine that photographs kids and prints their picture on sheets of tiny stickers to trade with friends.

The top-drawing music tour of 1997, Lilith Fair, featured only women; it was backed by sponsors chosen for their charitable or political views, including a bookstore chain, a women's shoe manufacturer, and a maker of skin-care products. The artists included Jewel, Sheryl Crow, Fiona Apple, Beth Orton, Mary Chapin Carpenter, Emmylou Harris, Shawn Colvin, Joan Osborn, and Cassandra Wilson. Tickets for Lilith's 32 dates sold quickly.

At Universal Studios Florida, *Hercules and Xena: Wizards of the Screen* is a live show that engages more than a dozen members of the audience to interact with cameras, costumes, creatures, and seven live cast performers. Anything can happen—and does—and the show has played to packed houses every day since it opened in early 1997.

Tony Christopher, cofounder of Landmark Entertainment, believes that all entertainment, including the new interactive media, is based on live theater and that understanding its various forms and using them will make urban entertainment a more compelling experience that brings audiences back again and again. Traditional theater also will benefit since technologies now being developed may allow a Broadway performance to be seen on stage in Los Angeles. Landmark Entertainment has created a new division called Landmark

Many new adult game centers have come out in the past few years, and several more are planned. This area of entertainment always has been male dominated, featuring shooting and scoring games. Brain research and opinion surveys indicate that women do not like games with violent themes. Entros in Seattle is an excellent example of an adult game center designed with women in mind. It encompasses 12,000 square feet and includes dining, a cocktail bar, an open kitchen, and games. However, the games are custom designed to encourage cooperation, teamwork, and socializing. They involve real time, real objects, and are extremely high touch/low tech. The customer base is split evenly between men and women. These types of games appeal to women.

Perhaps the most dramatic new female-targeted attraction in the United States today is the WNBA, which made its debut on June 21, 1997. The league is owned and operated by the NBA, and it plays during the summer. League attendance during its inaugural season was 1.1 million, an average of 9,700 per game. Sponsors include General

Top-Five Rates for Women's Participation in Sports and Fitness Activities

Activity	Percentage of Women Participating
Walking	85
Bicycling	63
Aerobics	61
Swimming	50
Bowling	33

Source: The Miller Lite Report on Sports and Fitness, *Working Woman,* March 1995.

Motors, Sears, Coca-Cola, Anheuser-Busch, Nike, and Lee. Games will be broadcast on NBC, ESPN, and Lifetime. Corporate America and major league sports believe the United States is finally ready for women to have a permanent, successful league of their own.

Implications for Entertainment Developers

What does all this mean to the leisure and entertainment industry? If you want to bring more women into your project and establish brand loyalty among your customers:

▼ Remember, God is in the details. Lights, sound, safety, and atmosphere are primary.

▼ Give customers intelligent, fun things to do with their children. Provide peaceful areas for mothers in entertainment centers.

▼ Design for women's preferences in how they spend their leisure time and money.

▼ Cater to women's time constraints through program and design.

▼ Ask women what they want through intercept interviews and focus groups. They will tell you.

▼ Keep the message optimistic and open ended. Women respond to creative, intelligent, expansive marketing and attractions.

Women of the 21st century have the potential to be the biggest, best-educated market yet. Please them and they will return often, bringing their family and friends with them.

Source: Jill Bensley, JB Research Company, Ojai, California.

Live! in New York that is considering creating an attraction in the 42nd Street area where the live stage and theme park technology will meet. The idea is to create a virtual show live on stage every hour on the hour.

As Nora Lee, editor of the *Entertainment Zone,* wrote, "The theater is not dead. It is, as its long history indicates, evolving, and urban entertainment centers are the next stop on the tour."

Entertainment developers will begin to target overlooked markets seriously.

A range of overlooked markets is evident from the current vantage point. Bob Rogers predicts that continuing immigration and the growth of ethnic populations will give rise to urban entertainment centers with an ethnic flavor that will cater to an increasingly multilingual and multiethnic society. Attractions and well as foods offered will reflect that diversity. At the same time, he predicts that the rise of a super-rich class will create demand for resort entertainment centers where guests are surrounded by a fantasy environment priced anywhere from $500 to $50,000 per guest.

The African American market, which has been overlooked consistently by traditional retailing, increasingly will be catered to in the entertainment realm. Black Entertainment Television (BET) has created the first of its spectacular entertainment-theme restaurants, BET SoundStage, targeting the African American community in suburban Prince Georges County, Maryland, the nation's wealthiest predominantly African American county.

Magic Johnson is successfully rolling out his chain of Magic Theaters in partnership with Sony/Loews in urban neighborhoods with large African American populations. The first one, in Crenshaw Plaza in Los Angeles's Baldwin Hills, is one of the top-grossing cineplexes in the country, demonstrating clearly that providing entertainment in underserved urban neighborhoods has incredible potential, which other enterprising developers will try to duplicate.

And women, who represent more than 50 percent of the population and make most of the retail spending decisions, have looked, often in vain, for entertainment attractions designed to appeal to them. That will have to change dramatically in the coming years if urban entertainment centers are to thrive. Already some entertainment companies are beginning to cater to the women's market: CD-ROM games for girls are now beginning to be developed, a music tour featuring women was held in 1997, adult arcade games that encourage cooperation and teamwork are beginning to be designed, and a women's professional basketball league has been formed. Because in the future the population of the United States will become increasingly diverse, developers must expand their efforts to cater to diverse audiences.

Conclusion

Three years ago, few people had heard the term "urban entertainment development" or recognized that a dynamic new form of development was being born. In this short

The proposed Harlem USA retail entertainment center on 125th Street in New York City has leased space to two anchors, the Disney Store and Cineplex Odeon. Construction is expected to begin in 1998.

period, the term has gone from being virtually unknown to being the buzzword of the real estate industry, like "plastics" in the 1970s-era film *The Graduate*. Does this form of development have staying power? Is it the wave of the future, the savior of America's downtowns, the miraculous rejuvenator of shopping centers that some people claim? Beyond the hyperbole and the inevitable smoke and mirrors that sometimes blight both the development and entertainment industries, several conclusions are clear. Something real *is* happening out there, and it has caught the imagination of a large number of savvy developers, entertainment companies, cities, and consumers. Projects open only a short while already are being expanded. New cineplexes, theme restaurants and stores, and specialized entertainment attractions are being built with increasing frequency. Attendance and sales figures are impressive. And the pent-up demand for exciting, innovative entertainment in a safe, public environment where people can interact with other people has now been demonstrated.

But the challenges are equally apparent. How many urban entertainment centers and attractions can the market support? What size and combination of features and attractions work best? Will people continue to be interested once the novelty wears off, or more important, can entertainment providers keep it from wearing off? What happens when the first few projects fail, as some inevitably will? Will investors run for the hills? Can these expensive creations be built and tenanted in smaller markets once the major markets are saturated in the next few years?

This book is the first comprehensive attempt to provide case-study-based information on the issues that are critical to the future of urban entertainment development. However, this book does not have all the answers to the questions posed in the previous paragraph because for many of them no answers currently exist. The industry is too new and the experience available is not yet

Sony will include a major entertainment component at Sony Center, its new European headquarters, on the Potsdamer Platz in Berlin.

deep enough. The book does create a base of information and insights that the entertainment development industry needs to move forward as it matures.

Where do we go from here? Stay tuned.

Note

1. Mitchell Pacelle, "Skeletons, Subs, and Other Restaurants Do Battle," *Wall Street Journal* (May 21, 1997), p. B1/2.

GLOSSARY

Bundling: The technique of combining specialized entertainment attractions, especially new-generation cinema complexes, with theme restaurants and retail shops in combinations that ensure the viability of an urban entertainment center.

Capitalization rate (cap rate): The current rate of return, derived by dividing the net operating income by the estimated property value or sale price, commonly expressed as a percentage.

Children's entertainment center (CEC): A center operated by a single business entity that charges admission for child-oriented games and attractions. It commonly includes modular play systems, party rooms, redemption games, arts and crafts, edutainment experiences, and concession stands. Examples include Club Disney, Discovery Zone, and Jeepers.

Circle of draw: The trade area from which a venue draws potential customers. May be broken down into primary, secondary, and tertiary trade or customer areas. Circles of draw and trade areas for entertainment venues are affected by many factors, including competition, changes in accessibility and visibility, and weather.

Consumer research: Research conducted by interviewing customers to determine needs, preferences, buying patterns, shopping patterns, and demographic profiles.

Demographics: Statistical information on characteristics of the population of an area, including but not limited to age, employment, income, expenditures, and persons per household.

Design day: The theoretical attendance level for an attraction, which is the average attendance for the top 20 to 40 days of the year, depending on the type of venue or attraction. Attractions and theme parks are designed for design day attendance levels, not for absolute peak level attendance, otherwise the venue would be oversized and underused much of the year.

EBDITA: Earnings before depreciation, interest, and taxes. Synonymous with net operating income for an attraction or other operating business. This measure permits earnings to be evaluated and compared without the influence of elements that bear little relationship to a company's operational performance. This calculation is often compared with the initial investment required to determine the viability of a potential business.

Entertainment-oriented retail (EOC): Retail stores with interactive and entertainment-oriented in-store displays and activities, from kiosks to cafés, that often act as brand-building marketing devices for manufacturers and entertainment companies. Examples are Barnes & Noble Bookseller, Niketown, REI Seattle, and Virgin Records Megastore.

Family entertainment center (FEC): An indoor and/or outdoor facility, operated by a single business entity, offering a traditional mix of games and attractions on a pay-as-you-go basis, commonly including video-game arcades, mini-golf, go carts, batting cages, and concession stands. Examples include Exhilarama, Fun Factory, and Q-City.

Feasibility study: A report that evaluates many factors that relate to an investment and provides an assessment of the investment's probable return.

Gate: A venue or attraction that charges admission. Often used as slang for the number of major theme parks in a market area or operated by the same company: for example, "Disney is opening a fourth gate in Orlando, Animal Kingdom; the other three are the Magic Kingdom, Epcot, and Disney MGM Studios."

Gross leasable area (GLA): In a UEC, the total of all rentable areas and all common areas of a building. A tenant's GLA is the total of the area of the tenant's suite and a proportional share of all common areas of the building. In retail centers, GLA is the total of all tenant suites. A tenant's GLA in a retail center is the measurement of the tenant's suite from the outside face of each exterior wall to the centerline of each demising wall.

In-grounds/in park simultaneous attendance: The number of people in a theme park at the peak time of day. Not all people attending a theme park during the course of a day are in grounds at the same time. Many theme parks expect a 70 percent to 80 percent in-grounds factor.

Internal rate of return (IRR): The discount rate applied to an investment that produces a net present value of zero. The IRR can be interpreted as the annualized rate of return on the investment.

Large-format film: (See specialty-format film)

Leisure entertainment center (LEC): *See urban entertainment center.*

Location-based entertainment (LBE): Any form of commercial out-of-home entertainment, especially a facility dedicated to one attraction type or a facility that does not fit within a more specialized category, like that for high-tech game centers. Examples include American Wilderness Experience, Dave & Busters, DisneyQuest, and Gameworks.

Market research: Research done to assess market conditions in a specified area.

Market segmentation: Population groupings based on various factors. Examples of market segments include the following: tourists staying with friends and relatives, tourists staying in the area, tourists staying outside the area, and the population living within a given radius of the project. Urban entertainment centers tend to attract a large number of market segments (seven to 12).

Megaplex: A grouping of more than 24 cinema screens under single management with a centralized, on-site location for ticket purchase.

Motion simulator: A ride simulation or ride film that includes a motion base (bench, seat, cabin, or platform) that moves the audience in synch with a film or video presentation, creating the illusion of participation in the experience.

Net operating income (NOI): Cash flow from a property after all expenses are deducted from gross income.

Occupancy cost: The total cost to a tenant of occupying its space. Derived for a retail tenant by adding rent, common area maintenance (CAM) charges, taxes, insurance, merchant association fees, and percentage rent. The total cost then can be divided by the sales of the tenant and expressed as a percentage to measure profitability.

Payback period: The amount of time required for an investor to recover the capital committed to a venture, attraction, or the acquisition of property.

Penetration rate or market capture: The percentage of a trade area population or various population segments that will visit a project or an attraction. This rate depends on the project's tenant mix (for retail), competition, alternative activities (for an attraction), and demographic profiles of the population.

Per-capita expenditures: The average amount spent by each visitor attending an attraction/venue over a certain amount of time (day, month, quarter, year). Per-capita expenditures are designated by category, for example:

Theme Park Expenditures	Movie Theater Expenditures
Admission and rides	Ticket price
Food and beverages	Concessions (popcorn, candy, drinks, etc.)
Merchandise	
Games	
Parking	
Miscellaneous	

Percentage rent: Rent computed as a percentage of retail sales above a breakpoint and paid by tenants. Usually paid instead of or in addition to a specified minimum base rent.

Psychographics: Characteristics of people, such as their personal interests and levels of aspiration, which can be used to determine tenant mix and center design.

Retail dining entertainment (RDE): *See urban entertainment center.*

Sales per square foot: Retail sales divided by the square footage of the tenant space. This measurement is used to determine profitability, to determine whether the tenant has reached the level over which it must pay percentage rent, and to compare the tenant with national standards for its tenant type.

Specialty-format film: A generic term for any imaging format that is not 2-D 35 mm film, the standard format. It most often refers to both a film and a projection system that may include large-format films (IMAX, Iwerks, Showscan), 360-degree presentations, 3-D films and videos, domes, and sometimes simulation.

Tenant mix: The combination of various tenant types in a leased property.

Theoretical capacity/capacity: The measurement of the processing power of an attraction. An example is the number of people who can be processed through a ride at a theme park in the course of an hour. If a vehicle carries ten people and launches every two minutes, the theoretical capacity for the ride would be 300. In most venues, it is impossible to keep to such a precise schedule and often all the seats in a vehicle are not filled, so that theoretical capacity almost never is obtained. Capacity, thus, takes into account an allowance for vacant seats and delays.

Throughput: The number of people that can be put through an attraction or venue over a period of time. Throughput also relates to capacity. Pulsed throughput is when an attraction has a surge of traffic at particular times, rather than a continuous flow. For example, when people must take an elevator or tram to get to an attraction, the number of people that can be processed is limited by how many can fit into the elevator or tram. When the elevator or tram arrives there is a surge of traffic, followed by a lull until the next tram or elevator arrives.

Urban entertainment center (UEC): Also referred to as an urban entertainment destination (UED), a leisure entertainment center (LEC), or retail dining entertainment (RDE). This type of center offers a synergistic combination of entertainment, food and beverage, and retail; it may take the form of a cohesively owned and operated complex with tenants or a downtown district of independent property owners and tenants. Examples of the former include Universal CityWalk, CocoWalk, the Entertainment Center at Irvine Spectrum, and the Mall of America; examples of the latter include Third Street Promenade and Times Square/42nd Street.

Urban entertainment destination (UED): *See urban entertainment center.*

Virtual reality: A computer-generated 3-D world that allows a user to inhabit it and interact in it by means of multiple sensory inputs such as headsets and data gloves.

Visitation or attendance: The number of people visiting a venue. That number is multiplied by per-capita expenditures to estimate demand for a project.

Source: Tsilah Burman, Westmark International and Westmark Realty Advisors, Inc., Los Angeles, California.